HOW TO RUN
Successful Projects
in Web Time

For a listing of recent titles in the *Artech House Computing Library,*
please turn to the back of this book.

HOW TO RUN
Successful Projects
in Web Time

Fergus O'Connell

Artech House
Boston • London
www.artechhouse.com

Library of Congress Cataloging-in-Publication Data
O'Connell, Fergus.
    How to run successful projects in Web time / Fergus O'Connell.
    p.   cm. — (Artech House computing library)
    Includes bibliographical references and index.
    ISBN 1-58053-165-2 (alk. paper)
    1. High technology industries—Management.   2. Industrial project
management.   I. Title.
    HD62.37 .O284   2000
    658.4'04—dc21   00-048094
                                                        CIP

British Library Cataloguing in Publication Data
O'Connell, Fergus
    How to run successful projects in Web time.— (Artech House
computing library)
    1. Industrial project management   2. High technology
    industries—Management
    I. Title
    658.4'04
    ISBN 1-58053-165-2

Cover design by Christina Stone
Text design by Darrell Judd

International Standard Book Number: 1-58053-165-2
Library of Congress Catalog Card Number: 00-048094

10 9 8 7 6 5 4 3 2 1

For Eamonn and Mandy

Contents

Preface

About five years ago, *DEC Computing*, a relatively obscure publication—and even more obscure now (!)—published an article I had written under the (editor's choice of) title *Silver Bullet Lies On Film*. In it, I tried to show that the problem of estimating, which still remains unsolved in the IT / software industry, has to a large part been solved in the film making industry. The article appeared and was promptly forgotten.

Many times after that, I found myself returning to this comparison of the two industries. I believe that the film making industry is, if anything, *even more complex* than the software development industry. This is particularly true in terms of its being part art part science, and also in terms of the level of perfection that is required in the finished product. Despite all of this, the problem of making it a predictable discipline has, to a large extent, been cracked. The notion continued to swim around in my head until a couple of other things happened.

One was that I read Alan Cooper's wise and wonderful book, *The Lunatics Are Running The Asylum*. In it I was delighted to find him making the same comparison. What's more, he was saying what I had been saying, that the key to the successful movie was not a successful production (i.e., shooting the movie) phase, but a comprehensively thought out pre-production phase (i.e., the project planning of the movie). He speculated what I had been speculating—that if we were to put more time into the project planning, we could shorten and cheapen the development time.

Now, to some extent, my company, ETP, had been teaching such a notion for years. My previous two project management books had been about this very idea. Put simply, the theory went that with no planning, everything became a firefight, but with a modest amount of planning, we could bring a lot more predictability to the process. But now we were talking about a lot more than just building the plan, giving it a quick review and update cycle, and off we go.

The final piece of the jigsaw fell into place at a European project management conference I attended in the last weeks of 1999. There I was fortunate enough to both hear a lecture by and—more importantly—have a two-hour conversation with Eli Goldratt. It turned out that the application of his Theory of Constraints to project management emerged with essentially the same conclusion. He just happened to call it "Critical Chain." He commented on the fact that everyone at the conference seemed happy with the state of things, despite the fact that many more projects fail than succeed.

I suddenly understood the reason why they were happy. Most project managers believe the project management war is unwinnable. They believe that provided they can hold the line and perhaps accomplish local successes now and again, that that is the best that can be achieved. I realized that the reason my previous two books and our company had been successful was that many people had believed it wasn't even possible to hold the line. In our small way, we had helped to stop the rout and stabilize the front—if I may continue with the military analogy.

I now realized that not only was it possible to hold the line, but it was possible to win the war. To use that hoary old chestnut, it would be over by Christmas.

This book is about winning the war.

Acknowledgements

For me, the nicest part of writing any book is this part. It is here that I get to recognize all of the people who contributed to making the book happen.

The trail starts with my editor at Artech House, the wonderful Viki Williams. It was her idea that we should do a book on this subject. Indeed, if Viki has her way, it'll only be a matter of time before the musical version appears. Viki's colleagues at Artech House, Suzanna 'Winona' Taggart helped to see it through the early stages, and Ruth Young, on one of her first assignments in publishing, showed that she's got the right stuff. The people at Artech House both in London and Boston, were a pleasure to work with: Val Moliere, Julie Lancashire, Darrell Judd, Jon Workman, and John Elwood.

Once again, Artech House's anonymous reviewer was Chuck 'Ming the Merciless' Howell. (Oh hell, Chuck, I've blown your cover!) His observations on how to improve the book were laser-like in their accuracy and correctness. I still owe Chuck dinner for the last book. I hope he'll be hungry when he comes to collect the dinner for this one.

On the subject of eating - particularly where large quantities of wine are involved - one of the most pleasant pieces of research I did for this book was to have a long lunch with Rob Quigley, Donal Geraghty, and Mick Walsh, producers at D-Rex Films. Rob, Donal, and Mick along with Tim O'Mahony, were kind enough to tell me how movies are made and to answer my stupid questions.

One rainy November day in Paris, I was fortunate enough to sit at the feet of a very great man— Eli Goldratt—for a few hours, and at the end of it he autographed my copy of *Critical Chain* with the words "Write to me when you think you are ready." This book is my way of saying that I think I'm ready now, Eli.

Other people played parts large and small in the unfolding of the book. Caroline Toland introduced me to the work of Alan Cooper. John Brackett of Boston University knows so much about so much and Paul Buckley at Warner Lambert reminded me of the importance of quality, and how it can get trodden on in the relentless drive to the deadline. Phil Chambers of the Institute of Business Analysts and Consultants showed me how, if you know what you're doing, a project can only have one result.

Though she won't know it until she reads this, my sister-in-law Paula McHugh taught me the importance of thinking in terms of sequences of events. (I always knew it was important—I just never realised how important.) The spreadsheets in Chapter 3 are derived from work done by Smith and Reinertsen in their book, *Developing Products in Half the Time*.

My colleagues at ETP share a dream of making the world a safer place for project managers. Every one of them has contributed at one time or another to this book. They are Colm Nolan, Jackie Costigan, Jonathan Dempsey, Elaine Scully, Bernadette Coleman, Trina Dunne, Tony O'Sullivan, Conor McCabe, Susan McHugh, Nancy Laureshen, Eimer Kernan, Alacoque McMenamin, Jim Seward, Clodagh Conway, Geraldine Myles, Shelly Burke, Val Downey, Karen Molloy, Tim O'Mahony, Brian Perse, Noel Kelly, Elaine Moore, and Sean McEvoy. My assistant, Sandra Foy, was selfless with *her* time so that I could spend mine on this.

In this book, as in all my previous ones, I cannot finish without mentioning my wife, business partner, and buddy Bernadette, and my two beautiful children, Hugh and Ferga, none of whom seem to mind that I don't have a proper job.

Introduction

There are many projects where shortening the project is not the primary consideration. In some cases, coming in within budget is the big issue. In others, smoothing the resources so that we don't have resourcing "spikes" is. However, in more and more projects these days, particularly in knowledge or high-tech industries, "shortening the project," "improving time to market," "doing the project in a Web year,[1]" "getting the product out in the window of opportunity," "running the project in Web-time[2]" are the phrases that are tripping off everyone's lips.

If your objective is to shorten your project then you must shorten the project's critical path. The critical path is shortest time in which the project can be done. A growing number of people use so-called "project management tools" to enable them to do this. If your interest is in shortening your project, then any tool you use has to be able to—above all else—show you the critical path of your project. There ought to be a red button on the tool which, when you select it, marks the critical path in characters of fire.

No tool that I'm aware of deals adequately with this business of the critical path. For example, there are more than three million users of Microsoft's Project product. Yet, in all recent versions of MS Project, the critical path function is safely tucked away in a reasonably anonymous

---

1   A "Web year" is loosely defined to be three calendar months.
2   I have taken the expression "running the project in Web-time" to mean *very significantly* shortening the project.

looking Wizard. Why do I mention this? Well, simply because if our wish is to shorten our projects, these project management tools may not help us all that much. We must look elsewhere.

An obvious place to begin looking is to ask ourselves whether anyone else has cracked this problem. If they have, then we ought to be able to adapt their solution and tools and processes to our own situation. Happily, there is indeed an industry that has cracked this problem, and as we indicated in the preface, that industry is the movie industry. There are two ideas we can lift directly from the movie industry that will help us enormously. One of these ideas applies to individual projects; the other is particularly significant when dealing with multiple projects.

Movies are developed in three phases:

1. Preproduction;

2. Production, that is, shooting the movie;

3. Postproduction.

By far the most expensive of these is the production phase. Because shooting a movie is so expensive, because every day's shooting costs so much, every attempt is made to keep this phase as short as possible. Work on keeping this phase as short as possible is begun during the preproduction phase. Here a plan is developed whose principle aim is to keep the production phase as short as possible. This plan is then implemented during the production phase. Is this starting to sound useful?

One of the key factors in implementing the plan is ensuring that people are available whenever they are needed—even if—horror of horrors!—this involves people waiting around for periods. Very few people on a movie do what is often referred to as "multitasking." For example, the Director of Photography doesn't spend Monday and Tuesday shooting Movie A, then Wednesday and half of Thursday on Movie B and the rest of the week on Movie C. Instead Movie A is shot and wrapped, followed by Movie B, followed by Movie C. This is also an idea we will use in this book and it is of immense significance in the multiple project situation.

Part 1 of the book is an Introduction. Chapter 2 describes in more detail the ideas we will be taking from the movie industry. Chapters 1 and 3 are about convincing firstly, yourself, and secondly, other people, that shortening projects is a good idea.

The remainder of the book describes a five-step approach that, if implemented, would enable you to run multiple shortened projects simultaneously.

Part 2 shows how all projects answer a need or solve a particular problem. The single most important consideration in having a successful project—never mind shortening it—is to establish that need, and identify the right problem to be solved. Part 1 shows how we can not only identify the correct need or problem, but also do so in the shortest possible time.

Having established the correct project to do, we then build a plan for the project. Part 3 describes how to do this, illustrating the approach with a fairly significant case study.

In Part 4 we describe the techniques and tools that enable us to shorten the project plan. We call this part "Turbocharging the Plan." Part 4 shows how we "sell" the plan to the other people involved in the project.

Part 5 describes monitoring, control, and reporting—in other words, how to execute the plan. It also deals with project post-mortems.

You may be responsible for running a number of projects using what the textbooks would call a "common resource pool," that is, the one bunch of people. In that case you need to read Part 6 about running (and shortening) multiple projects at the same time.

For those of you who read my earlier two books [1, 2] on project management, you may be wondering if I have jettisoned the famous "Ten Steps" which made appearances in both books. Far from it. They are alive and well. The work described in this book builds comfortably and neatly upon the Ten Steps. In particular, the steps are to be found, unchanged, in the following places:

Step 1: Visualize the goal	Chapter 4
Step 2: Make a list of jobs	Chapter 5
Step 3: There must be one leader	Chapter 6
Step 4: Assign people to jobs	Chapter 7
Step 5a: Have a margin for error	Chapters 8, 9
Step 5b: Manage expectations	Chapter 12
Step 6: Use an appropriate leadership style	Chapter 13
Step 7: Know what's going on	Chapter 13

If you have a project that you are interested in shortening, there are two possible "entry points." If you have not yet developed a plan for the project, you need to start at Chapter 3 and work your way through to Chapter 9. Then you can shorten the plan using Chapter 11. If you have already developed a plan, you need to check/correct it using Chapter 10 and then shorten it using Chapter 11.

Readers of my previous books will notice that unlike those books, this one is very prescriptive. Rather than saying "you could try this, or here are a bunch of ways to do that," it attempts to provide as foolproof a recipe as possible. As a result, while there may be a number of ways to do particular things, this book will, in general, say "do it this way," albeit giving sufficient justification for my stance (I hope).

Another aspect of trying to make the book as foolproof as possible, is that I have tried to ensure that there is no aspect of it where "it is left to the student as an exercise to complete this work." Everything is spelled out, and worked through as completely as possible. The worked example that appears in a number of chapters is intended as a complete and working model, which you can copy, modify, and use in your own work. The worked example is available, in its entirety on our Web site, www.etpint.com. I have a simple reason for trying to make things this straightforward. If you are going to run your projects in Web-time, then every minute counts. And the more I can help to stop you having to reinvent the wheel, the better that is.

Unlike my two previous books, this one contains a reasonable number of footnotes. While some of them deal with small points of clarification, quite a number of them serve to develop ideas that appear in the main text. I have deliberately laid things out in this way. The main text contains the basic idea and (sometimes) a few simple variants or enhancements of it. If there is an additional footnote, it generally describes further ways the idea can be used or extended. My intention is that if you find the basic idea useful, then you adopt it. Having done that and made it part of the way you operate, you can then return to the footnotes at a subsequent time and find further food for thought (and hopefully, action). Many of the footnotes are the suggestions of Chuck Howell, any author's dream reviewer.

The primary audience for the book is people involved in developing software or hardware-software, be they in software product development, information technology, telecommunications, or dot.com organizations. As a result, the worked example and many of the other examples are taken from the software development industry. However, I think anybody involved in a project in a high-tech or knowledge industry could benefit from this book, and could indeed run those projects in Web-time.

Finally, a note on the software used to create the examples in the text. The project plans were printed using Microsoft Project®, but were created using The Silver Bullet from ETP™. The movie industry examples in Chapter 2 were done with Movie Magic Scheduling.

References

1. O'Connell, F., *How To Run Successful Projects II—The Silver Bullet*, Hemel Hempstead, England: Prentice Hall, 1996.

2. O'Connell, F., *How To Run Successful High-Tech Project-Based Organizations*, Norwood: Artech House, 1999.

PART ONE
First Things First

In this part of the book we get some introductory stuff out of the way. Chapter 1 describes what you're letting yourself in for if you choose to run your projects in Web time. Chapter 2 explains the concepts we are taking from the movie making industry to apply to our own projects. Chapter 3 talks about convincing other people that all of this is a good idea. It shows how to calculate the effect of the project being both shortened and (especially inadvertently) lengthened.

1

You Must Really Want To Do It

> ➤ This chapter describes the different levels of planning that get done on typical projects. It shows that a decent level of planning is often quite unusual.

> ➤ It goes on to say that to significantly shorten projects, even more planning is needed. It notes that this notion may not always be attractive to people.

> ➤ This chapter also describes the principle reasons why projects have a tendency to take more, rather than less, time.

Introduction

I'm assuming that anyone turning to this chapter to see whether or not it would perhaps be worthwhile to buy this book, or take it from the library, or steal it (don't), is doing so for at least one reason. They want to know what the "catch" is. And indeed, not to disappoint you, I will explain shortly what the catch is. But first there is something which almost any project manager reading this will be thinking and so, rather than let it fester, let's get it out of the way.

I fully accept that sometimes projects get done in impossibly short periods of time with unbelievably inadequate resources and with scant planning. I have seen this happen myself; I have been involved in such projects. I know it is possible with a (generally small) highly motivated, extremely skilled, team.

However, many times more often, people who try to do projects in this way, screw them up completely.

3

And even if they don't screw them up, the completion of such a project is no guarantee that such a trick can be repeated. And who's to say that the project might not have been a whole lot easier or—heresy of heresies—even quicker, if there had been some halfway decent planning in the first place?

However, the fact remains that such impossible missions occasionally do happen, and I am not denying the fact. If however, you believe that all projects can and should be done like this, then DO NOT BUY THIS BOOK. You will find it upsetting and a waste of your money.

If however, you are being driven by the need for shorter and shorter time to market and would like to do something about it, I'd recommend that you read the rest of this chapter and then make your buying decision.

How Much Planning Do We Actually Do?

In my experience, one comes across a number of different grades of planning. The lowest grade, the F- of project planning, is where there is no plan at all. It's in the project manager's head—whatever that might mean—and, on a day-by-day basis, the plan is revealed to the team.

A step up from this is where there is a high level Gantt chart—perhaps no more than a page or two—showing high level milestones.

Stepping up from this again—we would now be grading these C or D—comes the document containing a fairly detailed Work Breakdown Structure and Gantt Chart, risk analysis, lists of deliverables and stakeholders.

Into the B student range, you can add in:

- Completion criteria;

- Acceptance criteria;

- Resources required—skill levels and resource loading;

- Project budget;

- Project organization chart.

You get a B+ if the plan is reviewed and signed off.

And finally, the A or A+ plan is where the project manager does everything the B student does, but then adds in one additional, crucial extra. After signoff, the plan is not just placed on file as a record of the fact that we passed certain criteria and were allowed to proceed to the next phase of the project. Rather it is used to steer the project and is continuously updated over its lifetime.

In general, project planning is not regarded as a fun activity—except perhaps by those whose idea of beauty is an exquisitely crafted MS Project chart. Rather it is treated as a necessary evil that has to be gone through so that the fun can begin. It is often thought of, or referred to as "the administrative side of the project."

And Now the Bad News

If you want to achieve the maximum amount of shortening possible on your project, then you may be upset to hear that even more planning is going to be needed. This is the "catch" we spoke of earlier. More will be needed at the beginning. However, the good news is that this may result in less project management actually being needed once the project gets rolling.

Once again, if you find this notion unattractive DO NOT BUY THIS BOOK. You will find it upsetting and a waste of your money.

So Why Do Projects Take So Much Time?

At this stage I'm assuming we're left with those people who really want to do something about shortening their projects. Now let's take a look at why the pesky things take so much time in the first place.

As I write this, I've just come from a little project to run a recruitment advertisement in the newspaper. This project has taken much longer than any of us intended, and the reasons why are very instructive, because this project exhibited most, if not all, of the things that cause projects to take more rather than less time. These things were:

1. The goal of the project wasn't clear. Sure we were running a recruitment ad, but current and potential customers would also see it. If we wanted it to, it could also say things to them. Once we realized this, it took us extra time we hadn't planned on to build in these other facets. In general, this can be described as the goal of the project not being properly defined, so that new things to be done are constantly coming to light or being identified.

2. The process by which the ad would be written and approved wasn't really worked through. In the end, many more people than we had originally imagined, had input to the review and signoff. In other words, many more jobs than we had originally expected needed to be done.

3. This business of the process is important. I once heard it said that projects were a bit like adultery—periods of frenzied activity interspersed with periods of just waiting around. This effect was certainly experienced on our project where a bout of furious activity was followed by a lull in the fighting while we waited for the next step to be carried out.

4. No one person was responsible for getting the ad done.

5. Nor was it 100% explicit who would be needed at what times to provide text for the ad or to review the results. In other words, not only was the process not clear, but the responsibilities at each stage of the process were not clear either. (And of course, if the process wasn't understood, how could the responsibilities be identified?)

6. A corollary of this was that since people didn't know they would be needed, they had arranged to do other things and so were unavailable when their time came. (It should be noted too that often, even when people do know they will be needed, they have inadvertently or otherwise overbooked themselves, and so are unavailable.)

7. Nobody had planned this little project and in particular, nobody had identified what the critical path was. (Remember that the critical path is the longest chain of dependent tasks in the project. It determines the time it will take to finish the project.) As a result, nobody was really focused on the effect a delay in one piece of the project might have on the rest of it.

8. A corollary of this is that nobody knew what, if any, advantages there might be to completing their bit of the project as quickly as possible.

9. And a second corollary was that, in general, people being people would leave their bit to as late as possible before starting. (Not knowing the critical path, this seems an innocent enough activity.)

10. Maybe it's a separate thing, maybe it's an accumulation of all of the preceding things, but I call it "Where did the week go?" syndrome.

Did you ever have one of those weeks when you get to the end of it, and you wonder where the days could have disappeared to, and what the hell you achieved? No? Lucky you!

As a result of these things, the ad drifted on and days were lost waiting for people to fit things into their schedule and come back with their piece done, so that the next bit could take place. It's important to say too that none of the things that had to get done was a surprise—once we thought about it. The problem was we didn't think about it.

The method we will describe in Parts 2 through 6 of this book will end up addressing precisely these issues. First, though, let us look at an industry where they do all of this rather well—with some well-publicized exceptions—and see what we can learn and whether there are any tools we can borrow. That industry is the film industry. We do it in Chapter 2.

2 How the Movies Do It

➤ This chapter shows how by converting the movie script (product to be built) into a series of strips, which are then analyzed on a strip board; movies are shot in the shortest time possible.

➤ It also discusses why "multitasking" does not really take place in movie production.

Shooting Movies in the Shortest Possible Time

If you have ever looked at the screenplay of a movie, you will have seen that it consists of anywhere up to two or three hundred scenes. Each scene is described in terms of:

- Setting (location);

- Whether the scene is an interior or exterior scene;

- The time of day at which it takes place;

- The people involved in the scene;

- What those people say and do.

Think of the script as the product to be built. Notice that, amongst many other things, the script gives us a feeling for "how much stuff there is"—how much work has to get done.

Now, when the time comes to plan the making of the film, somebody—say, an assistant director—goes through the script, scene by scene, and builds what are know as "breakdown sheets." There is a breakdown sheet per scene. An example of a breakdown sheet is given in Figure 2.1.

9

Breakdown Sheet

Scene # 1, 8, 211   Breakdown Page # 1

Script Page _____   Int/Ext: INT _____

Page Count2/8   Day/Night: Night

Scene Description: ____ Old man nearly burns his apartment down _____

Setting: _____

Location   _____

Sequence: _____ Script Day: _____

Cast Members	Extras	Props
1. Old man		Box of eggs Cast iron pot Cooker
	Stunts	**Vehicles**
Special Effects Cooker needs to catch fire	**Costumes**	**Makeup**
Set Dressing	**Greenery**	**Special Equipment**
Notes:		

Figure 2.1   Breakdown sheet.

Notice how potentially detailed the breakdown sheet is. For a particular scene it could tell us everything we need to know—interior/exterior, setting, time of day, cast members, extras, stunts, vehicles, props, special effects, costumes, makeup, set dressing, greenery, and special equipment—about shooting this particular scene. In addition, there are other categories—livestock, animal handler, music, sound, security, additional labor, optical effects, mechanical effects, and anything else—that can also appear on a breakdown sheet.

To schedule the movie a production board or strip board is created. (Typically, the process takes one person maybe five or six days.) An example is given in Figure 2.2.

Here a strip corresponds to each breakdown sheet. Notice a couple of important quantities on the strips—"Page Count" and "Shoot Day." Page Count tells us how much of the script gets shot in that particular breakdown sheet. Page Count is measured in units of eighths of a page. Shoot Day tells us which day that particular breakdown sheet gets shot. Note that once we have built a strip board, we can see exactly what bits of the movie, and how much of the movie will get shot on each particular day. That is to say, we know precisely which pieces of the product are being developed on precisely which days. Furthermore, the breakdown sheets tell us in excruciating detail, everything we need to know when we come to develop those particular pieces of the product. (Notice too how easy it is to monitor and control against such a scheme.)

Strip boards were developed so as to make it easy to move the strips around. By moving the strips around we determine the order in which the scenes in the movie get shot, that is, the schedule. More importantly though, we can optimize that order. We can for example, order the strips by set. This will enable us to shoot all of the scenes that take place on a particular set before moving on to the next set.

Finally, one other concept that is of interest: movies use the notion of a "held day." A held day is a day that somebody is being paid even though they're not scheduled to work.

To summarize then, movies are scheduled using the following technique:

1. A complete description (script) of the product to be built exists.

2. This description gives us an accurate feel for the amount of work to be done (number of scenes or pages to be shot).

3. Using this description, the work and other resources required to develop each particular piece of the product can be calculated.

Figure 2.2   Strip board.

		Night
	Day/Night:	Night
	Page Count:	2/8
	Int/Ext:	INT

		Scenes 1, 8, 211
Picture:		
Picture No.:		
Producer:		
Director:		
U.P.M.		
Asst. Director		
Script Dated:		
Timing:		
Prepared By:		
Old man	1	1
Extras:		
		n

4. These elements of work can then be chained together to form the schedule.

5. This schedule can be optimized.

We will use some of these ideas shortly.

Multitasking

Multitasking—where somebody works on a number of projects at the same time—doesn't really happen in the movie industry. When the crew gets assigned to one movie, then typically, they work on that movie until their work is complete. This is in fairly stark contrast to high tech industries where people can be spread across numerous projects—leading a project, involved in reviews on another one, supporting a third one, and so on.

If anything movies go to the other extreme. There are some people for whom there is only a possibility that their services may be needed on the movie. Nonetheless they are hired, are kept on the payroll and are available should they be required. The standby painter is an example. His job is to touch up the set should it get damaged during takes. It may be that this never happens and then he will never be required. But the alternative—where the entire project is held up while we wait for somebody to paint over some mark on a set—is clearly unthinkable.

And the Result of All This?

Picture a graph about any project ever run in a high-tech industry. On the horizontal axis is time, on the vertical axis are: stress, overtime, pressure, panic, or all-round, general angst. The graph starts out fairly level. Then, as we approach early milestones, the graph goes up. It continues to rise through mid-project milestones and by the time we are approaching the delivery date, the graph is going through the roof. With a reasonable amount of up-front planning, this graph can be flattened to a greater or a lesser extent. But the general shape of the curve is probably fairly constant over the vast run of high-tech projects.

In the movies the effect is quite the opposite. There may be some panics during the planning stage, but once the plan (as represented by the strip board) is in place, calm prevails. The shooting runs smoothly with very few panics. It is this level of calm we will aspire to on our projects.

3 Convincing the Others

➤This chapter shows how to convince those around you that shortening the project is a good idea. It describes how to calculate the reward if the project is done early and the loss if it runs late.

Introduction

Like anything new in life, one of the first things you'll find if you decide to shorten your project is that other people will want to see you fail. Ok, so I'm being too cynical. Let's be more precise and fair.

Some people may indeed want to see you fail—life is sometimes like that. However, some will probably want you to succeed. And the vast majority may be indifferent—as long as what you are planning to do doesn't affect them; as long as they don't have to change the way they do things. Unfortunately, some if not all, of the people involved in the project, are going to have to change the way they do things. We're not talking earth-shattering changes here, but we are talking changes.

Hopefully we will see, as the book proceeds, the various benefits that can flow from running your projects in Web time, but for the moment, let's go straight for the jugular. What's the quickest way to their hearts? What's the way that, if it's done right, is most convincing and people find hardest to argue with or refute? Why, show them the money, of course.[1] That's right, let's show them the savings if we do succeed in

---

1 Actually, there's another reason to shorten projects, which is perhaps as compelling as any, given the problems these days with finding and retaining good people: the shorter the project, the lower the exposure to key people leaving. Also the rapid pace and sense of achievement with a Web-time project may make it more attractive to star performers. (I'm grateful to Chuck Howell for this important observation.)

shortening the project. And we can also, while we're at it, show them the downside losses if the project runs over. (If nothing else, setting out to shorten your project is an action to reduce the risk—inherent in every project—that the project will actually run over schedule or budget.)

Building a Profit Model

In general, the savings realized by shortening a project are of two types: the savings due to being able to disband the team sooner and move them on to other work, and the revenue gained (or savings achieved) by having the product (or system) out in the field sooner. By developing a simple spreadsheet we can calculate what these are and, as a result, make the decision to support what we are doing, something of a no-brainer. The basic profit model spreadsheet to do this is shown in Figure 3.1.

In the rest of this section we describe it line by line. In their book, *Developing Products in Half the Time* [1], the authors talk of models like this being owned by "financial analysts." In an ideal world, this would indeed be the right way to go about things. However, in my experience, it is often the project manager who has to rough one of these spreadsheets together. Since all of the information you require may not be at your fingertips, we will describe, as we go, the various sources of the material you require. If an expected source can't come up with what you require, don't worry—what you do then is to make some assumptions on their behalf. That then puts the ball in their court to refute or support the assumptions.

Let's assume we are producing a software product. The current (unshortened) plan is to produce the product during a first year of development and then sell the product during two subsequent years. It is assumed that by the end of the second year of sales, the product will be coming/have come to the end of its life, and will need to be replaced by a new version or a new product.

1. Average sales price. We assume that the average sales price is $350. Sales or Marketing have figured this out. They have done so by doing projections of the number of units they expect to sell. Ideally they haven't just come up with a single figure, that is, we expect to sell 375,892 units (!), but rather, they have said something like this. There are a number of different price points, depending on how many licenses a customer buys. We expect to sell so many units at each of these price points. Multiplying each number of units by the

Calculation of savings due to shortening the project
(1) All figures in US$
(2) Figures shown in italics must be entered by the user

	Assumption	Development -Q4	-Q3	-Q2	-Q1	Year 1 Q1	Q2	Q3	Q4	Year 2 Q1	Q2	Q3	Q4
PRODUCT REVENUES													
Average sales price	*350*					350	350	350	350	350	350	350	350
Market size in units						40,000	40,000	50,000	60,000	80,000	120,000	120,000	120,000
Market share						20%	25%	25%	25%	20%	15%	15%	15%
Unit sales						8,000	10,000	12,500	15,000	16,000	18,000	18,000	18,000
Dollar sales						2,800,000	3,500,000	4,375,000	5,250,000	5,600,000	6,300,000	6,300,000	6,300,000
PRODUCT COSTS													
Units cost	*50*					50	50	50	50	50	50	50	50
Cost of goods sold						400,000	500,000	625,000	750,000	800,000	900,000	900,000	900,000
Gross margin (in $)						2,400,000	3,000,000	3,750,000	4,500,000	4,800,000	5,400,000	5,400,000	5,400,000
Gross margin (in %)						86%	86%	86%	86%	86%	86%	86%	86%
DEVELOPMENT COSTS													
Cost per team member	*100,000*	100,000	100,000	100,000	100,000	100,000	100,000	100,000	100,000	100,000	100,000	100,000	100,000
Number of team members		*2*	*6*	*6*	*4*	*2*	*1*	*0.5*	*0.5*	*0.5*	*0.5*	*0.5*	*0.5*
Development team cost		200,000	600,000	600,000	400,000	200,000	100,000	50,000	50,000	50,000	50,000	50,000	50,000
Marketing costs	*15%*					420,000	525,000	656,250	787,500	840,000	945,000	945,000	945,000
General & administrative	*5%*					140,000	175,000	218,750	262,500	280,000	315,000	315,000	315,000
Total costs		200,000	600,000	600,000	400,000	760,000	800,000	925,000	1,100,000	1,170,000	1,310,000	1,310,000	1,310,000
PROFIT / LOSS													
Profit(loss) before tax		−200,000	−600,000	−600,000	−400,000	2,040,000	2,700,000	3,450,000	4,150,000	4,430,000	4,990,000	4,990,000	4,990,000
Cumulative profit before tax (PBT)		−200,000	−800,000	−1,400,000	−1,800,000	240,000	2,940,000	6,390,000	10,540,000	14,970,000	19,960,000	24,950,000	29,940,000

Cumulative PBT   29,940,000

Figure 3.1   Profit model spreadsheet.

price point, adding them all up and dividing by the total number of units gives us the average sales price per unit. It is assumed that this price remains constant over the life of the product.

2. Market size, Market share, Unit sales. These are the Sales and Marketing projections. Ideally Sales and Marketing have done these projections by looking at the total market size and trying to estimate a market share. You can then calculate unit sales by multiplying market size by market share. Sometimes people just guess the unit sales!

3. Dollar sales. These are unit sales times unit price.

4. Unit cost. This is the cost to manufacture the product—duplication, packaging, shrink wrapping. You'll have to ask Finance for this figure. If they don't know (!), call up your local software duplication company and ask them. For simplicity, this is also assumed to be constant over the life of the product. In reality, you might be able to cut slightly better deals for manufacturing larger volumes.

5. Cost of goods sold. This is the total cost to us of the entire product that we sell over its life. It is calculated by multiplying unit cost by unit sales.

6. Gross margin (in $). This is dollar sales minus cost of goods sold.

7. Gross margin (in %). This is the gross margin in dollars divided by the dollar sales.

8. Cost per team member. If you're lucky, you'll be able to call the Finance people and they'll be able to give you chapter and verse on burdened and unburdened rates, and the price of a top software engineer versus a trainee versus a QA person versus a top of the range project manager. In reality you often have to make these numbers up for yourself. Then—and documenting your assumptions, of course—you might assume an average price per team member. To calculate this you might use a rule of thumb that said that anywhere from one and a half to two and a half times salary was a reasonable way to calculate the burdened labor rate. (I usually use double as it makes the sums as easy as possible.)

9. Number of team members. This is probably averaged out from your month-by-month staffing levels. For example, if the project runs for its first quarter like this:

Month 1	Month 2	Month 3
1	2	3

you would decide that the average for the quarter was 2. The example in Figure 3.1 shows that eventually, somebody ends up supporting the product half time.

10. Development team cost. This is cost per team member multiplied by number of team members.

11. Marketing cost for general and administrative. These are both calculated as a percentage of sales. Again the Finance people should be able to give you the numbers. If not, you could perhaps use the ones that are suggested here, that is, 15% for marketing and 5% for general and administrative.

12. Total costs. This is the sum of the development team cost, the marketing costs, and the general and administrative costs.

13. Profit (loss) before tax. This is the difference between dollar sales and total costs.

14. Cumulative profit (loss). This is the—in this case—profit accumulated over the life of the product. This is a simple measure of the success of the development project.

Show Them the Money

Now let's see what we can find out if we can shorten the project by a quarter—using the techniques that we will describe later in the book. (Note: 3 months in a 12-month project might or might not be regarded as a big savings. I have chosen 3 months here just to make the example easier to work. If you wanted to work in months rather than quarters, then you might want to denominate the spreadsheet columns in months.)

The result is shown in Figure 3.2.

The first thing that happens in this scenario is that all the revenues get pulled back a quarter. In addition, development costs are shortened by 3 months. Let's assume that this is achieved by adding an extra person at the beginning and staying at maximum project strength for the duration. (These assumptions would be replaced by facts once we had

Effect of shortening the project by 3 months on the basic profit model
(1) All figures in US$
(2) Figures shown in italics must be entered by the user

	Input	Development				Year 1				Year 2		
		-Q4	-Q3	-Q2	-Q1	Q1	Q2	Q3	Q4	Q1	Q2	Q3
PRODUCT REVENUES												
Average sales price	350				350	350	350	350	350	350	350	350
Market size in units					40,000	40,000	50,000	60,000	80,000	120,000	120,000	120,000
Market share					20%	25%	25%	25%	20%	15%	15%	15%
Unit sales					8,000	10,000	12,500	15,000	16,000	18,000	18,000	18,000
Dollar sales					2,800,000	3,500,000	4,375,000	5,250,000	5,600,000	6,300,000	6,300,000	6,300,000
PRODUCT COSTS												
Units cost	50				50	50	50	50	50	50	50	50
Cost of goods sold					400,000	500,000	625,000	750,000	800,000	900,000	900,000	900,000
Gross margin (in $)					2,400,000	3,000,000	3,750,000	4,500,000	4,800,000	5,400,000	5,400,000	5,400,000
Gross margin (in %)					86%	86%	86%	86%	86%	86%	86%	86%
DEVELOPMENT COSTS												
Cost per team member	100,000	100,000	100,000	100,000	100,000	100,000	100,000	100,000	100,000	100,000	100,000	100,000
Number of team members		3	6	6	2	1	0.5	0.5	0.5	0.5	0.5	0.5
Development team cost		300,000	600,000	600,000	200,000	100,000	50,000	50,000	50,000	50,000	50,000	50,000
Marketing costs	15%				420,000	525,000	656,250	787,500	840,000	945,000	945,000	945,000
General & administrative	5%				140,000	175,000	218,750	262,500	280,000	315,000	315,000	315,000
Total costs		300,000	600,000	600,000	760,000	800,000	925,000	1,100,000	1,170,000	1,310,000	1,310,000	1,310,000
PROFIT / LOSS												
Profit(loss) before tax		-300,000	-600,000	-600,000	2,040,000	2,700,000	3,450,000	4,150,000	4,430,000	4,990,000	4,990,000	4,990,000
Cumulative profit before tax (PBT)		-300,000	-900,000	-1,500,000	540,000	3,240,000	6,690,000	10,840,000	15,270,000	20,260,000	25,250,000	30,240,000

Cumulative PBT	30,240,000

Figure 3.2   Profit model spreadsheet shortened by a quarter.

shortened the plan.)   The net result of this is that the costs to do with supporting and marketing the product are also pulled back a quarter.

There are now some other possible effects to do with being in the market sooner that we have to make calls on:

- Does being there earlier mean we can charge a higher price until our competitors get there too?

- Will we get a higher market share by being there earlier?

- Can we assume that our product's lifetime is extended—say, for example, by that additional quarter that we saved?

However we answer these and similar questions, it is clearly easy to model them in our spreadsheet. Say, for example, we:

- Decide to charge a higher price ($400) for the first two quarters of sales;

- Assume we get a five percentage point higher market share;

- Assume that we get an additional quarter's sales but at half the volume of the quarter that precedes it.

Figure 3.3 shows the effect of these three changes. (They are shown in bold.)

What if it Runs Over?

Finally, our spreadsheet can be used to show the effect of the project running over. Let's assume it were to overshoot by a quarter. What would this do to the basic profit model from Figure 3.1? The answer is shown in Figure 3.4. (We have made the assumption that the team stays at full strength for an additional three months.)

First of all, the revenues get shunted out to the right. So too do the support and marketing costs. And the additional three months of development is dropped into the middle of the project. The resulting drop in cumulative profits is shown. In this case the drop is from $29,940,000 to $24,350,000, a loss of $5,590,000.

Doing something like this, at this stage, merely whets the appetites of the powers-that-be. It shows them the kind of paybacks that can be achieved, if they try to shorten a project. It also highlights for them the

Effect of some other changes
(1) All figures in US$
(2) Figures shown in italics must be entered by the user

	Effect	Development −Q4	−Q3	−Q2	−Q1	Year 1 Q1	Q2	Q3	Q4	Year 2 Q1	Q2	Q3	Q4
PRODUCT REVENUES													
Average sales price	*350*				400	400	350	350	350	350	350	350	350
Market size in units					40,000	40,000	50,000	60,000	80,000	120,000	120,000	120,000	120,000
Market share					25%	30%	30%	30%	25%	20%	20%	20%	10%
Unit sales					10,000	12,000	15,000	18,000	20,000	24,000	24,000	24,000	12,000
Dollar sales					3,500,000	4,200,000	5,250,000	6,300,000	7,000,000	8,400,000	8,400,000	8,400,000	4,200,000
PRODUCT COSTS													
Units cost	*50*				50	50	50	50	50	50	50	50	50
Cost of goods sold					500,000	600,000	750,000	900,000	1,000,000	1,200,000	1,200,000	1,200,000	600,000
Gross margin (in $)					3,000,000	3,600,000	4,500,000	5,400,000	6,000,000	7,200,000	7,200,000	7,200,000	3,600,000
Gross margin (in %)					86%	86%	86%	86%	86%	86%	86%	86%	86%
DEVELOPMENT COSTS													
Cost per team member	*100,000*	100,000	100,000	100,000	100,000	100,000	100,000	100,000	100,000	100,000	100,000	100,000	100,000
Number of team members		*3*	*6*	*6*	*2*	*1*	*0.5*	*0.5*	*0.5*	*0.5*	*0.5*	*0.5*	*0.5*
Development team cost		300,000	600,000	600,000	200,000	100,000	50,000	50,000	50,000	50,000	50,000	50,000	50,000
Marketing costs	*15%*				525,000	630,000	787,500	945,000	1,050,000	1,260,000	1,260,000	1,260,000	630,000
General & administrative	*5%*				175,000	210,000	262,500	315,000	350,000	420,000	420,000	420,000	210,000
Total costs		300,000	600,000	600,000	900,000	940,000	1,100,000	1,310,000	1,450,000	1,730,000	1,730,000	1,730,000	890,000
PROFIT / LOSS													
Profit(loss) before tax		−300,000	−600,000	−600,000	2,600,000	3,260,000	4,150,000	4,990,000	5,550,000	6,670,000	6,670,000	6,670,000	3,310,000
Cumulative profit before tax (PBT)		−300,000	−900,000	−1,500,000	1,100,000	4,360,000	8,510,000	13,500,000	19,050,000	25,720,000	32,390,000	39,060,000	42,370,000

Cumulative PBT	42,370,000

Figure 3.3   Profit model spreadsheet incorporating other changes.

Figure 3.4 Drop in profits due to three month delay in project
(1) All figures in US$
(2) Figures shown in italics must be entered by the user

	Input	Development				Year 1				Year 2			
		-Q4	-Q3	-Q2	-Q1	Q1	Q2	Q3	Q4	Q1	Q2	Q3	Q4
PRODUCT REVENUES													
Average sales price	*350*						350	350	350	350	350	350	350
Market size in units							40,000	40,000	50,000	60,000	80,000	120,000	120,000
Market share							20%	25%	25%	25%	20%	15%	15%
Unit sales							8,000	10,000	12,500	15,000	16,000	18,000	18,000
Dollar sales							2,800,000	3,500,000	4,375,000	5,250,000	5,600,000	6,300,000	6,300,000
PRODUCT COSTS													
Units cost	*50*												
Cost of goods sold							400,000	500,000	625,000	750,000	800,000	900,000	900,000
Gross margin (in $)							2,400,000	3,000,000	3,750,000	4,500,000	4,800,000	5,400,000	5,400,000
Gross margin (in %)							86%	86%	86%	86%	86%	86%	86%
DEVELOPMENT COSTS													
Cost per team member	*100,000*	100,000	100,000	100,000	100,000	100,000	100,000	100,000	100,000	100,000	100,000	100,000	100,000
Number of team members	*2*	*2*	*6*	*6*	*4*	*4*	*2*	*1*	*0.5*	*0.5*	*0.5*	*0.5*	*0.5*
Development team cost		200,000	600,000	600,000	400,000	400,000	200,000	100,000	50,000	50,000	50,000	50,000	50,000
Marketing costs	*15%*						420,000	525,000	656,250	787,500	840,000	945,000	945,000
General & administrative	*5%*						140,000	175,000	218,750	262,500	280,000	315,000	315,000
Total costs		200,000	600,000	600,000	400,000	400,000	760,000	800,000	925,000	1,100,000	1,170,000	1,310,000	1,310,000
PROFIT / LOSS													
Profit(loss) before tax		-200,000	-600,000	-600,000	-400,000	-400,000	2,040,000	2,700,000	3,450,000	4,150,000	4,430,000	4,990,000	4,990,000
Cumulative profit before tax (PBT)		-200,000	-800,000	-1,400,000	-2,000,000	-2,400,000	-360,000	2,340,000	5,790,000	9,940,000	14,370,000	19,360,000	24,350,000

Cumulative PBT | 24,350,000 |

Figure 3.4 Profit model spreadsheet showing overshoot.

risks they run should the project run over. What you are trying to do here is nothing more than get them interested in the notion that it might be a good idea. If you can do that, you then have to come back to them with the definitive numbers for your project, so that they can see the real picture. That is what Chapters 4 through 12 build toward and ultimately enable you to do.

Reference

1. Smith, P. G., and D. G. Reinertsen, *Developing Products in Half the Time*, New York: Wiley, 1998.

PART TWO
Answer the Need

In this part of the book we show how all projects answer a certain need. The key to a successful shortened project is to know exactly which project to launch and what its content should be. Chapter 4 describes how to identify and scope the right project.

4 Identify the Right Project

➤ Identifying the correct project boundary that will maximize the win conditions of the stakeholders is the key to a successful project, never mind a shortened project. Also the greatest savings in project elapsed time can be achieved during the early part of the project.

➤ This chapter describes how to ensure that the correct project gets done. It also introduces the worked example that we will use. The worked example will be added to at the end of every subsequent chapter.

Introduction

In their book, *Developing Products in Half the Time* [1], the authors Smith and Reinertsen refer to the beginning of the project as "the fuzzy front end." They say this:

> Time is an irreplaceable resource. When a month of potential development time is squandered, it can never be recovered ... each month of delay has a quantifiable cost of delay. Our goal as developers is to find opportunities to buy cycle time for less than this cost. These opportunities, large and small, appear throughout the development process. There is, however, one place that we could call the "bargain basement" of cycle time reduction opportunities. It is the place that we consistently find the least expensive opportunities to achieve large improvements in time to market. We call this stage of development the Fuzzy Front End of the development program. It is the fuzzy zone between when the opportunity is known and when we mount a serious effort on the development project.

27

While all of this is profoundly true, particularly the observation on time being an irreplaceable resource, it is also true that the greatest potential to get things badly wrong also occurs in the fuzzy front end. A project is (or should be) an answer to a need—the observation is Eli Goldratt's. Often, in deciding which project to run (i.e., what its scope and content should be), we are like people who are trying to give an answer without knowing the question.

As an example, let's assume a software company decides it needs to develop a new product. The Board says "the share price has been languishing. The company needs a new killer product." The CEO says "there's a window of opportunity and we're the people to go for it." Finance say "the product must have high margins and bring in this much profit over the next whatever." Marketing say "it's gotta beat these features that our competitors' products have." In the time-honored tradition, Sales announce the product, say it will demo at Comdex with general availability a few weeks later, and answer "yes" anytime a customer or potential customer asks if it will have the blah feature. Engineering say the product has to run on these platforms, have these features, be Web-enabled (whatever that might mean), and be written in Java.

Now, how do we launch a project that will achieve most or all of these aims? What should be its scope and content? When will the project be over? Is it when the project demos at Comdex? Is it when Engineering are finished QA? Or when Finance have put the money in the bank? Or when the share price (hopefully) soars? If we don't get the right answer here, we will end up doing the wrong project. And all the shortening in the world won't help if we've ended up doing the wrong thing.

The rest of this chapter shows you how to make the right call. There are two sections. The next one shows you how to max out the opportunity to shorten the project in the fuzzy front end. The one after that shows how to double-check that what you've decided to do is correct.

What's Our Project?

We saw in Chapter 1 how projects can often be very start-stop in nature. We do some stuff and then we have to wait, for example, for reviews, or approval, or for input from other people. Nowhere is this truer than in the fuzzy front end. Everyone believes they have something to contribute, lots of people want signoff, and there are always those who feel that their input is being ignored. At the same time, because the project hasn't really yet gotten off the ground, there are always a million and one things more immediate and pressing. The net result of all of this can be a long and frustrating period while requirements are identified, nailed down, and agreed.

We can circumvent all of this, and in the process begin running our project in Web-time, by trying to "concertina" all of this into one decisive event which we will call a project scoping session. I raised this notion in my first book, and I remember a reviewer at the time generally praising the book but saying that this notion of a mass brainstorming session was really a pretty passé idea. Newer things were there now—automatic requirements tracking, product definition methodologies and other great gizmos that relegated my idea to that great bin labelled "old-fashioned ideas." It may indeed be old fashioned. I couldn't necessarily say. All I know is that it's devastatingly effective. Here's how you do it.

1. Identify all of the people who are entitled to a say in the scope of the project. This needs to include those people who sometimes don't necessarily appear high on the organization chart, but have the power to change everything at the stroke of a pen.

2. Find a day when they can all come together. If all you're doing is scoping the project (as opposed to scoping it and planning it), then half a day to a day should be more than enough. (We'll come back to this idea again. In my experience, it is possible to do both the scoping, that is, the Chapter 4 stuff and the project planning (the stuff in Chapters 5 through 9) all in the same one 1–2 day session. However, for the moment, let's assume we're just concerned with the scoping.)

3. Make it clear that you will be regarding this day as day 1 of your project.

4. Make them do some preparation beforehand. Send them a memo along the lines of the one in Figure 4.1.

5. Once all the participants are in the room, take them through the following seven questions, noting down the answers on a flipchart.

   · How will we know when this project is over?

   · What constitutes its end point?

   · What physical things will it produce?

Figure 4.1   Briefing note for
scoping participants. (Also, it's
part of point 4.)

Briefing note for participants in the project scoping session

Essentially, the purpose of this session is to establish what the project is trying to achieve. The best way for individual participants to prepare for this is to try to do the following:

(a)   Document a goal for their piece of the project

You should need no more than half a day to do this preparation, and should limit yourself to whatever level of detail can be achieved in that time.

(a)   Goal

To do this, ask yourself questions like

- How will I know when the project is over?

- What will things be like? How will the company—or my piece of it—have changed?

- Who are the various people and/or groups (the stakeholders) affected by the project?

- For each of these individuals or groups, what would constitute a successful project from their point of view?

- Are these different views compatible? If not, is there a compromise set that we can live with?

Figure 4.1   Briefing note for scoping participants. (Also, it's part of point 4.)

- How will the quality of those things be determined?
- What things are definitely part of this project?
- What things are definitely not part of this project?
- Are there any people issues that we need to be aware of in connection with this project?

6.   Play back the answers to them—"So when this has happened, and this has happened, and this has happened, the project will be over, right? So if all this happened, we would class the project as a success, yes?" Add the additional detail that flows from this.

7.   When they have run dry, this is your first cut project scope.

Will This Keep the Stakeholders Happy?

To check on your first cut scope, do the following:

1.   Tape the flipchart pages containing the first cut scope up on the wall.

2. Now, armed with the flipchart again, ask them to help you make a list of all of the project stakeholders.

3. When you have done this, ask them now whether the project scope, as described around the walls, would make each stakeholder in turn happy?

4. If the answer is yes, then go on to the next stakeholder. If the answer is no, then add the additional things that get thrown up.

5. When you have finished the list of stakeholders, and you've played it back to them one more time, and nobody has anything more to add, then this is the final project scope.

6. Write it up and you're done.

Worked Example

A Note on the Worked Example

It had been my original intention in this part of the book to take a real live customer project (with their permission, of course), change the names to protect the innocent, and work it through. There would have been several advantages to this. It would have been a real industrial-strength project to which to apply our method. We would—of course (!)—have seen the method dramatically shortening the project, thereby proving that it worked.

However, there were also disadvantages. We would be stuck with whatever application area the project occurred in and I know myself that some people find this a bit of a turnoff. That is, unless they happen to be involved in that area themselves, in which case they find it riveting—so much so that they get caught up in the details of the application or the technology rather than the project management issues that we are trying to illustrate. In addition there were points I wanted to illustrate— particularly about Work Breakdown Structures (WBSs) that might not necessarily pop up in a naturally occurring project, or that I didn't want to be dictated by the circumstances of the project. And finally, if I wanted to prove that the method worked, I could use our Web site[1] to report on real-live applications and successes.

---

1   www.etpint.com

On balance therefore, I chose to go for a made-up example because this would give me more scope to show all the things I wanted to show. However, as regards the key issue—that of the example being industrial-strength, that is still very much intact. The book contains a full scale, end-to-end application of our method to a project that could indeed have produced a software product. The example is positioned vaguely in the financial area, but isn't necessarily intended to make sense as a software product. Again, I have done this on purpose. Rather than people fretting about whether the requirements are correct, or the systems analysis and design has been done properly, or the right software architecture, tools, and environment are being used, I have been deliberately vague and shadowy about the functionality of this product. Our concerns are project management concerns—not software engineering concerns.

Finally, purely from the point of view of keeping the worked example from getting too complicated, I have steered clear of issues in the project to do with configuration management (CM). On any project, CM is crucial. On a Web-time project, there is simply no room for disasters involving losing control of CM. Clear policies, use of good tools to avoid destroying each others' work, baselining to allow recovery from false steps, backup, and recovery are all essential elements of the CM side of the project. All project deliverables, not just code, can be kept under CM. Again however, our concerns in this book are project management, not configuration management concerns. If you are unsure of this area, and have nobody on your team who knows much about it, invest in some tools and training, and buy a few books to understand the issues. Then give somebody the responsibility and allow them one mistake.

Identify the Right Project

Okay, so it's day 1 of your project. You manage to get all of the right people together. You have given them their preparation to do. Whether they have done it or not is another question, but in my experience, it doesn't seem to make all that much difference to the quality of what gets done at the scoping session. What it does seem to do is slow the session down somewhat and make everything take a bit longer.

You start to ask the questions.

You: How will we know when this project is over?

Engineering: The product is out the door.

CEO: It's selling in droves.

Finance: It has added five million dollars to the bottom line (Pause) in year 1.

Marketing: When the reviews say it's the best of breed.

Sales: When it demos at Comdex (in case you'd forgotten!). No, no. When the (thousands of) orders we take at Comdex have shipped.

You: Which?

A general discussion ensues. You guide them to the conclusion that all of these points might constitute possible endings of the project. And that in fact, what these different endings give you is your first cut of a project plan or timeline. These various points are milestones in the life of the project, which might look something like this:

Start;

Product demos at Comdex;

Product leaves Engineering;

Product reviews occur;

End of year 1 revenues.

You: So what constitutes its end point?

Again you lead them to the notion that all of these are valid end points, depending on your point of view. What is of concern to you today is that you pick one that you can all buy into and work with. More discussion. The group finally makes the following choices, but notice that they are precisely that—choices—which means you could have chosen differently and still be correct.

1. The group decides that the year 1 revenues one is too far away to really think about. After all, if you're thinking in Web-time, then a calendar year is more like four years.

2. Next it decides that while reviews are important, what's more important is that those first users of the product like it. It's clear that those people who buy the product at Comdex will be its first users and so you revise your milestones like this:

    Start;

    Product demos at Comdex;

Beta version of the product leaves Engineering and ships to Comdex buyers. (A beta test period follows during which customers are closely monitored and supported, bugs and change requests are reported, and Engineering fix some while adding others to the Release 2 wish list.);

Beta test period ends when (a) no more killer bugs[2] exist and at least 50% (the number is chosen arbitrarily) of customers have ordered more copies;

End.

3. You make a final decision whose sole purpose is to suit the author of this book! You decide that for your present purposes, you will treat the end of the project as the day on which the Beta version leaves Engineering. Marketing is happy with that. They say: "Don't worry. You let us worry about the Beta test program. We've done dozens of these before. You just get the product to us as quickly as you can and we'll take it from there."

You (looking the Marketing guy right in the eye): So the Beta test program will be the subject of a separate plan?

Marketing: Yes.

You write this down on a sheet of flipchart paper that you label "Actions."[3] It has three columns— what, who, when. It now reads: 1 Develop Beta test plan/Marketing guy/To be filled in (ideally before you leave the room). The list of milestones now reads:

Start;

Product demos at Comdex;

---

2   Presumably you have the normal scheme for classifying severity of bugs where killer bugs are showstoppers for which there is no reasonable workaround.

3   This isn't going to be one of those meetings that end in vague consensus but nothing firm in writing. (No meeting should be!) And while we're on the subject, why not have a bunch of set meeting times in the week? Looking for a day that suits everybody is a simple, unobtrusive way that schedules can slip out a day or two. Having fixed times for say, dealing with, change requests or configuration management issues or technical issues, means that:
(a) We can often accumulate these issues and deal with them all at once;
(b) The meetings act as little deadlines which people feel they have to "make";
(c) We don't get slippage as a result of waiting for a meeting.

Beta version of the product leaves Engineering;

End.

Just before we proceed, I'd like to return to this question of the wrong project, which we touched on at the beginning of the chapter. If the objective we had started out with had been to make so much profit in a given period, then the project we have just defined is the wrong project. To put it another way, if the question is "how do we make so much profit in a given period?" then this project is not the correct answer. This project *may* be part of the answer. If we included within its scope, marketing, sales, and various other bits and pieces, we might end up with a project whose goal would be to "make so much profit in a given period." But this project by itself will not do that. Please note that this is not just a semantic difference. It is a fundamental difference; and a difference which it is easy to lose sight of. We will show how we ensure that we don't in the final section of this chapter. For the moment, let's return to our scoping session.

Next question.

You: What physical things will the project produce?

Let's assume you get to the answers without too much difficulty, and that the list of deliverables is:

- The software itself—in a form whereby it can be distributed;

- User Manual in hardcopy;

- Online tutorial.

Again, the list isn't necessarily as complete as it would be for a real product. (This is a book on project management, not on how to develop winning software.)

Question number four.

You: How will the quality of those things be determined?

There follows much talk of reviews, code walkthroughs, focus groups, QA, automated test tools, signoff, prototyping, the demo at Comdex, and so on. Eventually you settle on the following. You will build a prototype that Marketing will show to some users to get feedback. There will be peer reviews of the requirements and designs. (You point out to them, in case they hadn't already noticed, that this session is going to be the review of the requirements. They hadn't noticed! And the realization has a somewhat sobering effect on the conversation!) A separate group will QA the product and they will be the people who decide whether the product is fit to go into the Beta test program. The prototype is considered important enough that it is added to the list of milestones.

Start;

Prototype available;

Product demos at Comdex;

Beta version of the product leaves Engineering as soon as QA completes;

End.

You: What things are definitely part of this project?

This is the part of the show when everyone gets a chance to talk about features, and the attendees go at it for all they're worth. Eventually you end up with ten features. (Your product is going to be small and elegant and containing what you believe to be killer features.)

1. Pricing;

2. Foreign exchange;

3. Euro support;

4. 3rd party payments;

5. Settlement;

6. Reporting;

7. Web interface;

8. Security;

9. Tutorial;

10. Online help.

For good measure, Engineering throw in the fact that it'll run in Windows 98 or 2000 environments only, and be written in C++. Also they make the point that this will be an English language only version.

They do this to wind up the Marketing guy, who promptly obliges by leaping out of his seat and saying that the product has to be available in FIGS (French, Italian, German, Spanish)—oh, and Japanese, Chinese, Thai, and Indonesian. A bit of a tussle ensues in which the Marketing guy restates his case, and Engineering just keeps saying "you want it when?" What is eventually agreed is that this release will be English only. However, this release will contain all the facilities necessary for multilingual support. The actual availability in the other languages will follow as part of Release 2.

You: What things are definitely not part of this project?

More spirited argument ensues until finally, the following is agreed. There will be no training course developed—the tutorial is considered to be adequate. A whole list of features that Marketing had hoped to get included is battered into Release 2. The justification for this is the following.

In their book, *Microsoft Secrets: How the World's Most Powerful Software Company Creates Technology, Shapes Markets and Manages People* [2], the authors discuss the "Microsoft Triangle" where feature richness, time to market, and product quality are three sides of a triangle. In a situation where we are trying to shorten time to market as much as possible, we must be prepared to focus then on the other two sides of the triangle—feature richness and product quality. If we assume that we never compromise on quality, then that leaves feature richness as the only remaining area that can be attacked. The meeting attacks it vigorously and while Marketing gulps every time another feature disappears into Release 2, they console themselves with the lure of the shortened time to market.

Final question.

You: Are there any people issues that we need to be aware of in connection with this project?

A few surface. The right people are hard to get and harder to keep. This is especially true in the Web area. Existing people have been working large amounts of continuous overtime, and some may be borderline burnout cases. Most of the attendees shrug. Welcome to the world. It's just another day in paradise.

"So, okay," you say, finally summarizing. "If we were to get these ten features (you show them the feature list); out the door in this kinda timeline (you show them the list of milestones); with these deliverables (you show them the list of deliverables); in English only—then every-body'd be happy?"

A reasonably lengthy silence follows, which is broken when the Sales guy says, "As long as it was within 30 days of Comdex." Shucks! Still it was worth a try.

You repeat your assertion with the desired amendment. "Okay, so, get these ten features (you show them the feature list); out the door in this kinda timeline (you show them the list of milestones); with these deliverables (you show them the list of deliverables); in English only and within 30 days of Comdex—then everyone'd be happy." There is nodding and general agreement. You're there. You remind them one more time that this is the plan for the Engineering part of the project only, and that other plans will be required for the other bits—marketing, sales, and so on. They all nod, you add to your action list precisely which plans will be needed. (The lure of a break makes them do this very quickly.) Then it's time to break for coffee. Or lunch. Or dinner, depending on how long all of this has taken you.

Keep the Stakeholders Happy

After the break, caffeined up to our eyeballs and ready to fight the good fight once more, we set out to check that what we did earlier is correct. We do this by making a list of all the project stakeholders, identifying what they would regard as a successful project (their win condition[4]), and then trying to see if the project we scoped earlier satisfies all of these win conditions. If it turns out that it does, fine. If not we may have to make some modifications to the scope.

We start with the list of stakeholders (see Table 4.1). Now we add each stakeholder's win conditions (see Table 4.2).

When the list is complete, you ask whether the project, as scoped in the previous section, meets all of these conditions. It is generally agreed that it does, provided that the sales and marketing plans are also developed and rolled into the equation. Notice again how crucial this is. (Remember that I removed sales and marketing from the equation only to limit the scope of this example, and to enable it to fit within the confines of the book. Had you been doing this for real, you would almost certainly *not* have excluded these two areas from the project scope—if

---

4   This notion of win conditions is described in Barry Boehm's paper *Theory W Software Project Management: Principles and Examples* [3]. I'm grateful to Jon Brackett for drawing attention to this.

Table 4.1 List of Stakeholders

Stakeholder	
The shareholders	
The board	
The CEO	
The customers	
The heads of Marketing, Sales, Engineering	
You (the Project Manager)	
The team	

Table 4.2 Stakeholder's Win Conditions

Stakeholder	Win Conditions
The shareholders	Grow market share
	Meet profit targets
The Board	Grow market share
	Meet profit targets
	Make them look good
The CEO	Grow market share
	Meet profit targets
	Make him look good
The customers	Good quality product
	Solves a real need for them i.e. adds value
The Heads of Marketing, Sales, Engineering	Grow market share
	Meet profit targets
	Make them look good
	Help them to keep their jobs
You (the Project Manager)	An interesting piece of work
	Make you look good
	You keep your job
The team	Interesting work
	Make them look good

for no other reason, than having asked the relevant people along, it would then have been fairly outrageous to exclude them from the proceedings.) Without these two other plans, notice that the number of stakeholders whose win conditions are satisfied is hugely reduced. Without them, the only people whose win conditions might potentially have any chance of being satisfied would be those of the Head of Engineering, you, the Project Manager, and the team. I say "might" because you might produce the greatest product the world had ever seen, but if sales and marketing didn't do their bits, then the product might only be remembered as a turkey.

Anyway, back to our session. It is generally agreed that provided Sales and Marketing can scope their projects as effectively as the Engineering plan has just been scoped, then all of the stakeholders' win conditions would be satisfied.

As you start gathering up the sheets of flipchart paper to document the proceedings, you mentally add two other win conditions, one for you and one for the team. They are win conditions that, for all sorts of reasons, you wouldn't particularly have wanted to add to the public list. For yourself, you add

"Put you in a position to ask for a raise and some more stock options" and for the team,

"Get the product out the door working reasonable (i.e., 40 hours or so) working weeks."

References

1. Smith, P. G., and D. G. Reinertsen, *Developing Products in Half the Time*, New York: Wiley, 1998.

2. Selby, R. W., and M. A. Cusumano, *Microsoft Secrets: How the World's Most Powerful Software Company Creates Technology, Shapes Markets and Manages People*, New York: Simon & Schuster 1998.

3. Boehm, B. W. and R. Ross, "Theory-W Software Project Management: Principles and Examples," *IEEE Transactions on Software Engineering*, Vol. 15, No.7, July 1989, pp. 902–916.

PART THREE
Build the Plan

Having figured out the correct project to do, we now have to build a plan for that project. We begin to do that here, and will work a step at a time, through the next five chapters. Only when we have done all of this will we be in a position to look at shortening our project. Chapter 5 shows how to figure out what has to be done, both in terms of which jobs and how much work those jobs entail. Chapter 6 ensures that we add in jobs and effort for the project management tasks. Chapter 7 is all about the people who will do the work we have identified in Chapter 5, that is, those who will do the jobs. In Chapter 8 we will put contingency into our plan. Chapter 9 shows how to do a simple risk analysis on our plan.

5 Identify the Work To Be Done

➤ This chapter describes how to build a complete Work Breakdown Structure (WBS). It says that, at this stage, you are only trying to find out three things—what jobs are to be done, how much effort (not elapsed time) is in each of those jobs, and the dependencies between jobs.

➤ It shows that no matter what project you are engaged in, WBSs can be built very quickly from reusable components.

➤ It talks about who should do the estimating, how to do it, and the units in which people should estimate.

➤ It shows how to build a WBS that supports both seeing the big picture and being able to focus on the detail.

➤ It shows the advantages of a deliverable-oriented WBS over an activity-oriented one.

➤ It explains how to ensure that jobs don't get forgotten.

➤ Finally, it describes how to ensure that sufficient tasks for checking product quality are built into the WBS.

➤ The worked example is added to.

How to Build a Work Breakdown Structure (WBS)

Introduction

Once you've scoped the correct project, that is, figured out which project to launch and what its content should be, the next thing you have to do is to identify all the jobs that have to be done to make the project happen. Specifically, what you're looking for at this point is three things:

- The jobs;

- The effort (or work) in those jobs (not the elapsed time);

- The dependencies between jobs.

The reason for this is that project management is a problem in supply (people available to do the work) and demand (work to be done), and a successful project requires these to be matched. By identifying these three things—jobs, dependencies, and effort estimates—we calculate the demand. What we have here are the beginnings of what is conventionally called a Work Breakdown Structure (WBS).

At the risk of stating the obvious, there is a big problem with building the list of jobs. That problem is that you essentially have to predict the future.

And maybe they didn't tell you this when they thrust greatness on you and made you a project manager. Up until then, perhaps you were beavering away as maybe a software engineer, a designer, or a business analyst. Each day you practiced your craft you learned more and became a better engineer, designer, or analyst. Then they made you a project manager. Now your job would be to predict the future. If you did it well, you would be showered (!) with rewards while, if you did it badly —in an extreme case—you might be fired. But maybe they didn't quite point this out to you. Sometimes, when I'm teaching courses in this stuff, I hold up a lottery ticket and a Gantt chart and say "what do these have in common?" (Somebody once answered this question by saying "If I won the lottery I wouldn't have to do this stupid stuff any more!") What they have in common is that they're both predictions of the future. We'd like to feel that the odds on the Gantt chart are better than those on the lottery ticket, but there's a sobering thought—that they might not be. I've certainly seen Gantt charts where the smart money would have been on the lottery ticket.

Anyway, all of that's the bad news. The good news is that there are tools to help you develop WBSs and we will discuss some of them here. Specifically, we will discuss four that we call

- Make the journey in your head;

- Open up black box jobs;

- Use knowledge and assumptions;

- Count the bricks in the wall.

We will tend to use all four together as we build our WBS.

Make the Journey in Your Head

The most effective way to build a WBS is to think the project through "from left to right" i.e., from start to finish, making very small jumps and asking—all the way—"who does what?" People have a tendency, in building a WBS, to say things like requirements, design, code, and so on. They take big jumps and write down words that are at best, ambiguous. For example, the word "code," what does it mean? Here are—and the list is not intended to be exhaustive—seven possible meanings:

1.   Type the software into the computer;

2.   Do 1 plus compile the software;

3.   Do 2 plus type in '0' and '–1' and see if it crashes;

4.   Do 3 plus write a test plan;

5.   Do 4 plus execute the test plan;

6.   Do 5 plus execute the test plan plus fix the bugs;

7.   Do 6 plus continue to execute the test plan and fix bugs until no more occur.

The problem with the big jumps and the ambiguous words approach is that we miss too much. We end up with a WBS that has gaping holes in it. Of course, we only find this out much later— generally, after we have made commitments based on the WBS with the gaping holes.

A much more trustworthy approach, which is much more likely to result in a WBS that we can be confident about, is the small jumps and "who does what" approach. It goes like this.

Try and imagine the day the project starts. Who does what? Somebody writes a document, or calls a meeting, or sends out a memo or something. Now based on that first event, a second event happens. Or maybe several events happen in parallel. What are those events? Who does what? Don't tell me something vague like "determine requirements." Tell me "Charlie and Catherine work on writing the requirements document. The document follows the normal company format, so that it has 10 sections. On average, each section will take them a day and the document can be split evenly between them. And when they're finished, the document will have to go for review."

How do I know all this stuff? Because I've gone to the trouble of thinking about it. That's all. Nothing more. I'll have to think about it sooner or later. Why not do it now? I'll save myself all sorts of trouble as a result.

And so you carry on like this chaining little jobs together. To be very precise, when I say "small jumps," I mean that every job that we identify should be somewhere between 1–5 person-days of effort, and certainly not more than 5 person-days.

Open Up Black Box Jobs

"Open up black box jobs" means whenever you find yourself having taken a big jump, you write down, for example, "integrity test," then you back up and try to open up this particular job. In opening it up, you are trying to see the intricate mechanism inside it, breaking it down to the 1–5 person-day unit we discussed earlier.

Use Knowledge and Assumptions

I fear you may be already spluttering and saying "there's no way I can break my entire project down to that level of detail." There was a time when I used to think that. There was a time when I had this idea of a project being like a folded map. The analogy was with the way most normal people use maps when they're driving. Rather than having the entire map unfolded and spread across the passenger seat, dashboard, and part of the windscreen, they fold it up so they can see in lots of detail the next piece of the journey (i.e., the next few weeks of the project). Then when they get to the edge of the map (the next milestone), they can flip the map over and see in detail the next piece of the journey and so the project proceeds in this way. To the best of my knowledge, many project management methodologies still use this notion in some shape or form.

I no longer feel we need to be limited in this way, and the magic thing that enables us to remove this limitation is the use of assumptions. If we run into a brick wall, where we say "I just have no idea what is involved in that—I don't know what jobs I have to do, never mind how much work might be involved in those jobs," you make an assumption.

Take the "integrity test" job from the previous section. It could mean almost anything, right? So rather than leave it like that, let's have it mean something pretty definite. Let's make some assumptions, even if those assumptions need to be changed subsequently. The assumptions have the effect of replacing vagueness by definiteness, which is all to the good if we are trying to build and estimate WBSs.

So we might say (assume) that integrity test is actually the following:

• Follow test script and record errors;

- Make required software corrections.

Notice that this immediately triggers a couple of other issues. A test script must get written so there'd better be a job here or somewhere else in the WBS to make that happen. Also, are we assuming that once the software corrections are made, we're finished? Yes? No, the answer is no. It wouldn't make sense in terms of what would be happening on the ground. This is because once the software corrections are made, we will have to test again. Thus, at the very least, integrity test would have to look like this:

- Follow test script and record errors;

- Make required software corrections;

- Repeat test scripts.

And we're still not finished, because now another implicit assumption pops out. That is that there will be no more errors when we run the test scripts for a second time. Likely? Maybe. Depends on lots of things. A pointer as to whether it's correct or not might be our experience on previous projects, assuming we had recorded or can remember such experience. (This is a subject on which we'll be saying more later.)

Anyway, for the purposes of this little example, we might assume that there will be no more errors second time out, and so our final integrity test piece of the WBS ends up as the following with notes attached to the first and third items mentioning what we have already discussed:

- Follow test script and record errors;

- Make required software corrections;

- Repeat test scripts.

Count the Bricks in the Wall

Software estimating is no different from estimating in any other discipline, in the sense that you need to understand how much stuff has to get done. People in software often tend to forget this, focussing on the activities they will be doing—requirements, design, codes and so on—instead of how much of a particular activity is needed. When we go to build our WBS later in the worked example, we will constantly be asking ourselves the question "How much stuff is there to be done?" along with related questions like "How do I know this? On what basis am I making this estimate?

Perhaps this is a good point to dwell for a moment on these related questions and the associated (and dreaded) condition known as "programmer optimism." If bitter experience has not already taught you that programmers are optimists, then making it a working assumption for the rest of the time that you are employed in the software industry would not be a bad thing. Given that it is true, then it is a good idea when people propose estimates, to question their estimate. There are a number of ways you can do this. Here are a few of them:

1. You could ask "what are the odds that you might finish 25% sooner? Or 25% later?"

2. How much would you bet that your estimate is correct? (A personal favorite of mine.)

3. Are you assuming you'll be successful first time, or will you require iterations of some task or set of tasks? (Particularly useful in relation to testing type activities.)

4. Why? (Bald questions are often the best!)

Summary

These four tools—make the journey in your head, open up black box jobs, use knowledge and assumptions, count the bricks in the wall—provide powerful techniques to build WBSs. But we're not finished yet. In the next section, we will discuss even more powerful ones.

How to Build a WBS From Reusable Components

Introduction

Software people are great individualists. Nowhere is this truer than in the project plans software people build. Look at a typical software project plan and you would imagine that nobody had ever remotely attempted what was being attempted here. The plan would be unique, an absolute one of a kind.

I don't know why this should be. Because my experience has led me to believe that there is actually very little difference from one software plan to the next. We do the same things—requirements, design, develop prototype, code, test, and so on—and so we would expect software project plans to be remarkably similar. And indeed they are, provided we look for the similarities. Not only that, but once we recognize these similarities, we can build software project plans very quickly. Let's look at what I mean.

Reusable Components

Let's imagine that as a result of a scoping session as we described in the previous chapter, we had come up with a set of high level tasks as shown in Figure 5.1.

Many of the tasks here, notably numbers 1–5, involve us in writing a document and then reviewing that document. The review cycle might look as in Figure 5.2.

Once we have established this sequence, we can re-use it every time a review cycle on a document is required. Notice that, for the moment, we are focussing only on the jobs and the dependencies, and not on the effort in those jobs. We will get to the business of the effort in a while. In the meantime, the examples show every job having an elapsed time of 1 day.

Here are some other possible reusable components. Here's one (in Figure 5.3) to develop a piece of software for a particular module, or

ID	①	Task name	1, 2000		Qtr 2, 2000			Qtr 3, 2000			Qtr 4, 2000			Qtr 1, 2001			Qtr 2, 2001			Qtr 3, 2001			Qtr 4, 2001		
			Feb	Mar	Apr	May	Jun	Jul	Aug	Sep	Oct	Nov	Dec	Jan	Feb	Mar	Apr	May	Jun	Jul	Aug	Sep	Oct	Nov	Dec
1		Produce requirements document																							
2		Produce system/acceptance test plan																							
3		Produce high level design (HLD)																							
4		Produce low level design (LLD)																							
5		Produce integration test plan																							
6		Write code																							
7		Produce user documentation and Help system																							
8		Integrate system																							
9		Execute system test																							
10		Carry out beta test																							
11		Project management tasks																							
12		Training																							
13		Release to manufacturing																							
14		End of project review																							

Key: ····· Today's date

Figure 5.1   High level tasks.

ID		Task name	1, 2000		Qtr 2, 2000			Qtr 3, 2000			Qtr 4, 2000			Qtr 1, 2001			Qtr 2, 2001			Qtr 3, 2001			Qtr 4, 2001			Qtr 1, 2002		
			Feb	Mar	Apr	May	Jun	Jul	Aug	Sep	Oct	Nov	Dec	Jan	Feb	Mar	Apr	May	Jun	Jul	Aug	Sep	Oct	Nov	Dec	Oct	Nov	Dec
1		**Review cycle**																										
2		Circulate																										
3		Individual review																										
4		Review meeting																										
5		Changes to document																										
6		Circulate again																										
7		Second review																										
8		Signoff																										
9		Document complete																										

Key: ▼▼ Summary task
       ↳   Detailed task

Figure 5.2   Review cycle.

ID		Task name	14 Feb '00	21 Feb '00	28 Feb '00	06 Mar '00	13 Mar '00
			M T W T F S S	M T W T F S S	M T W T F S S	M T W T F S S	M T W T F S S
1		Code and unit test					
2		Write code element (including clean compile)					
3		Document code element					
4		Unit test code					

Key: ▦ Detailed task
       ↴ Dependency

Figure 5.3   Develop a piece of software.

unit, or feature. Figure 5.4 gives one to write some tests for a piece of software. Figure 5.5 gives one to code and unit test a piece of software.

Figure 5.6 shows one for testing a piece of software. It assumes that one round of testing will be enough to uncover all the bugs and that the second round is merely to confirm this. Note that if we thought that one round of testing wouldn't be enough, we could add as many iterations as we liked or thought would be necessary.

ID		Task name	14 Feb '00	21 Feb '00	28 Feb '00	06 Mar '00	13 Mar '00
			M T W T F S S	M T W T F S S	M T W T F S S	M T W T F S S	M T W T F S S
1		**Write navigation tests**					
2		Define test sequence					
3		Write test scripts					
4		Define expected results					

Key: ▦ Detailed task
       ↴ Dependency
      ▼▼ Summary task

Figure 5.4   Write some tests.

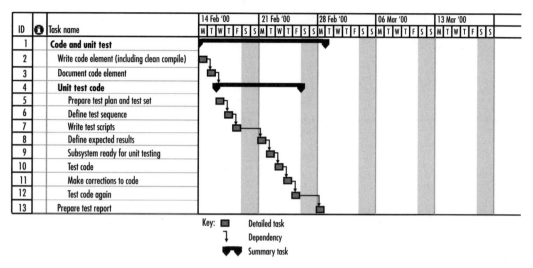

Figure 5.5   Code and unit test.

Figure 5.6   Test a piece of software.

And notice another interesting thing here. Imagine that we had several different types of testing that we intended to carry out say, for example as in Figure 5.7.

Then, we could put an iteration of the component or block in Figure 5.6 under each of the items in Figure 5.7.

Thus, when we come to build our WBS, using the techniques we outlined in Section 5.1, we do not have to build it all from the ground up. There will be times when, in making the journey in our head, we can make a biggish jump, simply by bolting on one of our reusable blocks.

Now, let's look at the next question—that of estimating effort.

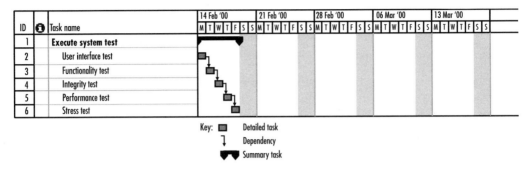

Figure 5.7   Different types of testing.

Estimating

Who Should Do It

The obvious answer is "those who are going to have to do the work." And indeed, the obvious answer is the right answer in this case. There is no substitute for it—assuming the people are known. Maybe some are known and some aren't. In that case, you'll just have to make do with whoever is known. If you find yourself in a position where nobody is known, then you'll just have to make do. Try to get some people whose judgement you trust. The absolute worst thing you can do is to do it by yourself. So if it looks like you think you're going to end up in that situation, find a "buddy" project manager and do a deal—if she's prepared to spend time helping you on your project, you'll do the same whenever she needs it. In my experience, it's an offer you'll find readily accepted.

The Jobs

Using the techniques that we've described, you're now in a position to identify the jobs. Begin by taking those small (1–5 person-day) jumps. Whenever you find you've taken too big a jump, back up, and do it again. Whenever you feel you've run into a brick wall, make an assumption and jump the wall. Whenever, you see an opportunity, make a series of little jumps, using one of our reusable blocks of jobs. If you find other blocks appearing more than once, add those to your little store of reusable blocks. Insert the milestones you've identified from scoping the project into the WBS at the appropriate points.

Dependencies

A lot of the dependencies will have ended up in the WBS as a result of building the list of jobs. Often, dependencies are so self-evident that it's as easy to put them in at the time when you identify the jobs. However, it's no harm, once, to make a separate pass to ensure that you have caught them all.

Effort Estimates

Now add in the effort estimates to the jobs on the job list, noting down any assumptions you made as you proceed. Notice that you are estimating in normal working days, not in some kind of supercharged day that consists of 5.37 (or whatever) hours of raw productivity. (This is a notion that often pops up—how many productive hours are there in a day? In my view, it's a fairly fruitless discussion. Apart from the question of whether one can accurately calculate what the number of productive hours is, I believe this is not a unit in which people can intuitively estimate. Far better, I think, to stay with normal 8-hour, 5 of them per week, days.)

Conclusion

While I have described the business of identifying the jobs, dependencies, and effort as three separate operations. In reality, it often happens that all three are done together. This is illustrated in the worked example that follows next.

Worked Example

Introduction

In this section, we will take the project scope arrived at in the previous chapter and work it right through, establishing jobs, dependencies, and efforts. In the course of doing so, we will make some additional general observations on things that we have learned.

So let's return to our friends from the previous chapter. In fact, let's rewrite part of that chapter slightly before we begin. Specifically, let's make some changes to where we scoped the project.

In the previous chapter, we said that we were gathering the people together to scope the project. In fact, I have found that it is much more effective to both scope and plan the project in the format we described in the previous chapter. It might be that if you were estimating the Engineering parts, the non-Engineering people might want to butt out. However, in my experience, not only do they not want to do that, but they provide valuable input which the techies often overlook.

Let's assume then that you had gathered the people together for a planning and scoping session. To do so, you would have sent out a longer memo than that described in Chapter 4. Your revised memo would look something like Figure 5.8.

In addition, you will have brought along an additional person to the scoping session. That person—a sidekick of yours, in all likelihood—is what we will call a "scribe." Armed with a PC containing Word, Excel, and MS Project (or their equivalents), their job is to record the deliberations of the group.

Now, with the project scoped, we are ready to begin the planning. Specifically, we are ready to begin identifying jobs, dependencies, and effort. You could record all of this work perfectly adequately on a flipchart and then transcribe it to a computer. I have done this and it works fine. However, on this occasion, we will use the PC with MS Project. Thus, we will record our work as shown in Figure 5.9.

Jobs, Dependencies, Effort

You (nodding to your scribe who writes down the word "start"): "Okay, who does what? What happens first?"

"This meeting," somebody pipes up. (Ah, so they were awake.) You nod to your scribe and he does the necessary, adding in the fact that the meeting is a day elapsed, but given that there are nine participants (you, scribe, CEO, Marketing guy, Sales guy, Engineering guy, a couple of other engineers, Finance guy), it is 9 days, effort.

Now the Marketing guy puts a spanner in the works by saying that they need to survey potential users and competitive products. You groan inwardly. You assumed they would have done this prior to this meeting. Otherwise how could the marketing input be valid? Tactfully, you say nothing, but begin to put in place the sequence of events that will fold in (a) the input from today, (b) the results of the competitive analysis, and (c) the user questionnaires into a Requirements Document.

Figure 5.8   Revised brief note.

Briefing note for participants in the 2-day project scoping and planning session

Essentially, the purpose of the 2-day session is to:

(a)   Establish what the project is trying to achieve—the goal;
(b)   Create a plan for reaching the goal.

The best way for individual participants to prepare for this is to try to do the following:

(a)   Document a goal for their piece of the project.
(b)   Prepare a plan to achieve this goal.

You should need no more than half a day to do this preparation, and should limit yourself to whatever level of detail can be achieved in that time.

(a) Goal

To do this, ask yourself questions like these. (Give yourself no more than an hour.)

- How will I know when the project is over?

- What will things be like? How will the company—or my piece of it—have changed?

- Who are the various people and/or groups ('the stakeholders') affected by the project?

- For each of these individuals or groups, what would constitute a successful project?

- Are these different views compatible? If not, is there a compromise set that we can live with?

(b)   Plan

To do this, do the following. (Plan to spend no more than 2–3 hours in total on the first three points and no more than an hour on the last two.)

- Make a list of all the jobs that you can think of that need to be done to reach the goal.

- Mark any dependencies between jobs (or dependencies on other projects or groups).

- Try to estimate how much work is involved in each job and therefore, the project as a whole.

- Try to identify people who will do the work.

- Document any assumptions you make or unresolved issues you have.

ID	❽	Task Name	Work	Predecessor	Notes
1		1 The project	457.75 days		
2		1.1 START	0 days		
3	▦	1.2 Project planning and scoping meeting	9 days	2	9 people for 1 day
4		1.3 Produce requirements document	27 days	3	
5	▦▦	1.3.1 Research user requirements	7 days		
6	▦	1.3.1.1 Gather info on competitive products	0.5 days		Charlie'll do it
7	▦	1.3.1.2 Review with marketing	2 days	6	Assume 3 marketing people and Charlie @ 1/2 day each gives 2 days work. It's a…
8	▦	1.3.1.3 Identify users	0.5 days	7	Marketing guy—his estimate
9	▦	1.3.1.4 Prepare user questionnaires	2 days	8	Charlie says he'll do it. Take him a coupla days.
10	▦	1.3.1.5 Distribute questionnaires	0.5 days	9	An Admin. person. Estimate is on the basis that 1/2 day is the smallest unit we recognize…
11	▦	1.3.1.6 Retrieve questionnaires	0.5 days	10FS + 1 wk	Half a days work chasing; Probably 5 days elapsed time to get it done
12	▦	1.3.1.7 Analyze information	1 day	11	Charlie and a marketing person @ 1/2 day each
13	▦	1.3.2 Write requirements document	9 days	12	Charlie. Use company standard 9 section format @ 1 day person section
14		1.3.3 Review cycle	10.5 days	13	
15	▦	1.3.3.1 Circulate	0.5 days		Admin. person—basis for estimate is same as for 'Distribute questionnaires' above
16	▦	1.3.3.2 Individual review	2.5 days	15	5 reviewers, half day each, allow 1 week elapsed time in which it has to happen
17	▦	1.3.3.3 Review meeting	3 days	16	Charlie and 5 reviewers @ 1/2 day each
18	▦	1.3.3.4 Changes to document	2.5 days	17	Charlie—his estimate
19	▦	1.3.3.5 Circulate again	0.5 days	18	Same as earlier 'Circulate'
20	▦	1.3.3.6 Second review	1.5 days	19	5 reviewers, 1–2 hours each, try and do it ASAP—so give reviewers a deadline to…
21	▦	1.3.4 Signoff	0.5 days	14	Assume there will be no substantial changes. Admin. person chases signoffs
22		1.3.5 Requirements complete	0 days	21	
23		1.4 Produce system/acceptance test plan	39.75 days	4	
24		1.4.1 Research	5 days		
25		1.4.2 Write navigation tests	3 days	24	
26		1.4.2.1 Define test sequence	1 day		
27		1.4.2.2 Write test scripts	1 day	26	
28		1.4.2.3 Define expected results	1 day	27	
29		1.4.3 Write functionality tests	3 days	25	
30		1.4.3.1 Define test sequence	1 day		
31		1.4.3.2 Write test scripts	1 day	30	
32		1.4.3.3 Define expected results	1 day	31	
33		1.4.4 Write integrity tests	3 days	29	
34		1.4.4.1 Define test sequence	1 day		
35		1.4.4.2 Write test scripts	1 day	34	
36		1.4.4.3 Define expected results	1 day	35	

Figure 5.9   Full detail.

ID	ⓘ	Task Name	Work	Predecessor	Notes
37		**1.4.5 Write performance tests**	**3 days**	33	
38		1.4.5.1 Define test sequence	1 day		
39		1.4.5.2 Write test scripts	1 day	38	
40		1.4.5.3 Define expected results	1 day	39	
41		**1.4.6 Write stress tests**	**3 days**	37	
42		1.4.6.1 Define test sequence	1 day		
43		1.4.6.2 Write test scripts	1 day	42	
44		1.4.6.3 Define expected results	1 day	43	
45		**1.4.7 Write installation tests**	**3 days**	41	
46		1.4.7.1 Define test sequence	1 day		
47		1.4.7.2 Write test scripts	1 day	46	
48		1.4.7.3 Define expected results	1 day	47	
49		**1.4.8 Review cycle**	**16.25 days**	45	
50		1.4.8.1 Circulate	0.5 days		
51		1.4.8.2 Individual review	5 days	50	Assume 5 reviewers @ 1 day each. …
52		1.4.8.3 Review meeting	3.5 days	51	
53		1.4.8.4 Changes to document	5 days	52	
54		1.4.8.5 Circulate again	0.5 days	53	
55		1.4.8.6 Second review	1.75 days	54	
56		1.4.9 Signoff	0.5 days	49	
57		1.4.10 System/acceptance tests written	0 days	56	
58	▦	**1.5 Prototype**	**22 days**	4	Assuming people are available immediately to review the work. So the 22 days effort…
59		**1.6 Write code**	**184 days**	58	
60		1.6.1 Pricing	**8 days**		
61	▦	1.6.1.1 Write code element (including clean…)	4 days		
62		1.6.1.2 Document code element	0.5 days		
63		**1.6.1.3 Unit test code**	**3.5 days**	62	
64		**1.6.1.3.1 Prepare test plan and test set**	1 day		
65		1.6.1.3.1.1 Define test sequence	0.25 days		
66		1.6.1.3.1.2 Write test scripts	0.5 days	65	
67		1.6.1.3.1.3 Define expected results	0.25 days	66	
68		1.6.1.3.2 Subsystem ready for unit testing	0 days	67	
69		1.6.1.3.3 Test code	1 day	68	
70		1.6.1.3.4 Make corrections to code	0.5 days	69	
71		1.6.1.3.5 Test code again	0.5 days	70	
72		1.6.1.3.6 Prepare test report	0.5 days	71	
73		**1.6.2 Settlement**	**8 days**		
74		1.6.2.1 Write code element (including clean…)	4 days		

Figure 5.9 (continued)

How to Run Successful Projects in Web Time

ID	ⓘ	Task Name	Work	Predecessor	Notes
75		1.6.2.2 Document code element	0.5 days		
76		**1.6.2.3 Unit test code**	**3.6 days**	75	
77		**1.6.2.3.1 Prepare test plan and test set**	**1 day**		
78		1.6.2.3.1.1 Define test sequence	0.25 days		
79		1.6.2.3.1.2 Write test scripts	0.5 days	78	
80		1.6.2.3.1.3 Define expected results	0.25 days	79	
81		1.6.2.3.2 Subsystem ready for unit testing	0 days	80	
82		1.6.2.3.3 Test code	1 day	81	
82		1.6.2.3.4 Make corrections to code	0.5 days	82	
84		1.6.2.3.5 Test code again	0.5 days	83	
85		1.6.2.3.6 Prepare test report	0.5 days	84	
86		**1.6.3 Reporting**	**8 days**		
87		1.6.3.1 Write code element (including clean...)	4 days		
88		1.6.3.2 Document code element	0.5 days		
89		**1.6.3.3 Unit test code**	**3.5 days**	88	
90		**1.6.3.3.1 Prepare test plan and test set**	**1 day**		
91		1.6.3.3.1.1 Define test sequence	0.25 days		
92		1.6.3.3.1.2 Write test scripts	0.5 days	91	
93		1.6.3.3.1.3 Define expected results	0.25 days	92	
94		1.6.3.3.2 Subsystem ready for unit testing	0 days	93	
95		1.6.3.3.3 Test code	1 day	94	
96		1.6.3.3.4 Make corrections to code	0.5 days	95	
97		1.6.3.3.5 Test code again	0.5 days	96	
98		1.6.3.3.6 Prepare test report	0.5 days	97	
99		**1.6.4 Foreign Exchange**	**16 days**		
100		1.6.4.1 Write code element (including clean...)	8 days		
101		1.6.4.2 Document code element	1 day		
102		**1.6.4.3 Unit test code**	**7 days**	101	
103		**1.6.4.3.1 Prepare test plan and test set**	**2 days**		
104		1.6.4.3.1.1 Define test sequence	0.5 days		
105		1.6.4.3.1.2 Write test scripts	1 day	104	
106		1.6.4.3.1.3 Define expected results	0.5 days	105	
107		1.6.4.3.2 Subsystem ready for unit testing	0 days	106	
108		1.6.4.3.3 Test code	2 days	107	

Figure 5.9   (continued)

ID	☎	Task Name	Work	Predecessor	Notes
109		1.6.4.3.4 Make corrections to code	1 day	108	
110		1.6.4.3.5 Test code again	0.5 days	109	
111		1.6.4.3.6 Prepare test report	0.5 days	110	
112		**1.6.5 Euro support**	**16 days**		
113		1.6.5.1 Write code element (including clean...)	8 days		
114		1.6.5.2 Document code element	1 day		
115		**1.6.5.3 Unit test code**	**7 days**	**114**	
116		**1.6.5.3.1 Prepare test plan and test set**	**2 days**		
117		1.6.5.3.1.1 Define test sequence	0.5 days		
118		1.6.5.3.1.2 Write test scripts	1 day	117	
119		1.6.5.3.1.3 Define expected results	0.5 days	118	
120		1.6.5.3.2 Subsystem ready for unit testing	0 days	119	
121		1.6.5.3.3 Test code	2 days	120	
122		1.6.5.3.4 Make corrections to code	1 day	121	
123		1.6.5.3.5 Test code again	1 day	122	
124		1.6.5.3.6 Prepare test report	1 day	123	
125		**1.6.6 3rd party payments**	**16 days**		
126		1.6.6.1 Write code element (including clean...)	8 days		
127		1.6.6.2 Document code element	1 day		
128		**1.6.6.3 Unit test code**	**7 days**	**127**	
129		**1.6.6.3.1 Prepare test plan and test set**	**2 days**		
130		1.6.6.3.1.1 Define test sequence	0.5 days		
131		1.6.6.3.1.2 Write test scripts	1 day	130	
132		1.6.6.3.1.3 Define expected results	0.5 days	131	
133		1.6.5.3.2 Subsystem ready for unit testing	0 days	132	
134		1.6.6.3.3 Test code	2 days	133	
135		1.6.6.3.4 Make corrections to code	1 day	134	
136		1.6.6.3.5 Test code again	1 day	135	
137		1.6.6.3.6 Prepare test report	1 day	136	
138		**1.6.7 Tutorial**	**16 days**		
139		1.6.7.1 Write code element (including clean...)	8 days		
140		1.6.7.2 Document code element	1 day		
141		**1.6.7.3 Unit test code**	**7 days**	**140**	
142		**1.6.7.3.1 Prepare test plan and test set**	**2 days**		
143		1.6.7.3.1.1 Define test sequence	0.5 days		
144		1.6.7.3.1.2 Write test scripts	1 day	143	

Figure 5.9 (continued)

ID	ⓘ	Task Name	Work	Predecessor	Notes
145		1.6.7.3.1.3 Define expected results	0.5 days	144	
146		1.6.7.3.2 Subsystem ready for unit testing	0 days	145	
147		1.6.7.3.3 Test code	2 days	146	
148		1.6.7.3.4 Make corrections to code	1 day	147	
149		1.6.7.3.5 Test code again	1 day	148	
150		1.6.7.3.6 Prepare test report	1 day	149	
151		**1.6.8 Web interface**	**16 days**		
152		1.6.8.1 Write code element 1 (including clean com...)	3 days		
153		1.6.8.2 Write code element 2 (including clean com...)	3 days	152	
154		1.6.8.3 Write code element 3 (including clean com...)	3 days	153	
155		1.6.8.4 Write code element 4 (including clean com...)	3 days	154	
156		1.6.8.5 Document code element 1	1 day		
157		1.6.8.6 Document code element 2	1 day		
158		1.6.8.7 Document code element 3	1 day		
159		1.6.8.8 Document code element 4	1 day		
160		**1.6.8.9 Unit test code**	**16 days**	159	
161		**1.6.8.9.1 Prepare test plan and test set**	**4 days**		
162		1.6.8.9.1.1 Define test sequence	1 day		
163		1.6.8.9.1.2 Write test scripts	2 days	162	
164		1.6.8.9.1.3 Define expected results	1 day	163	
165		1.6.8.9.2 Subsystem ready for unit testing	0 days	164	
166		1.6.8.9.3 Test code	6 days	165	
167		1.6.8.9.4 Make corrections to code	2 day	166	
168		1.6.8.9.5 Test code again	2 day	167	
169		1.6.8.9.6 Prepare test report	2 day	168	
170		**1.6.9 Security**	**32 days**		
171		1.6.9.1 Write code element 1 (including clean com...)	3 days		
172		1.6.9.2 Write code element 2 (including clean com...)	3 days	171	
173		1.6.9.3 Write code element 3 (including clean com...)	3 days	172	
174		1.6.9.4 Write code element 4 (including clean com...)	3 days	173	
175		1.6.9.5 Document code element 1	1 day		
176		1.6.9.6 Document code element 2	1 day		
177		1.6.9.7 Document code element 3	1 day		
178		1.6.9.8 Document code element 4	1 day		

Figure 5.9 (continued)

ID	ⓘ	Task Name	Work	Predecessor	Notes
179		**1.6.9.9 Unit test code**	**16 days**	178	
180		**1.6.9.9.1 Prepare test plan and test set**	**4 days**		
181		1.6.9.9.1.1 Define test sequence	1 day		
182		1.6.9.9.1.2 Write test scripts	2 days	181	
183		1.6.9.9.1.3 Define expected results	1 day	182	
184		1.6.9.9.2 Subsystem ready for unit testing	0 days	183	
185		1.6.9.9.3 Test code	6 days	184	
186		1.6.9.9.4 Make corrections to code	2 day	185	
187		1.6.9.9.5 Test code again	2 day	186	
188		1.6.9.9.6 Prepare test report	2 day	187	
189		**1.6.10 Online Help**	**16 days**		
190		1.6.10.1 Write code element 1 (including clean com...)	3 days		
191		1.6.10.2 Write code element 2 (including clean com...)	3 days	190	
192		1.6.10.3 Write code element 3 (including clean com...)	3 days	191	
193		1.6.10.4 Write code element 4 (including clean com...)	3 days	192	
194		1.6.10.5 Document code element 1	1 day		
195		1.6.10.6 Document code element 2	1 day		
196		1.6.10.7 Document code element 3	1 day		
197		1.6.10.8 Document code element 4	1 day		
198		**1.6.10.9 Unit test code**	**16 days**	197	
199		**1.6.10.9.1 Prepare test plan and test set**	**4 days**		
200		1.6.10.9.1.1 Define test sequence	1 day		
201		1.6.10.9.1.2 Write test scripts	2 days	200	
202		1.6.10.9.1.3 Define expected results	1 day	201	
203		1.6.10.9.2 Subsystem ready for unit testing	0 days	202	
204		1.6.10.9.3 Test code	6 days	203	
205		1.6.10.9.4 Make corrections to code	2 day	204	
206		1.6.10.9.5 Test code again	2 day	205	
207		1.6.10.9.6 Prepare test report	2 day	206	
208		**1.7 Produce user documentation and Help system**	**99 days**	58	
209		1.7.1 Research requirements	5 days		
210		1.7.2 Set up environment and tools	5 days		
211		1.7.3 Define style sheet and produce prototype	5 days		

Figure 5.9 (continued)

How to Run Successful Projects in Web Time

ID	🛈	Task Name	Work	Predecessor	Notes
212		**1.7.4 Write user documentation or Help text**	**53 days**	211	
213		1.7.4.1 Structure into chapters	1 day		
214		1.7.4.2 Produce Table of Contents	1 day	213	
215		1.7.4.3 Review Table of Contents	1 day	214	
216	▦	1.7.4.4 Write documentation	50 days	215	Based on ten features @ 5 days per feature
217		**1.7.5 Edit User documentation or Help text**	**21 days**	212	
218	▦	1.7.5.1 Review documentation (incl. validation...)	10 days		
219	▦	1.7.5.2 Edit documentation	10 days	218	
220		1.7.5.3 Produce index	1 day	218, 219	
221		1.7.6 Final integration of online Help system	5 days		
222		1.7.7 Final preproduction of manuals	5 days	221	
223		**1.8 Execute system test**	**72 days**	23, 59	
224		**1.8.1 Test pass #1**	**48 days**		
225	▦	1.8.1.1 Follow test script and record errors	24 days		
226	▦	1.8.1.2 Make requires s/w corrections	24 days	225	
227		**1.8.2 Test pass #2**	**17 days**	224	
228		1.8.2.1 Follow test script and record errors	8 days		
229	▦	1.8.2.2 Make requires s/w corrections	9 days	228	Assume takes a bit longer than testing time
230		**1.8.3 Test pass #3**	**5 days**	227	
231		1.8.3.1 Follow test script and record errors	2 days		
232	▦	1.8.3.2 Make requires s/w corrections	3 days	231	Assume takes a bit longer than testing time
233		1.8.4 Finalize test documentation	2 days		
234		1.8.5 System test complete	0 days	233	
235	▦	**1.9 End of project review**	**5 days**	223	10 people for 1/2 day
236		**1.10 END**	**0 days**		

Figure 5.9   (continued)

You: "What happens next?"

"Gather info on competitive products?"

"Sure it is. Any idea of an estimate?"

"Half a day on the Net should do it," mutters Charlie, one of the engineers. "If I do it," he adds ominously. You accept his offer—even if it wasn't intended as one. (Charlie is a somewhat untypical software person. While he has some of the normal traits—grumpiness (especially with Sales and Marketing people), an unwillingness to suffer fools gladly, a tendency to wear the same T-shirt several days in a row—he cares passionately not just about software engineering, but about producing good products.)

"Next?"

"Review the stuff with Marketing."

"Estimate?"

You note (in the Notes field) what they intend to do and move on. For the next few lines the Notes field shows the conclusions you come to.

"That's gonna need a review cycle," you say, "once you've covered 1.3.2 Write requirements document." Everyone agrees, so now you throw in one of your reusable blocks. Again you note down in the Notes field the estimates associated with the various tasks.

OK, so now we're starting to make some progress. "What's next?" you ask.

"Well, once we've got the requirements," says the other engineering type—Charlie's buddy, Engineer #2, "given the level of detail we do requirements at in this organization, we'll be able to write an Acceptance Test Plan." Engineer #2 is one of those people who, if you asked them what time it was, he'd tell you how to build a watch. He does this somewhat now. "So," he continues, "we'll have to do some kinda research first." Your ears prick up at the sound of this. When a software person says "research," you suspect that what it really means is that they want to take a bit of a breather before getting stuck into a big chunk of work. However, you let it go. It serves your purposes too. It provides you with a potential little bit of contingency in your plan. Whenever you see these offered to you, you *never* turn them down. Engineer #2 is in full flight. "Then we'll have to do Navigation, Functionality, Integrity, Performance, Stress and Installation Tests." Your scribe is furiously writing. Engineer #2 finishes, well satisfied with his contribution. The Sales, Marketing, and Finance people look at Engineer #2 with either deep respect or deep contempt—you can't really tell which. You say "and so, Engineer #2, give us the estimates." Engineer #2 is stumped for a moment, before falling back on the age-old fallback of software people when asked for an estimate. "I dunno," he says, "how long is a piece of string?" But you're not buying this. You push a little harder. "For each type of test, what do we have to do—Engineer #2?" Engineer #2 hesitates before continuing. "Define the tests ... write the scripts ... define the test data and expected results." You nod furiously drawing him on. Your scribe scribes. "Estimates, Engineer #2?" Engineer #2 is either going to get very angry with you or wrestle with the problem. He is like a train coming up to a set of points. The points click. He goes down the wrestle-with-the-problem line. "I really don't know," he says. "How about assume 1 day's work for each of the three aspects and do as much as you can in that day." You can't really come up with a better idea yourself, so you go with that. You throw in a review cycle and a signoff. That's it for the System Test Plan.

You feel you're starting to get onto a bit of a roll. "Next up?"

"High Level Design," the engineering people chorus. You propose going at it the same way as the previous two documents, the Requirements and System Test Plan. But now Engineer #2 decides to get his own back. "Aw, I think this waterfall model type approach really isn't appropriate to what we're doing here. That may have been OK when you were designing software," he says to you, "but prototyping and RAD is where it's at the moment. Anyway, didn't we say we'd do a prototype?" He sits back and crosses his arms. Check! Not to be outdone, Charlie throws in another one. "Engineer #2, weren't we talking about using the Unified Process [1] on this one?"

While Engineer #2 and Charlie start to work this one into a firestorm—to the irritation of the rest of the people in the room—you decide it's time for a bit of winging it. "Prototyping" and "RAD (Rapid Application Development)" you had. "Unified Process" has you stumped completely. You take a chance.

"Sure," you say, sounding completely unphased, "it's a good way to go." Addressing the other occupants in the room, you say "What Engineer #2 and Charlie are essentially saying—correct me if I picked you up wrong, guys—is that there's a lot to be said for adopting the we'll-know-it-when-we-see-it approach. So that instead of writing and reviewing a document, we'll build a prototype as a proof of concept, let you guys review it, change it, review it again, and so on. Let's be clear too, that this is not just a mock-up of the user interface, but that the underlying design concepts, structure, architecture, will be worked out. That right, guys?" Engineer #2 and Charlie are disappointed. They nod, smiling limply. "So let's look at doing that. We would then have a sequence of jobs that went,"

1. Build prototype.

2. Review with Marketing and note changes.

3. Go back to 1.

You go over to the counter-attack. "So can you estimate this for us, guys?" They're grumpy now and start to sulk. You blaze ahead without them. "Say 5 days for the first build, a day to review. Now a second iteration ... and a third iteration ... assuming eight iterations." You have scribbled something on the flipchart that looks like this (Table 5.1).

Table 5.1 Build and review prototyp. (All estimates in person-days.)

Job/Iteration	1	2	3	4	5	6	7	8	Totals
1. Build/revise prototype	5	3	2	2	2	1	1	1	17
2. Review with Marketing	1	1	0.5	0.5	0.5	0.5	0.5	0.5	5
Total per iteration	6	4	2.5	2.5	2.5	1.5	1.5	1.5	22

"What makes you think it'll only be eight iterations?" asks Engineer #2. He regrets the question as soon as it pops out of his mouth. "We're *assuming* it's eight iterations, Engineer #2," you say patiently. "It can be any number you like. Do you think it should be more? Less?" Silence. You hold his gaze. Finally, he mumbles "Leave it at eight for the moment." Checkmate!

Your scribe is looking expectantly over his laptop's screen at you. "Let's put in one line item," you say "Prototype, 22 days' effort. And note that as well as assuming eight iterations, we're also assuming people are available immediately to review the work. So the 22 days' effort is also 22 days' elapsed time." You call a break to let Engineer #2 and Charlie get over it.

During the break, you point out to your scribe three important points that arose during the prototype discussion. One we've seen already—we saw it in Figure 5.6—is the notion that you can have several iterations of a sequence of jobs. The second point is related to this. It's something that we might call "scaling." On a first iteration, we might give certain estimates for the particular jobs in the sequence. On a second iteration, it might happen that the estimates would be different—either larger or smaller. In the case we have just seen we expect them to reduce because we are in a scenario where we are converging (hopefully) on something. Thus, in the table above we see the estimates gradually reducing with the iterations. And thirdly, we saw that sometimes it is convenient for us, i.e., less long-winded, to "package" a bunch of jobs together in a single job. In the case of "Prototype," we packed sixteen little jobs—the eight iterations of "Build/revise prototype" and the eight iterations of "Review with Marketing" into a single job. While the single job—at 22 person-days—is outside our 1–5 person-days rule of thumb, its sixteen components aren't. Provided we remind ourselves—which we did with a note in the Notes field—of the existence of the components, this is often a good thing to do. We will see a slightly different use of the concepts of scaling and packaging in the next piece of the worked example.

The group reassembles and we move on. The next milestone we identified in Chapter 4 was the demo at Comdex. It is now agreed that the prototype will constitute the demo. Marketing will take the final prototype resulting from iteration eight and make it the basis for the demo. It will be their job to get it to Comdex and it is agreed that that project is outside the scope of this one. Marketing asks to have Charlie or Engineer #2 on hand during Comdex, and this is agreed. (Subsequently—during the shortening of the project in Chapter 11—this gets changed to Charlie or Engineer #2 not going to Comdex but being available on the end of phone line with remote access to the demo machine on the stand.)

"Who does what next?" you ask. "Code," Engineer #2 says. He's happy again. He's had a very large espresso, he's nursing a Coke and anyway, with "Code" we're back on his home turf. "OK," you say, "let's estimate it." "Won't know till we've done the Design—eh, the prototype," says Charlie, somewhat warily. Mentally, you shake your head. Wrong again. Reminding yourself a bit of Margaret Thatcher giving a speech, you say "We have ten features, right?" You write them down on the left-hand side of a flipchart page.

1. Pricing;

2. Foreign exchange;

3. Euro support;

4. 3rd party payments;

5. Settlement;

6. Reporting;

7. Web interface;

8. Security;

9. Tutorial;

10. Online help.

General agreement. "Are they all the same size and complexity?" General agreement that they aren't necessarily. "So can we try and figure out which is which?" Nodding. You (as though the idea has just this very minute popped into your head): "Could we maybe rate them according to some scheme or other?" Nodding. "How about this? We'll class them as small (S), medium (M), or large (L) and then try to estimate them?" More nodding. Also some skepticism. Still, there seems to be a general air of "it can't hurt." You run down the list and people propose their various views. There is good discussion because often what Marketing had in mind for a particular feature bears no relation to what Engineering were intending to do. All the decisions about what a particular feature is or isn't gets recorded in our notes from the scoping part of the day. We finally end up with our flipchart page looking like this.

1. Pricing (S);

2. Foreign exchange (M);

3. Euro support (M);

4. 3rd party payments (M);

5. Settlement (S);

6. Reporting (S);

7. Web interface (L);

8. Security (L);

9. Tutorial (M);

10. Online help (L).

"OK, now for each of these items, what jobs do we have to do?" You flip the flipchart page, reorder the features, and draw a table. It's in Table 5.2. "Write Code, Document Code, Test Code?" somebody suggests. It sounds reasonable enough. (You realize that the "Document Code" will probably never happen, but that may well be okay by you, since you will see it as a few more juicy morsels of contingency.)

Table 5.2 Jobs to develop the software.

Feature	Size	Write Code	Document Code	Test Code
Pricing	S			
Settlement	S			
Reporting	S			
Foreign exchange	M			
Euro support	M			
3rd party payments	M			
Tutorial	M			
Web interface	L			
Security	L			
Online help	L			

"Estimates?" you ask briskly. "We'd only be guessing," says Engineer #2, earnestly. "Guess away," you say. They do, occasionally you question an estimate and when in doubt you always increase it, again there is discussion on the way particular features will appear or be implemented. You propose a couple of assumptions, namely that you will assume that a Medium feature takes twice as long to code as a Small one, and that a Large feature takes three times as long. (The value of doing this is that if, when you run the project, the first three features you code are a Small, a Medium, and a Large one, you can soon see how valid this assumption was. This in turn acts as a form of early warning about your estimates.[1]) You plug in a reusable component for the testing, and estimating its individual components makes you more comfortable with the overall estimate. For the Large components, you assume that when they come to be done, each will break down into four major elements which have to get done. (The value of doing this is again to do with early

---

[1] This is a very important point and one worth highlighting. Chuck Howell told me how NASA uses the term "dark areas" to describe those areas of a big software development that have the most technical uncertainty or technical risk. By deliberately front loading development of these areas, the associated risks and uncertainties can be winkled out at the beginning of the project. Thus, not only might we schedule certain activities early in order to calibrate the accuracy of our estimates, we might also do it to "defuse" technical risk or uncertainty.

A variant of this idea, which often has merit, would be to take one thread of the project all the way through development and test to shake out the technical infrastructure. If your project relied on delivery of certain components by third parties, then doing this would be a good way of forcing early delivery dates on them. This would check their ability to meet commitments as well as resulting in one less set of things to go wrong.

warning. If, when the prototype has been done and the design is clear, it turns out that the Large components are much larger (e.g. one of them has *ten* major components, not four) than we anticipated, then we again know that there may be a problem with our estimates.)

Finally your table looks like the one in Table 5.3. (And you'll forgive me if all of the estimates look a *little* too good to be true, but this was done in the interests of not making the worked example too ungainly to follow.) Notice again that we are doing scaling and packaging here.

Table 5.3 Estimates to develop software. (All estimates in person-days.)

Feature	Size	Assumption	Write Code	Document Code	Test Code	Totals
Pricing	S		4	0.5	3.5	8
Settlement	S		4	0.5	3.5	8
Reporting	S		4	0.5	3.5	8
Foreign exchange	M	M = 2S	8	1	7	16
Euro support	M	M = 2S	8	1	7	16
3rd party payments	M	M = 2S	8	1	7	16
Tutorial	M	M = 2S	8	1	7	16
Web interface	L	L = 3S	12	4	16	32
Security	L	L = 3S	12	4	16	32
Online help	L	L = 3S	12	4	16	32

You're going to need a technical author to work on this project, but that person hasn't been identified yet, and there's nobody in the room with a background in that discipline. All you can do is try as best you can. You ask the question. "OK, so what happens next?"

Somebody fronts up with another "Research" and you happily accept this. The two jobs that follow it are pure guesses. You can't help feeling that the people who proposed the estimates had just heard the terminology and wanted to show off their knowledge. Talk about the blind leading the blind! Still, your take on it is this. If push came to shove, somebody could just write the text in Word, pretty it up, and send it out. These 10 person-days may or may not be needed. At worst they are, at best it's a bit more contingency.

The four jobs under "Write user documentation or Help text" are again guesses. You notice that there's going to be a large amount of over-lap between the feature "Online help" and these jobs. There are issues to be sorted out there. For example, can the technical author write one lot of text that can be used in both the hardcopy manual and the online help? It seems likely. If so, there could be a great heap of contingency buried inside these jobs. However, you judge correctly that it's something you don't have to waste everybody's time with today. You slap down your estimates and press on. You can smell the finish line.

Somebody pipes up about editing and integrating the user documentation and help text. Another five jobs spatter onto the plan. Again, these can be cleaned up later.

The final act in the drama is the System Testing. You suggest an assumption that three passes will be enough. (You do this to facilitate the author of this book. In reality, you'd probably want more.) You make a couple of assumptions to enable you to estimate the first pass and you "package" the estimates. Then you "scale" from there to the other two passes.

An end of project review completes the show.

Summary

In applying the ideas in this chapter, we have begun the process of building an accurately estimated WBS. Because of the way we have gone about it, the WBS has a number of characteristics—over and above those already mentioned—which make it attractive.

First, we can see both the detail and the big picture. We built the WBS in chunks, first identifying each new chunk that needed to be done, and then delving down into the detail to give us accurate estimates. As a result of this approach, we can now see, for example, only the high level, as in Figure 5.10.

Or we can see all of the detail as in Figure 5.9. Or we can see bits of the detail that might interest us, as in Figure 5.11.

Next, notice that our WBS is a deliverable-oriented one, rather than an activity-oriented one. Rather than being built around what we as product developers are doing (write code, unit test software, and so on), we focus on the things that are being delivered—the features, the user manual, the prototype/demo for Comdex. In terms of visibility, especially to stakeholders outside the team, this can only be a good thing.[2]

---

2   My thanks to John Brackett for this concept.

ID	⊕	Task name	Work	Predecessor	Notes	2000 J F M A M J J A
1		1 The project	457.75 days			
2		1.1 START	0 days			
3	▦	1.2 Project planning and scoping meeting	9 days	2	9 people for 1 day	
4		1.3 Produce requirements document	27 days	3		
23		1.4 Produce system/acceptance test plan	39.75 days	4		
58	▦	1.5 Prototype	22 days	4	Assuming people are available immediately to review the work. So the...	
59		1.6 Write code	184 days	58		
208		1.7 Produce User documentation and Help system	99 days	58		
223		1.8 Execute system test	72 days	23, 59		
235	▦	1.9 End of project review	5 days	223	10 people for 1/2 day	
236		1.10 END	0 days			

Key: ▪ Detailed task
⊣ Dependency
◥◤ Summary task

Figure 5.10   High level picture.

Third, notice that by building up the WBS in the way we described—
"making the journey in your head"—we made the journey end to en,d
i.e. from the absolute start of the project to the point at which the scoping session had determined the project would be over. This maximized
our chances that nothing would be overlooked in our WBS.

Finally, as part of the scoping, we decided what quality assurance
checks were required, and these were then easily built into the WBS.[3]

We are now ready to press on with the next piece of the business,
which—mercifully—is a quick one. We do so in Chapter 6.

---

3   One technique for reducing defects and thereby ensuring quality is inspections. There is a lot of evidence that they are a cost-effective way to reduce defects, especially by catching them early, before
they soak up huge amounts of effort to fix. In my experience, there is also a lot of evidence that
inspections are one of those things that get thrown by the wayside, particularly if there is a rush
on to finish the project. Inspections have also gained a bit of a bad reputation as being very
time-consuming and luxuries that perhaps can only be afforded in big companies.

Like many of these things, this is a case where we don't want to throw out the baby with the bath
water. Inspections are a good idea. If you would like to use them in perhaps as efficient a way as
possible then you could look at two papers mentioned in the References [2, 3]; Bibliography [8,9].
Their titles speak for themselves: *Does Every Inspection Need a Meeting* and *Anywhere, Anytime
Code Inspections: Using the Web to Remove Inspection Bottlenecks in Large-Scale Software
Development.*

ID	⬛	Task Name	Work	Predecessor	Notes
1		**1 The project**	**457.75 days**		
2		**1.1 START**	0 days		
3	▦	**1.2 Project planning and scoping meeting**	9 days	2	9 people for 1 day
4		**1.3 Produce requirements document**	27 days	3	
23		**1.4 Produce system/acceptance test plan**	**39.5 days**	4	
24		1.4.1 Research	5 days		
25		**1.4.2 Write navigation tests**	**3 days**	24	
29		1.4.3 Write functionality tests	**3 days**	25	
33		1.4.4 Write integrity tests	**3 days**	29	
37		1.4.5 Write performance tests	**3 days**	33	
41		1.4.6 Write stress tests	**3 days**	37	
45		1.4.7 Write installation tests	**3 days**	41	
49		**1.4.8 Review cycle**	**16 days**	45	
50		1.4.8.1 Circulate	0.5 days		
51	▦	1.4.8.2 Individual review	5 days	50	Assume 5 reviewers @ 1 day each. …
52		1.4.8.3 Review meeting	3.5 days	51	
53		1.4.8.4 Changes to document	5 days	52	
54		1.4.8.5 Circulate again	0.5 days	53	
55		1.4.8.6 Second review	1.5 days	54	
56		1.4.9 Signoff	0.5 days	49	
57		1.4.10 System/acceptance tests written	0 days	56	
58	▦	**1.5 Prototype**	**22 days**	4	
59		**1.6 Write code**	**184 days**	58	
60		**1.6.1 Pricing**	**8 days**		
73		**1.6.2 Settlement**	**8 days**		
86		**1.6.3 Reporting**	**8 days**		
87		1.6.3.1 Write code element (including clean…)	4 days		
88		1.6.3.2 Document code element	0.5 days		
89		**1.6.3.3 Unit test code**	**3.5 days**	88	
90		**1.6.3.3.1 Prepare test plan and test set**	**1 day**		
91		1.6.3.3.1.1 Define test sequence	0.25 days		
92		1.6.3.3.1.2 Write test scripts	0.5 days	91	
93		1.6.3.3.1.3 Define expected results	0.25 days	92	
94		1.6.3.3.2 Subsystem ready for unit testing	0 days	93	
95		1.6.3.3.3 Test code	1 day	94	
96		1.6.3.3.4 Make corrections to code	0.5 days	95	
97		1.6.3.3.5 Test code again	0.5 days	96	
98		1.6.3.3.6 Prepare test report	0.5 days	97	

Figure 5.11   Partial detail.

How to Run Successful Projects in Web Time

ID	⊕	Task Name	Work	Predecessor	Notes
99		1.6.4 Foreign exchange	16 days		
112		1.6.5 Euro support	16 days		
125		1.6.6 3rd part payments	16 days		
138		1.6.7 Tutorial	16 days		
151		1.6.8 Web interface	32 days		
170		1.6.9 Security	32 days		
189		1.6.10 Online help	32 days		
208		1.7 Produce User documentation and Help system	99 days	58	
223		1.8 Execute system test	72 days	23, 59	
235	▦	1.9 End of project review	5 days	223	10 people for 1/2 day
236		1.10 END	0 days		

Figure 5.11   (continued)

References

1. Kruchten, P., *The Rational Unified Process*, Reading, MA: Addison-Wesley, 1998.

2. Votta, L. G. Jr., "Does Every Inspection Need a Meeting," *ACM Sigsoft*, 1993.

3. Perpich, et al., "Anywhere, Anytime Code Inspections: Using the Web to Remove Inspection Bottlenecks in Large-Scale Software Development," *ICSE*, 1997.

6

Add In the Project Management

➤ Project management is crucial to shortening the project. This chapter shows how to calculate and set aside enough time for project management.

➤ It also discusses what to do when the project is too big for one person to run.

➤ The worked example is continued.

Introduction

At the risk of stating the blindingly obvious, project management is important on all projects. It is also one of those things that software people, especially, tend to regard as something of an optional extra. It's a break from the real work, or an irritant (the administrative work on the project), or a chance to put in some extra contingency, which can then be used on those tasks that were underestimated.

On a dramatically shortened project, project management—the shepherding or "trailbossing" [1] of the project forward is mandatory and essential to ensuring that nothing falls between the cracks and that no time is wasted.

The next section gives a rule of thumb for adding in the project management. The net result of doing this is one extra job on the list of jobs developed in the previous chapter. You could argue that I could have just done this in Chapter 5. I would argue in return that this issue is so important, it deserves a chapter to itself.

A Rule of Thumb

Before I drop my rule of thumb on you, I should say the following. It may be that you already have a rule of thumb that you use for this aspect of your projects. Or it may be that your company has a standard that everybody follows (in theory, at least) for how much project management to put into a project. If so, that's fine—just follow those rules here. They are much more likely to be right in your organization, for your projects than anything I might propose.

If, however, you don't have any such rule of thumb or standard, then go with the following.

Take 10% of the total project effort (work) identified in Chapter 5 and add that in (i.e., this is an additional 10%) to cover the various project management tasks on your project. This 10% is intended to cover all aspects of the project management of your project as described in Chapters 4 through 15 of this book. To put it another way, anything I suggest you do in Chapters 4 through 15 will have been accounted for, budgeted for, set aside for in this 10%.

You may be wondering where this 10% comes from. There are really two sources. One is our own company's experience over the last eight years, where we would have looked at literally, thousands of projects. The other is that this 10% figure tallies pretty well with other sources. See for example [2] where Boehm proposed between 6% and 8% depending on the size and complexity of the project. (If our slightly higher 10% causes you to have a little extra contingency as a result, you won't hear me complain.)

Worked Example

As we saw in the previous chapter, in Figure 5.10, the total effort identified in the project is 457.5 person-days. Our rule of thumb thus gives us 46 person-days for project management. This is shown, added in, in Figure 6.1.

What If I Don't Have Enough Time?

It can sometimes happen that, having done the project management effort calculation, the result shows you that there is more work than can be done by one person. For example, say your project was 180 person-

ID	❶	Task name	Work	Predecessor	2000	2001
1		1 The project	503.5 days			
2		1.1 START	0 days			
3	▦	1.2 Project planning and scoping meeting	9 days	2		
4		1.3 Produce requirements document	27 days	3		
23		1.4 Produce system/acceptance test plan	39.5 days	4		
58	▦	1.5 Prototype	22 days	4		
59		1.6 Write code	184 days	58		
208		1.7 Produce User documentation and Help system	99 days	58		
223		1.8 Execute system test	72 days	23, 59		
235	▦	1.9 End of project review	5 days	223		
236		1.11 Project management	46 days			
237		1.11 END	0 days	235		

Key: ■ Detailed task
      ↧ Dependency
     ◣◢ Summary task

Figure 6.1   Plan including project management effort.

months, (3,600 person-days using 1 person-month = 20 person-days) effort (30 people for an average of 6 months), so that the project management required is 360 person days over 6 elapsed months, then clearly this cannot be done by one person. Then you must introduce a structure into your team so that the project management is spread across, and done by, more than one person.

In this example, you might decide to have 5 teams of 6 people each with the 5-team leaders reporting to you. Then, you can do this 10% calculation at two levels. For each of the team leaders, they are running a 36 person-month (6 people for 6 months) project. 36 person-months are 720 person-days. 10% of this gives 72 person-days project management. You in turn, are now running a 5-person team (the 5 team leaders). Thus your project is 30 person-months (5 people for 6 months). This equals 600 person-days; so your project management is 60 person-days.

This, in theory, is how the calculation goes. And, in a perfect world, this is what would happen. In reality, the fact that there is now a two-layer structure through which information must flow means additional effort on the part of yourself and the team leaders. In that case, what I think I would do—I've found it the cleanest thing—is to leave their 10% unchanged and increase yours to something more like 15% or 20% to allow for this. This recognizes the fact that the project is still your responsibility, so that if there are problems with one or more of the team leaders, it is you who has to take up the slack.

A final point: the situation of not having enough time can also arise where you are going to be project manager on the project but also have technical responsibilities. This is a very common situation, particularly on small teams working in technically complex areas. We will discuss this problem, not just in relation to project management effort, but in general in the next chapter where we talk about peoples' availability.

References

1. O'Connell, F., *How To Run Successful High-Tech Project-Based Organizations*, Norwood: Artech House, 1999.

2. Boehm, B., *Software Engineering Economics,* Englewood Cliffs, NJ: Prentice Hall, 1981.

7

Get People To Do the Work

➤ This chapter shows how, by calculating team member's availability and dividing this into the effort (from Chapter 5) we get the elapsed time for a particular job, and ultimately the project elapsed time.

➤ One of those people is you and we look at that.

➤ The chapter shows how to calculate the supply parameter in our supply-demand equation.

➤ It shows how to identify the strengths and weaknesses of the team.

➤ We continue the worked example.

Introduction

You now need people to do the work identified in Chapters 5 and 6. Here, your project will stand or fall on three issues:

1. People being there to do the work;

2. Those peoples' availability;

3. The strengths and weaknesses of those people.

We look at them in turn.

People

You need people to do the work. It's quite common that at the beginning of a project, you don't know who some or all of those people are, and then it is customary to indicate these on the plan with so-called "generic resources." These are names like "A. N. other," "New hire,"

"Contractor #3," "Java Programmer," and so on. No problem with this, except that before the job starts there has to be a real person in place to replace the generic resource.

All so obvious, you might say, it's ludicrous to even be writing it. However, an enormous number of projects go wrong because all the jobs didn't get done—because there weren't people doing them. Hmmm. Something wrong somewhere.

Your first job then is to track down the people who are going to do the work. For real people, you stick them in the plan and that's the end of it. For generic resources, you put them in with some kind of mental (or better still, written) note to yourself that you'll need to do some legwork to find those people. This work will be accounted for under the project management heading we identified in the last chapter.

Peoples' Availability

Imagine Bozo shows up one day on your project. He's been sent by central casting and announces that he's to be your Java programmer. Great. Your first question is to ask Bozo whether he's available full time. Sure, he nods enthusiastically. This is a project he really wants to work on. He's got no other project on the go at the moment. Great. Oh, there is the Project Y wind-down that's going on, but that's just gonna be 1 or 2 days for the next week or two. Okay. "And I've gotta go to a meeting with a customer that Marketing's arranged," adds Bozo brightly. Okay. "I've booked some vacation," says Bozo, somewhat more uncertainly. You ask when and he tells you. Enough already.

You sit Bozo down and say "Okay Bozo, we're going to do a Dance Card for you." "A what?" he asks. "A Dance Card." You explain that you're going to help Bozo figure out how much of his time he has already sold to other projects. (The term "Dance Card" is a reference to those more gentile days—I don't remember them myself!—where, when ladies went to dances, they were issued dance cards. To dance with a particular lady, you wrote your name in a particular slot on her dance card. When that dance was taken, that slot was booked, and could not be given to anyone else. If Bozo has allocated some of his time to the Project Y wind-down, then that time is not available to you—unless you can cut some deal with the Project Y people.)

So you do Bozo's Dance Card with him and it ends up looking something like in Figure 7.1.

#	Project	Basis		01/11	08/11	15/11	22/11	29/11	06/12	Total
1	Project Y wind-down	2	dpw	2	2	2	2			8
2	Meeting with customer	1	day	1						1
3	PLC Conference	3	days			3				3
4	Support of Project X	0.5	dpw	0.5	0.5	0.5	0.5	0.5	0.5	3
5	Reviews of other designs	4	days	1	1	0.5	0.5	0.5	0.5	4
6	Admin. / Inbox / Interruptions	1.5	hpd	1	1	1	1	1	1	6
7	Training others	1.5	hpd	1	1	1	1	1	1	6
9	Support of Project Z	1	dpw	1	1	1	1	1	1	6
10	Holidays	5	days				5			5
	Available	30	days							
				7.5	6.5	9	11	4	4	42
	Notes:									
	(1) 'dpw' = days per week									
	(2) All figures in person-days									

Figure 7.1   Bozo's Dance Card.

It shows that over the next six weeks, when the Java work on your project was intended to be lifting off, Bozo has no time at all available to work for you. In a period of 30 working days, Bozo has 42 days work to do—even before he begins to include your project. Also—to put it mildly—he looks like he's having a few heavy weeks. Bozo looks at it in stunned silence. You lift the phone and call central casting.

Now obviously, I made Figure 7.1 come out a certain way to make a certain point. In my experience, however, getting people to do Dance Cards is almost always a sobering experience. For you it is an invaluable tool to enable you to establish the real availability of individual people to your project.

(Just as an aside, if you find on one of your projects any of the following symptoms:

- Jobs are not getting done;

- People working longer and longer hours;

- Projects falling further and further behind,

then a possible cause of this is that you're not getting the effort that was originally budgeted for in the plan. A Dance Card check would be a good way to establish this.)

Dance Cards raise an interesting issue that is worth exploring. How many things (projects) can somebody reasonably work on? Let's assume that everyone has their "Admin./Inbox/Interruptions" just like Bozo. In my experience, for even the most focused and brutally able time manager, these blow away about 1–1.5 hours a day. That's the best part of one day of any given week. That leaves four other days. If we go with our proposition that half a day is the smallest unit of time we recognize, then potentially somebody could work on eight different things—Bozo's got seven.

Now, can somebody reasonably work on eight projects at the same time? (I'm referring specifically here to workers on projects—people responsible for getting the stuff done. For managers of projects we've already discussed the issue in Chapter 6.) If they were eight projects to dig eight separate holes, for example, then the answer is probably yes. You would finish a half day's shovelling at one hole, and then saunter across to the next one where you would do another half-day's shovelling. However, if you're involved in a knowledge or high-tech industry, then this is clearly a joke. The put-down-pick-up time in switching from one project to another makes this a monstrously inefficient use of someone's time.

One project I'll buy. I'll even buy two. Pushed far enough, I'd maybe buy up to four—one day apiece—even though at that point I think things are falling apart. Ideally give me one—the person is available full-time, or two—the person is available half-time and, for God's sake, let's leave it at that.[1]

This issue of so-called "multitasking" is very important and we will return to it later in the book, especially in Chapter 15.

One final thing: Remember that if, on your project, you have both jobs or technical work to do and you are also the project manager, your availability to do jobs or technical work is limited because you must set time aside for project management.[2]

---

1   If this idea is too radical for you, then here's a much-watered down version of it. You might consider asking your management that on a crunch project or phase of a project, your people don't have to attend the normal all hands, team building, and other events that companies, especially large ones, run.

2   I know I said that was the final point, but there are still more useful things you can do with Dance Cards and I'm grateful to Chuck Howell for pointing them out. He calls them "finding the join" and "defragmenting the liveware."

Finding the Join

When you have Dance Cards for all of the staff allocated to your project, you can see all of the other projects with which your team members are involved. Meeting the managers of those other projects, either altogether or singly over coffee would almost certainly be valuable. You could understand their schedule, risks, needs, and surprises that they think are going to happen. There's no fun when they say something like "Charlie didn't tell you we'd be in crunch mode for all of March because of the April deadline? Hmmm, must've slipped his mind," but better to find out now than at the beginning of March.

Meeting with the other project managers, especially in large organizations, also helps to establish some rules of engagement for resolving inevitable surprises and competing demands for people. Also it is useful to understand who is at the "join" on the organization chart, that is, who is the person to break impasses, decide deadlocks, and determine the definitive allocation of resources among competing projects and project managers.

Defragmenting the Liveware

When all the project managers sit together and look at how they are using staff, it may be the case that there are some opportunities for reducing the fragmentation among staff. For example, Fred may be scheduled to do test development and execution on projects A and B one day per week each, and development the rest of the time. Mary may be scheduled to do test development and execution on projects B and C one day per week each and development the rest of the time. Perhaps one of them would be interested in becoming a tester full time on projects A, B, and C (assuming one day per week allocated to overhead and miscellaneous swill). The potential improvements in efficiency and opportunities for synergy may be worth the shuffling if mutually agreeable.

Strengths and Weaknesses

People are good at some things and not good at others. To assume that people are "plug and play"—just drop them into a slot and they'll work out—would be very foolish indeed. I'd like to think that not a lot of people would consciously make such a mistake. But I think many people do it unconsciously. Or perhaps, phrased a different way, they neglect to think about the issue at all.

The point is, though, that we have to. How you use or misuse the talents (and weaknesses) of your team will have everything to do with the outcome of your project. There are lots of ways one could approach this. A way I've used for a long time that I find works well is to rate the assignments of people to jobs according to the following scheme:

- The person has the necessary skill and experience to do the job and likes to do it.

- The person has the necessary skill and experience to do the job and is prepared to do it.

- The person has the necessary skill and experience to do the job but is not prepared to do it.

- The person can be trained or instructed into doing the job.

- The person cannot do the job.

While the project manager can do this, an even better way is to have both the project manager do it and each individual team member do it for the jobs to which they have been assigned. Then compare the results. They are always interesting. Misconceptions you may have had about a particular person, or that they may have had about themselves, inevitably surface and may well result in some reassignments.

Worked Example

To begin figuring out how many and what kinds of people we're going to need, the plan is as good a place as any to start. We begin by putting in the names—either peoples' names where they're known or generic resources where they're not—against jobs. Our notes from earlier steps also assist us here. We begin to build up, line by line, the picture in Figure 7.2.

We are adding three extra things to the plan. The three are:

- who,

- availability,

- duration.

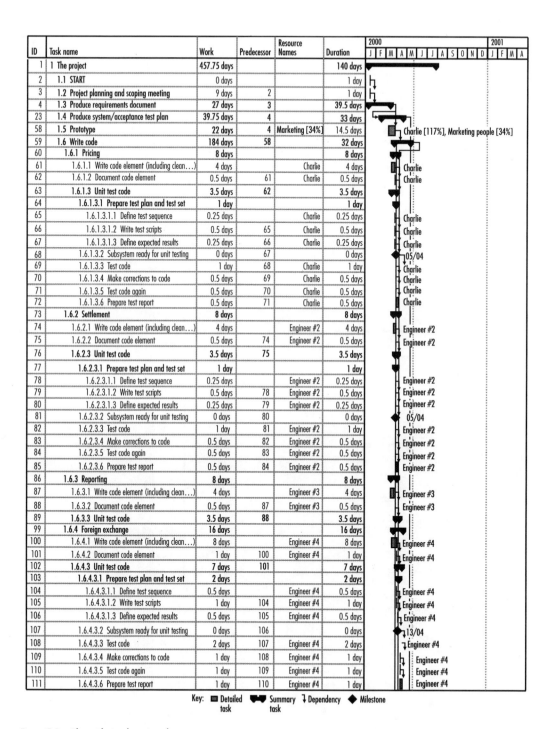

ID	Task name	Work	Predecessor	Resource Names	Duration	2000 / 2001
1	1 The project	457.75 days			140 days	
2	1.1 START	0 days			1 day	
3	1.2 Project planning and scoping meeting	9 days	2		1 day	
4	1.3 Produce requirements document	27 days	3		39.5 days	
23	1.4 Produce system/acceptance test plan	39.75 days	4		33 days	
58	1.5 Prototype	22 days	4	Marketing [34%]	14.5 days	Charlie [117%], Marketing people [34%]
59	1.6 Write code	184 days	58		32 days	
60	1.6.1 Pricing	8 days			8 days	
61	1.6.1.1 Write code element (including clean...)	4 days		Charlie	4 days	Charlie
62	1.6.1.2 Document code element	0.5 days	61	Charlie	0.5 days	Charlie
63	1.6.1.3 Unit test code	3.5 days	62		3.5 days	
64	1.6.1.3.1 Prepare test plan and test set	1 day			1 day	
65	1.6.1.3.1.1 Define test sequence	0.25 days		Charlie	0.25 days	Charlie
66	1.6.1.3.1.2 Write test scripts	0.5 days	65	Charlie	0.5 days	Charlie
67	1.6.1.3.1.3 Define expected results	0.25 days	66	Charlie	0.25 days	Charlie
68	1.6.1.3.2 Subsystem ready for unit testing	0 days	67		0 days	05/04
69	1.6.1.3.3 Test code	1 day	68	Charlie	1 day	Charlie
70	1.6.1.3.4 Make corrections to code	0.5 days	69	Charlie	0.5 days	Charlie
71	1.6.1.3.5 Test code again	0.5 days	70	Charlie	0.5 days	Charlie
72	1.6.1.3.6 Prepare test report	0.5 days	71	Charlie	0.5 days	Charlie
73	1.6.2 Settlement	8 days			8 days	
74	1.6.2.1 Write code element (including clean...)	4 days		Engineer #2	4 days	Engineer #2
75	1.6.2.2 Document code element	0.5 days	74	Engineer #2	0.5 days	Engineer #2
76	1.6.2.3 Unit test code	3.5 days	75		3.5 days	
77	1.6.2.3.1 Prepare test plan and test set	1 day			1 day	
78	1.6.2.3.1.1 Define test sequence	0.25 days		Engineer #2	0.25 days	Engineer #2
79	1.6.2.3.1.2 Write test scripts	0.5 days	78	Engineer #2	0.5 days	Engineer #2
80	1.6.2.3.1.3 Define expected results	0.25 days	79	Engineer #2	0.25 days	Engineer #2
81	1.6.2.3.2 Subsystem ready for unit testing	0 days	80		0 days	05/04
82	1.6.2.3.3 Test code	1 day	81	Engineer #2	1 day	Engineer #2
83	1.6.2.3.4 Make corrections to code	0.5 days	82	Engineer #2	0.5 days	Engineer #2
84	1.6.2.3.5 Test code again	0.5 days	83	Engineer #2	0.5 days	Engineer #2
85	1.6.2.3.6 Prepare test report	0.5 days	84	Engineer #2	0.5 days	Engineer #2
86	1.6.3 Reporting	8 days			8 days	
87	1.6.3.1 Write code element (including clean...)	4 days		Engineer #3	4 days	Engineer #3
88	1.6.3.2 Document code element	0.5 days	87	Engineer #3	0.5 days	Engineer #3
89	1.6.3.3 Unit test code	3.5 days	88		3.5 days	
99	1.6.4 Foreign exchange	16 days			16 days	
100	1.6.4.1 Write code element (including clean...)	8 days		Engineer #4	8 days	Engineer #4
101	1.6.4.2 Document code element	1 day	100	Engineer #4	1 day	Engineer #4
102	1.6.4.3 Unit test code	7 days	101		7 days	
103	1.6.4.3.1 Prepare test plan and test set	2 days			2 days	
104	1.6.4.3.1.1 Define test sequence	0.5 days		Engineer #4	0.5 days	Engineer #4
105	1.6.4.3.1.2 Write test scripts	1 day	104	Engineer #4	1 day	Engineer #4
106	1.6.4.3.1.3 Define expected results	0.5 days	105	Engineer #4	0.5 days	Engineer #4
107	1.6.4.3.2 Subsystem ready for unit testing	0 days	106		0 days	13/04
108	1.6.4.3.3 Test code	2 days	107	Engineer #4	2 days	Engineer #4
109	1.6.4.3.4 Make corrections to code	1 day	108	Engineer #4	1 day	Engineer #4
110	1.6.4.3.5 Test code again	1 day	109	Engineer #4	1 day	Engineer #4
111	1.6.4.3.6 Prepare test report	1 day	110	Engineer #4	1 day	Engineer #4

Key: ■ Detailed task   ◤◥ Summary task   ↲ Dependency   ◆ Milestone

Figure 7.2   Plan with people assigned.

ID	Task name	Work	Predecessor	Resource Names	Duration	2000 / 2001 (timeline)
112	1.6.5 Euro support	16 days			16 days	
113	1.6.5.1 Write code element (including clean…)	8 days		Engineer #4	8 days	Engineer #4
114	1.6.5.2 Document code element	1 day	113	Engineer #4	1 day	Engineer #4
115	1.6.5.3 Unit test code	7 days	114		7 days	
116	1.6.5.3.1 Prepare test plan and test set	2 days			2 days	
117	1.6.5.3.1.1 Define test sequence	0.5 days		Engineer #4	0.5 days	Engineer #4
118	1.6.5.3.1.2 Write test scripts	1 day	117	Engineer #4	1 day	Engineer #4
119	1.6.2.5.1.3 Define expected results	0.5 days	118	Engineer #4	0.5 days	Engineer #4
120	1.6.2.5.2 Subsystem ready for unit testing	0 days	119		0 days	13/04
121	1.6.2.5.3 Test code	2 days	120	Engineer #4	2 days	Engineer #4
122	1.6.2.5.4 Make corrections to code	1 day	121	Engineer #4	1 day	Engineer #4
123	1.6.2.5.5 Test code again	1 day	122	Engineer #4	1 day	Engineer #4
124	1.6.2.5.6 Prepare test report	1 day	123	Engineer #4	1 day	Engineer #4
125	1.6.6 3rd party payments	16 days			16 days	
126	1.6.6.1 Write code element (including clean…)	8 days			8 days	Engineer #4
127	1.6.6.2 Document code element	1 day	126	Engineer #4	1 day	Engineer #4
128	1.6.6.3 Unit test code	7 days	127		7 days	
129	1.6.6.3.1 Prepare test plan and test set	2 days			2 days	
130	1.6.6.3.1.1 Define test sequence	0.5 days		Engineer #4	0.5 days	Engineer #4
131	1.6.6.3.1.2 Write test scripts	1 day	130	Engineer #4	1 day	Engineer #4
132	1.6.6.5.1.3 Define expected results	0.5 days	131	Engineer #4	0.5 days	Engineer #4
133	1.6.6.5.2 Subsystem ready for unit testing	0 days	132		0 days	13/04
134	1.6.6.5.3 Test code	2 days	133	Engineer #4	2 days	Engineer #4
135	1.6.6.5.4 Make corrections to code	1 day	134	Engineer #4	1 day	Engineer #4
136	1.6.6.5.5 Test code again	1 day	135	Engineer #4	1 day	Engineer #4
137	1.6.6.5.6 Prepare test report	1 day	136	Engineer #4	1 day	Engineer #4
138	1.6.7 Tutorial	16 days			16 days	
139	1.6.7.1 Write code element (including clean…)	8 days		Engineer #3	8 days	Engineer #3
140	1.6.7.2 Document code element	1 day	139	Engineer #3	1 day	Engineer #3
141	1.6.7.3 Unit test code	7 days	140		7 days	
142	1.6.7.3.1 Prepare test plan and test set	2 days			2 days	
143	1.6.7.3.1.1 Define test sequence	0.5 days		Engineer #3	0.5 days	Engineer #3
144	1.6.7.3.1.2 Write test scripts	1 day	143	Engineer #3	1 day	Engineer #3
145	1.6.7.5.1.3 Define expected results	0.5 days	144	Engineer #3	0.5 days	Engineer #3
146	1.6.7.5.2 Subsystem ready for unit testing	0 days	145		0 days	13/04
147	1.6.7.5.3 Test code	2 days	146	Engineer #3	2 days	Engineer #3
148	1.6.7.5.4 Make corrections to code	1 day	147	Engineer #3	1 day	Engineer #3
149	1.6.7.5.5 Test code again	1 day	148	Engineer #3	1 day	Engineer #3
150	1.6.7.5.6 Prepare test report	1 day	149	Engineer #3	1 day	Engineer #3
151	1.6.8 Web Interface	32 days			32 days	
152	1.6.8.1 Write code element 1 (including clean…)	3 days		Charlie	3 days	Charlie
153	1.6.8.2 Write code element 2 (including clean…)	3 days	152	Charlie	3 days	Charlie
154	1.6.8.3 Write code element 3 (including clean…)	3 days	153	Charlie	3 days	Charlie
155	1.6.8.4 Write code element 4 (including clean…)	3 days	154	Charlie	3 days	Charlie
156	1.6.8.5 Document code element 1	1 day	155	Charlie	1 day	Charlie
157	1.6.8.6 Document code element 2	1 day	156	Charlie	1 day	Charlie
158	1.6.8.7 Document code element 3	1 day	157	Charlie	1 day	Charlie
159	1.6.8.8 Document code element 4	1 day	158	Charlie	1 day	Charlie
160	1.6.8.9 Unit test code	16 days	140		16 days	
161	1.6.8.9.1 Prepare test plan and test set	4 days			4 days	

Key: ■ Detailed task   ◤◢ Summary task   ↧ Dependency   ◆ Milestone

Figure 7.2   (continued)

How to Run Successful Projects in Web Time

ID	Task name	Work	Predecessor	Resource Names	Duration	2000 J F M A M J J A S O N D	2001 J F M A
162	1.6.8.9.1.1 Define test sequence	1 day		Charlie	1 day	Charlie	
163	1.6.8.9.1.2 Write test scripts	2 days	162	Charlie	2 days	Charlie	
164	1.6.8.9.1.3 Define expected results	1 day	163	Charlie	1 day	Charlie	
165	1.6.8.9.2 Subsystem ready for unit testing	0 days	164		0 days	26/04	
166	1.6.8.9.3 Test code	6 days	165	Charlie	6 days	Charlie	
167	1.6.8.9.4 Make corrections to code	2 days	166	Charlie	2 days	Charlie	
168	1.6.8.9.5 Test code again	2 days	167	Charlie	2 days	Charlie	
169	1.6.8.9.6 Prepare test report	2 days	168	Charlie	2 days	Charlie	
170	**1.6.9 Security**	**32 days**			**32 days**		
171	1.6.9.1 Write code element 1 (including clean…)	3 days		Engineer #2	3 days	Engineer #2	
172	1.6.9.2 Write code element 2 (including clean…)	3 days	171	Engineer #2	3 days	Engineer #2	
173	1.6.9.3 Write code element 3 (including clean…)	3 days	172	Engineer #2	3 days	Engineer #2	
174	1.6.9.4 Write code element 4 (including clean…)	3 days	173	Engineer #2	3 days	Engineer #2	
175	1.6.9.5 Document code element 1	1 day	174	Engineer #2	1 day	Engineer #2	
176	1.6.9.6 Document code element 2	1 day	175	Engineer #2	1 day	Engineer #2	
177	1.6.9.7 Document code element 3	1 day	176	Engineer #2	1 day	Engineer #2	
178	1.6.9.8 Document code element 4	1 day	177	Engineer #2	1 day	Engineer #2	
179	**1.6.9.9 Unit test code**	**16 days**	178		**16 days**		
180	**1.6.9.9.1 Prepare test plan and test set**	**4 days**			**4 days**		
181	1.6.9.9.1.1 Define test sequence	1 day		Engineer #2	1 day	Engineer #2	
182	1.6.9.9.1.2 Write test scripts	2 days	181	Engineer #2	2 days	Engineer #2	
183	1.6.9.9.1.3 Define expected results	1 day	182	Engineer #2	1 day	Engineer #2	
184	1.6.9.9.2 Subsystem ready for unit testing	0 days	183		0 days	26/04	
185	1.6.9.9.3 Test code	6 days	184	Engineer #2	6 days	Engineer #2	
186	1.69.9.4 Make corrections to code	2 days	185	Engineer #2	2 days	Engineer #2	
187	1.6.9.9.5 Test code again	2 days	186	Engineer #2	2 days	Engineer #2	
188	1.6.9.9.6 Prepare test report	2 days	187	Engineer #2	2 days	Engineer #2	
189	**1.6.10 Online Help**	**32 days**			**32 days**		
190	1.6.10.1 Write code element 1 (including clean…)	3 days		Engineer #3	3 days	Engineer #3	
191	1.6.10.2 Write code element 2 (including clean…)	3 days	190	Engineer #3	3 days	Engineer #3	
192	1.6.10.3 Write code element 3 (including clean…)	3 days	191	Engineer #3	3 days	Engineer #3	
193	1.6.10.4 Write code element 4 (including clean…)	3 days	192	Engineer #3	3 days	Engineer #3	
194	1.6.10.5 Document code element 1	1 day	193	Engineer #3	1 day	Engineer #3	
195	1.6.10.6 Document code element 2	1 day	194	Engineer #3	1 day	Engineer #3	
196	1.6.10.7 Document code element 3	1 day	195	Engineer #3	1 day	Engineer #3	
197	1.6.10.8 Document code element 4	1 day	196	Engineer #3	1 day	Engineer #3	
198	**1.6.10.3 Unit test code**	**16 days**	197		**16 days**		
199	**1.6.10.3.1 Prepare test plan and test set**	**4 days**			**4 days**		
200	1.6.10.3.1.1 Define test sequence	1 day		Engineer #3	1 day	Engineer #3	
201	1.6.10.3.1.2 Write test scripts	2 days	200	Engineer #3	2 days	Engineer #3	
202	1.6.10.5.1.3 Define expected results	1 day	201	Engineer #3	1 day	Engineer #3	
203	1.6.10.5.2 Subsystem ready for unit testing	0 days	202		0 days	26/04	
204	1.6.10.5.3 Test code	6 days	203	Engineer #3	6 days	Engineer #3	
205	1.6.10.5.4 Make corrections to code	2 days	204	Engineer #3	2 days	Engineer #3	
206	1.6.10.5.5 Test code again	2 days	205	Engineer #3	2 days	Engineer #3	
207	1.6.10.5.6 Prepare test report	2 days	206	Engineer #3	2 days	Engineer #3	
208	**1.7 Produce User documentation and Help System**	**99 days**	58		**83.5 days**		
223	**1.8 Execute system test**	**75 days**	23, 59		**27.25 days**		
235	**1.9 End of project review**	**5 days**	223	Team members	**5 days**	Team members	
236	**1.10 Project management**	**46 days**		You [33%]	**140 days**	You [33%]	
237	**1.11 END**	**0 days**	235		**1 day**		

Key: ■ Detailed task   ◤◥ Summary task   ↓ Dependency   ◆ Milestone

Figure 7.2   (continued)

How to Run Successful Projects in Web Time

In the column labelled "Resources Names" we are adding:

- Who will do the work;

- Those peoples' availability.

Sometimes this is enough and the duration is automatically calculated. This is the case in task 6. Other times, we want to enter explicit elapsed times, that is, we want to give people an elapsed time in which the work must get done. This is the case in tasks 7 and 12, for example.

As we begin to build up the plan, notice how "starring" and "minor" players start to emerge. Charlie is clearly one of the stars of the show. On the other hand, the Marketing people and the Administrative Assistant, for instance, will be playing minor roles. However, these are roles, which, if there were nobody available to fill them, could still mess things up for us.

In putting in people at this stage, we may well be aware of the likely number of people we'll have on our project. On the other hand, it might be that we don't yet know and then we have to make some sort of assumption. This is what we do here. Our assumptions as regards numbers and types of people builds up like this:

- You as Project Manager;

- Charlie, the Requirements person and Head Designer;

- Tester #1;

- Tester #2;

- Engineer #2;

- Engineer #3;

- Engineer #4; (You're being wildly optimistic—you're assuming that you can get 4 engineers in total to work on your project. You also note that Engineers #3 and #4 can be somewhat less senior than Charlie and Engineer #2.)

- Technical Author.

In choosing which engineer is going to work on which piece, you obviously try to match skill levels and experience to the particular task.

Notice that the project management effort represents about a third of your time, that is, somewhere between 1.5 and 2 days per week.

While we're at it, let's also do a quick analysis on the strengths of our team, using the classification scheme we described earlier. Again to simplify the worked example, let's grade the people, rather than the people as they are assigned to particular jobs. What we are, in effect, saying is that person X is equally good at any of the tasks he gets assigned to. This may not be quite so straightforward in reality. For example, Engineer #3 may be great at developing software but lousy at fixing bugs. It is purely in the interests of keeping the worked example manageable that we do this (see Table 7.1).

Table 7.1 Analysis of the Strengths of the team.

You as Project Manager	1
Charlie, the Requirements person and Head Designer	1
Tester #1	2
Tester #2	4
Engineer #2	2
Engineer #3	4
Engineer #4	4
Technical Author	2

Finally, and this is again in the interests of making the worked example manageable, I have assumed that all the starring players—Charlie, the three other engineers, the two testers and the technical author—are available full-time from the time they start on the project to the time they walk off. To be quite precise, this means that apart from their "Admin./Inbox/Interruptions", they are not working on anything else when they are working for us. And you'll recall from Chapter 5 that we took "Admin./Inbox/Interruptions" into account when we chose to estimate in normal human being days rather than raw productivity type days.

8 Put Contingency Into the Plan

➤ This chapter gives the three reasons why contingency is mandatory on projects and shows the best way to put contingency in on projects that are to be shortened.

➤ We extend the worked example further.

Introduction

There are three reasons why contingency is and should be mandatory on projects and in project plans. Any one of them by itself would, in my view, be sufficient to warrant me making this statement. Taken together, they are a "no-brainer" and are an irrefutable argument for the need for contingency. They are:

1. If there is no contingency in your plan, then the only logical conclusion we can come to with you is that you believe your plan will work out exactly like you said. The only logical conclusion we can draw from that is that you're insane!

2. If, like most organizations, you run your project from a common resource pool (i.e., the same bunch of people), then if your plans don't have contingency, a slip in one project cannot be localized in that project, but will have to effect some other project. This, in turn, will effect another project, and so on, domino style. With contingency in the plans, slips in projects can—up to a point—be contained, and not effect other projects.

3. Contingency can be used—again, up to a point—to deal with change control issues on your projects. With no contingency in the plan, then every time a change occurs on the project, you must go back to your boss or customer announcing a change to the plan. With contingency, some of these changes can be "absorbed" without affecting commitments to others.

I will phrase it as bluntly as I can. With no contingency in your plan, your project is doomed to fail.

Putting Contingency in the Plan

There are all sorts of inventive ways that contingency can be put in plans. I discussed a number of them in one of my previous books [1]. For our purposes here, the single best way to do it is to add some extra time onto the end date. It has loads of advantages. It is very visual, very easy to track against, very simple to spot drift, hugely effective as an early warning system—all sorts of things. There are also some disadvantages to deal with how the contingency is presented both to the troops and to the powers that be and we will discuss these in Chapter 12. In the next section we add contingency to the worked example.

Worked Example

Figure 7.2 showed our plan having an elapsed time of 140 days. There are actually over allocations of some of the people in the plan, that is, they are working more than 100% of their time. This means that the elapsed time would almost certainly end up greater than 140 days by the time these had been sorted out.

If we were not planning to shorten the project, we would have to resolve these over allocations. Because we have other plans, then we can leave these for the moment—they will be resolved during the shortening process in Chapter 11.

We now simply add on an additional say, 10% (14 days), giving a new elapsed time of 154 days. The corresponding plan is shown in Figure 8.1.

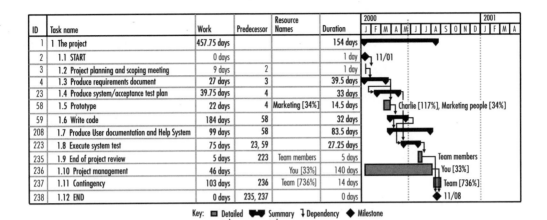

ID	Task name	Work	Predecessor	Resource Names	Duration	2000 J F M A M J J A S O N D	2001 J F M A
1	1 The project	457.75 days			154 days		
2	1.1 START	0 days			1 day	11/01	
3	1.2 Project planning and scoping meeting	9 days	2		1 day		
4	1.3 Produce requirements document	27 days	3		39.5 days		
23	1.4 Produce system/acceptance test plan	39.75 days	4		33 days		
58	1.5 Prototype	22 days	4	Marketing [34%]	14.5 days	Charlie [117%], Marketing people [34%]	
59	1.6 Write code	184 days	58		32 days		
208	1.7 Produce User documentation and Help System	99 days	58		83.5 days		
223	1.8 Execute system test	75 days	23, 59		27.25 days		
235	1.9 End of project review	5 days	223	Team members	5 days	Team members	
236	1.10 Project management	46 days		You [33%]	140 days	You [33%]	
237	1.11 Contingency	103 days	236	Team [736%]	14 days	Team [736%]	
238	1.12 END	0 days	235, 237		0 days	11/08	

Key: ▣ Detailed task   ◣▆◢ Summary task   ⬇ Dependency   ◆ Milestone

Figure 8.1   Plan with contingency.

Reference

1. O'Connell, F., *How To Run Successful Projects II—The Silver Bullet*, Hemel Hempstead, England: Prentice Hall, 1996.

9 Do a Risk Analysis

➤ This chapter shows how to do a risk analysis and feed the results into the plan, updating the plan accordingly.

➤ The worked example continues.

Introduction

In the previous chapter we implicitly took the view that all parts of our project were equally risky. By putting contingency into our plan, we were, in effect, saying that the whole thing was so volatile we had to reduce the chances of its blowing up in our faces.

In reality, things are not as scary as that. Some parts of our project may indeed be as unstable as TNT. There will be other parts, however, where we can be reasonably confident in our predictions. A risk analysis tries to uncover the unexploded bombs and make them as safe as possible. The result of this will be that some will never go off. Some will—despite our best efforts—but then our risk analysis will have ensured that we are all safely far away when they do.

Doing a Risk Analysis

A simple and very effective way to do a risk analysis is to go through the following steps.

1. Identify—in a brainstorming session—the risks to the project;

2. For each risk, grade it in terms of the likelihood of its happening. We use a three point scale—3 = high, 2 = medium, 1 = low;

3. For each risk, grade it in terms of, if it were to happen, what would its effect be? We use the same three-point scale;

4. Multiplying (2) by (3) gives you your exposure to that particular risk, the larger the number the greater the risk;

5. For each risk, identify what action(s) you can take to reduce that risk;

6. For each risk identify how you will know if that risk is actually starting to happen. Tom DeMarco calls these "early transition indicators."

The result of this will almost certainly be some additional jobs that must then be put back into the plan—in the list of jobs and processed from there, i.e., effort estimated, dependencies established, people identified to do them. This will in turn affect the project management effort calculation.

Worked Example

We're back live at the 1- or 2-day planning and scoping session and you ask the group to turn their attention to the business of risk analysis. You rule a flipchart page as in Table 9.1 and ask them to start proposing risks. To kick-start the proceedings you have a list (see Figure 9.1) in one of your back pockets, of the ten most common reasons why projects fail—here it is:[1]

Figure 9.1   Ten most common reasons why projects fail.

1. The goal of the project isn't defined properly.
2. The goal of the project is defined properly, but then changes to it aren't controlled.
3. The project isn't planned properly.
4. The project isn't led properly.
5. The project is planned properly but then it isn't resourced as was planned.
6. The project is planned such that it has no contingency.
7. The expectations of project participants aren't managed.
8. The project is planned properly but then progress against the plan is not monitored and controlled properly.
9. Project reporting is inadequate or nonexistent.
10. When projects get in to trouble, people believe the problem can be solved by some simple action e.g., work harder, extend the deadline, add more resources.

---

1   See ETP's Web site : http://www.etpint.com/whyfail.htm

Table 9.1 Risks with corresponding exposure.

Risk	Likelihood	Impact	Exposure = L × I	Action(s)	Early Transition Indicators
1. The latent burnout kicks in	3	3	9		
2. Scope creep	1	3	3		
3. Poor or inadequate project management	2	3	6		
4. Inadequate resources	3	3	9		
5. People leave	3	3	9		
6. Charlie leaves	2	3	6		
7. Estimates are wrong	2	3	6		
8. Project is technically infeasible	1	3	3		

In your other back pocket, you have a number of the "core risks indicated by past industry experience"[2]—things such as scope creep, underestimation, and staff turnover—that you vaguely remember from a talk you once heard Tom DeMarco give.[3]

The group eventually comes up with 8 risks. (Again, this is intended to be illustrative, rather than exhaustive.) They are graded in Table 9.1.

1. It could happen that the borderline burnout we spoke of in Chapter 4 could suddenly catch fire causing people either to leave or productivity to nose dive. In your view this is a major issue and your exposure is very high here.

2. Scope creep—Marketing ask for "just one more feature" and Engineering agree to slip it in. Or, more dangerously, Marketing people creep down to Engineering and ask individual engineers. Or, more dangerously still, some engineer suddenly thinks "this would be

---

2   The phrase is Tom DeMarco's who, in my view, is the oracle on such matters.
3   Two other risks that are often well worth giving an outing to are problems with the technical infrastructure and delivery of project components by third parties. Technical infrastructure risks include bugs in the compiler, the operating system, database, application server, and so forth that are the infrastructure of the project. To offset these you could consider, for example, checking bug reports for the various elements of the technical infrastructure. Third party delivery risks are where you outsource the development of particular components to supposed experts and then they let you down. To reduce these risks, you can do things like check their references and put in explicit milestones to check status.

really neat." You got burned on this one before and it's a calamity when it happens. You're going to watch it like a hawk.

3. You're deeply offended when they suggest the next one—poor project management. Perhaps it shows on your face, because one of the more sensitive of them hastily adds something to the effect that it's "sometimes been a problem in the past in other parts of Engineering." You come out fighting. This project is going to be different—though you're not sure yet exactly how. You let them leave the likelihood at 2, even though you know in your heart that this project is going to be managed like no project has ever been managed.

4. You don't get enough supply to match the demand. This is your big fear. You are convinced that doing a proper project management job is the key to risks 2, 4, and 5.

5. This is another of your big fears—people leave. Maybe it's already covered to some extent by number 1, but you want it highlighted.

6. And this is your third big one. It all falls apart if Charlie leaves. To put it in technobabble, Charlie is the SPOFITL—the single point of failure in the liveware. You're reasonably close to Charlie and don't think he's job hunting at the moment. But you never can tell.

7. Estimates are wrong—always a fear on software projects. You don't grade it 3 because you believe that the approach you used to build the WBS and work estimates are sound.

8. The project turns out to be technically infeasible. Low risk—you're not really blazing a technical trail here. The sophistication is in the set of features you've packaged together, not the technology or software architecture you're using.

Next you add in the risk reduction actions (see Table 9.2):

1. You still haven't mentioned it to anybody, but you're going to try and make this project both a happy one and a short one, that is, you're going to try to run the project in Web-time. (One of the possible beneficial side effects of running projects in Web-time is that sometimes projects can be over before anybody has a chance to get too disgruntled!) As regards the people being happy, you haven't fully thought that one through yet, but somewhere in the back of your head lurks a half-formed idea that it must be possible to run projects without endless amounts of continuous overtime. You've

Table 9.2 Risks with risk reduction actions.

Risk	Likelihood	Impact	Exposure = L × I	Action(s)	Early Transition Indicators
1. The latent burnout kicks in	3	3	9		People leave Morale plummets Project starts to run late
2. Scope creep	1	3	3	Project manager stops it from happening	Project starts to run late
3. Poor or inadequate project management	2	3	6	It won't happen	Project starts to run late
4. Inadequate resources	3	3	9	It won't happen	Project starts to run late
5. People leave	3	3	9	HR to get in some resumes Possible incentives	People leave
6. Charlie leaves	2	3	6	Possible incentives	Charlie leaves
7. Estimates are wrong	2	3	6	Monitor estimated against actuals to ensure early warning	Project starts to run late
8. Project is technically infeasible	1	3	3		Design or code phases take longer than estimated

read Tom De Marco's book *The Deadline* [1] and it's confirmed what you've suspected for a long time—that continuous overtime doesn't give extra productivity. It isn't even neutral on productivity. *It actually reduces it.* However, in terms of risk reduction actions, you want to keep these cards close to your chest for the moment. Nobody else can come up with a plausible action here. They make threatening noises about "finding a project manager who *can* manage them." But ultimately, it's summed up by the CEO who says bluntly, "If that happens we might as well all go home."

2.   You reckon you can keep a lid on this one.

3.   "It won't happen," you say looking them in the eye while your stomach churns. They watch unimpressed while you write it down.

4.   You write it down again. This time you're the one who stares intimidatingly at them.

5.   You suggest that HR open up a recruitment pipeline, so that there are at least some resumes from likely candidates in the hopper. It's not much but it's something. (If you are intending to run projects in Web-time, then people leaving is really a kiss of death. Given the normal 3-month (i.e., a Web-year) average time required to get a new hire in the door—never mind train them and bring them up to speed—you need to do everything you can to try to ensure continuity.) You make some noises about stock options and bonuses and the powers that be don't appear to shut the door completely on that one. You quickly write it down and make a mental note to yourself to go talk to your boss so that, now that you've managed to get the issue on the table, it doesn't fall off again.

6.   The incentives will be the key here.

7.   You need to be on the lookout for the first sign of drift between what was estimated and what actually starts happening.

8.   This is another "we may as well all go home" one.

You note the additional risk reduction actions into the plan. They are:

• Talk to the powers that be about incentives.

• Talk to HR about recruitment.

For our own convenience in keeping the plan as clear as possible, we won't put them as separate items in our Gantt chart, but rather assume that you deal with them under the general heading of "Project Management."

Reference

1.   DeMarco, T., *The Deadline—A Novel About Project Management*, New York: Dorset House, 1997.

PART FOUR
Turbocharge the Plan

In this part of the book we show how to shorten the plan. Chapter 10 is for those people who already have a plan that was not necessarily developed using the process described in the preceding chapters. The chapter shows what has to be done to get the project ready for the shortening process described in Chapter 11. Chapter 11 shows you how to shorten the plan for your project. Chapter 12 talks about getting buy-in from everybody for the shortened plan.

10 Prepare To Shorten the Plan

➤ Shortening the plan is a two-step process. Here we present the first of those two steps.

➤ If you have been building your plan by applying the ideas in Chapters 5–9, then this chapter is your next logical step.

➤ However, you may already have a project plan that *wasn't* developed using the techniques described in Chapters 5–9. This chapter explains how to take such a plan and prepare it so that the shortening techniques to be described in Chapter 11 will work.

➤ In either of the above cases, the tool we will use will be our equivalent of a movie strip board, which is introduced here.

➤ We illustrate the strip board by applying it to our worked example.

Introduction

If you have been following our method, chapter by chapter, and building your plan, then you are ready for the next step. It is described in the Worked Example and you should go straight there.

You may however, have come to this chapter from a different starting point. You may already have a plan. You may have developed it yourself using the skills, experience, method, and native cunning that have served you well in the past. Or the plan may have been foisted on you—passed on by some uncaring boss or from one of your colleagues who has gone on to new pastures. However it has arrived, if you are interested in shortening it, there will almost certainly be some massaging you have to do before you can move on to apply the shortening techniques to be described in Chapter 11. Essentially, the massaging you will have to do will involve creating the equivalent to a movie strip board based on the Gantt chart and the Dance Cards of team members.

The best way to illustrate all of this is with an example. Imagine that you have been handed the Gantt chart that appears in Figure 10.1.

No resources are listed on the Gantt chart but you are given an additional list of the people who are going to be involved in the project. The question is—is this a plan that can be shortened? The answer, at this stage, must be that we don't know. We don't know yet for the simple reason that we don't know if this plan makes sense. For it to make sense, the Work, Duration, and Resources parameters in the plan have to tally with what is happening on the ground on the project.

For example, suppose we have a task whose Work = 10 person-days and Duration = 5 (elapsed) days. If two people are indeed working, or have been earmarked to work on this task, then this task makes sense. Here are Work and Duration numbers that might not necessarily make

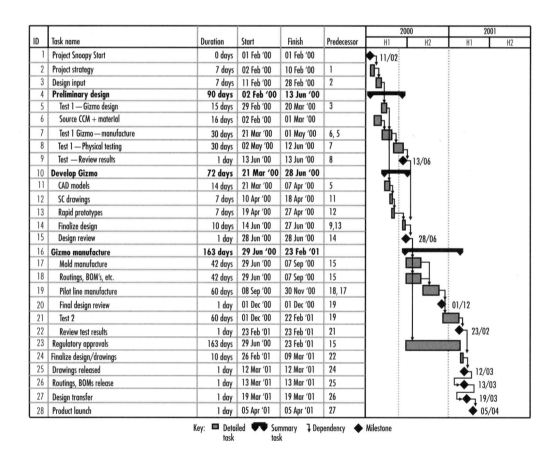

ID	Task name	Duration	Start	Finish	Predecessor
1	Project Snoopy Start	0 days	01 Feb '00	01 Feb '00	
2	Project strategy	7 days	02 Feb '00	10 Feb '00	1
3	Design input	7 days	11 Feb '00	28 Feb '00	2
4	**Preliminary design**	**90 days**	**02 Feb '00**	**13 Jun '00**	
5	Test 1 — Gizmo design	15 days	29 Feb '00	20 Mar '00	3
6	Source CCM + material	16 days	02 Feb '00	01 Mar '00	
7	Test 1 Gizmo — manufacture	30 days	21 Mar '00	01 May '00	6, 5
8	Test 1 — Physical testing	30 days	02 May '00	12 Jun '00	7
9	Test — Review results	1 day	13 Jun '00	13 Jun '00	8
10	**Develop Gizmo**	**72 days**	**21 Mar '00**	**28 Jun '00**	
11	CAD models	14 days	21 Mar '00	07 Apr '00	5
12	SC drawings	7 days	10 Apr '00	18 Apr '00	11
13	Rapid prototypes	7 days	19 Apr '00	27 Apr '00	12
14	Finalize design	10 days	14 Jun '00	27 Jun '00	9,13
15	Design review	1 day	28 Jun '00	28 Jun '00	14
16	**Gizmo manufacture**	**163 days**	**29 Jun '00**	**23 Feb '01**	
17	Mold manufacture	42 days	29 Jun '00	07 Sep '00	15
18	Routings, BOM's, etc.	42 days	29 Jun '00	07 Sep '00	15
19	Pilot line manufacture	60 days	08 Sep '00	30 Nov '00	18, 17
20	Final design review	1 day	01 Dec '00	01 Dec '00	19
21	Test 2	60 days	01 Dec '00	22 Feb '01	19
22	Review test results	1 day	23 Feb '01	23 Feb '01	21
23	Regulatory approvals	163 days	29 Jun '00	23 Feb '01	15
24	Finalize design/drawings	10 days	26 Feb '01	09 Mar '01	22
25	Drawings released	1 day	12 Mar '01	12 Mar '01	24
26	Routings, BOMs release	1 day	13 Mar '01	13 Mar '01	25
27	Design transfer	1 day	19 Mar '01	19 Mar '01	26
28	Product launch	1 day	05 Apr '01	05 Apr '01	27

Key: ▣ Detailed task   ◤◥ Summary task   ↧ Dependency   ◆ Milestone

Figure 10.1   Existing plan.

sense. Work = 10 person-days, Duration = 10 (elapsed) days. Are ten people working on this for 1 day each? They may well be. I have to say though, that in my experience of knowledge or high-tech projects, such tasks tend to be somewhat uncommon.

This then is the question: Do the numbers in the plan we have been given make sense? Is there a way we can check? Clearly there are several ways we can check. One would be to use our buddies from Chapter 5:

- Make the journey in your head.

- Open up black box jobs.

- Use knowledge and assumptions.

- Count the bricks in the wall.

- Use reusable components.

- Rebuild the plan from scratch.

Then we could see whether what we came up with tallied with the plan we had been handed. This would be one way to proceed.

However, if our intention is to shorten our project, then wouldn't it be good if we could take a step in that direction during this "checking" operation? We can indeed do this, but to do so we must first introduce our equivalent of the movie industry's strip board.

The Strip Board

Figure 10.2 shows the framework that we will refer to from now on as a strip board. Down the extreme left-hand side are day numbers. Each of these represents another day spent on the project. In the next column comes dates. The strip board I have shown here only shows normal Monday through Friday working days. There is another version of this column of the strip board that shows 7-day weeks. (If you've ever read J.R.R. Tolkien's *The Lord of the Rings* [1], you'll know that the ring that Frodo has to get rid of can be used for good or evil. The 7-day week version of the strip board is a bit like that—we'll return to the concept of the 7-day week in the later chapters.) Across the top of the strip board are cells where we can enter the names of our "cast members" and some are shown in this example.

Perhaps you can see what our intention is. The strip board is a very simple way of representing our project plan. At its most elementary, it

Day #	Date	Cast (Jobs)													
		Charlie	Engineer #2	Engineer #3	Engineer #4	Technical author	Marketing people (3)	Admin. assistant	Reqs. reviewers (5)	Test and design reviewers (2)	Tester #1	Tester #2	Users	Project management	
1	3-Jan-00														
2	4-Jan-00														
3	5-Jan-00														
4	6-Jan-00														
5	7-Jan-00														
6	10-Jan-00														
7	11-Jan-00														
8	12-Jan-00														
9	13-Jan-00														
10	14-Jan-00														
11	17-Jan-00														
12	18-Jan-00														
13	19-Jan-00														
14	20-Jan-00														
15	21-Jan-00														
16	24-Jan-00														
17	25-Jan-00														
18	26-Jan-00														
19	27-Jan-00														
20	28-Jan-00														
21	31-Jan-00														
22	1-Feb-00														
23	2-Feb-00														
24	3-Feb-00														
25	4-Feb-00														
26	7-Feb-00														
27	8-Feb-00														
28	9-Feb-00														
29	10-Feb-00														
30	11-Feb-00														
31	14-Feb-00														
32	15-Feb-00														
33	16-Feb-00														
34	17-Feb-00														
35	18-Feb-00														
36	21-Feb-00														
37	22-Feb-00														
38	23-Feb-00														
39	24-Feb-00														
40	25-Feb-00														
41	28-Feb-00														
42	29-Feb-00														
43	1-Mar-00														
44	2-Mar-00														
45	3-Mar-00														
46	6-Mar-00														
47	7-Mar-00														
48	8-Mar-00														

Figure 10.2   Strip board framework.

Day #	Date	Cast (Jobs)														
		Charlie	Engineer #2	Engineer #3	Engineer #4	Technical author	Marketing people (3)	Admin. assistant	Reqs. reviewers (5)	Test and design reviewers (2)	Tester #1	Tester #2	Users	Project management		
49	9-Mar-00															
50	10-Mar-00															
51	13-Mar-00															
52	14-Mar-00															
53	15-Mar-00															
54	16-Mar-00															
55	17-Mar-00															
56	20-Mar-00															
57	21-Mar-00															
58	22-Mar-00															
59	23-Mar-00															
60	24-Mar-00															
61	27-Mar-00															
62	28-Mar-00															
63	29-Mar-00															
64	30-Mar-00															
65	31-Mar-00															
66	3-Apr-00															
67	4-Apr-00															
68	5-Apr-00															
69	6-Apr-00															
70	7-Apr-00															
71	10-Apr-00															
72	11-Apr-00															
73	12-Apr-00															
74	13-Apr-00															
75	14-Apr-00															
76	17-Apr-00															
77	18-Apr-00															
78	19-Apr-00															
79	20-Apr-00															
80	21-Apr-00															
81	24-Apr-00															
82	25-Apr-00															
83	26-Apr-00															
84	27-Apr-00															
85	28-Apr-00															
86	1-May-00															
87	2-May-00															
88	3-May-00															
89	4-May-00															
90	5-May-00															
91	8-May-00															
92	9-May-00															
93	10-May-00															
94	11-May-00															
95	12-May-00															
96	15-May-00															

Figure 10.2   (continued)

Day #	Date	Charlie	Engineer #2	Engineer #3	Engineer #4	Technical author	Marketing people (3)	Admin. assistant	Reqs. reviewers (5)	Test and design reviewers (2)	Tester #1	Tester #2	Users	Project management		
97	16-May-00															
98	17-May-00															
99	18-May-00															
100	19-May-00															
101	22-May-00															
102	23-May-00															
103	24-May-00															
104	25-May-00															
105	26-May-00															
106	29-May-00															
107	30-May-00															
108	31-May-00															
109	1-Jun-00															
110	2-Jun-00															
111	5-Jun-00															
112	6-Jun-00															
113	7-Jun-00															
114	8-Jun-00															
115	9-Jun-00															
116	12-Jun-00															
117	13-Jun-00															
118	14-Jun-00															
119	15-Jun-00															
120	16-Jun-00															
121	19-Jun-00															
122	20-Jun-00															
123	21-Jun-00															
124	22-Jun-00															
125	23-Jun-00															
126	26-Jun-00															
127	27-Jun-00															
128	28-Jun-00															
129	29-Jun-00															
130	30-Jun-00															
	28-Jun-00															
	29-Jun-00															
	30-Jun-00															
	6-Jul-00															

Figure 10.2   (continued)

How to Run Successful Projects in Web Time

will show in terms of both elapsed project days, and actual calendar days, who on our team is working on what on which particular day. If we were to write into the cells of the strip board, some sort of task identifier, then our strip board would show

- Who was working;

- On what task;

- On every project day/calendar day of our project.

In terms of correcting the plan we saw in the previous section, it would do precisely that. It would remove any lack of clarity as to which and how many people were working on what tasks.

Now you might argue that a plan done in MS Project would enable us to do this too. "It would and it wouldn't" has to be the answer. Theoretically it would. In reality, I'm not convinced that MS Project (or any Gantt charting tool) offers this much clarity. There is the added disadvantage that it might require a level of capability with MS Project that not everyone possesses. In my view, Excel (or any spreadsheet) is a better choice. It is a lowest common denominator, and I mean the phrase in a very positive, rather than a disparaging sense.

So, if we had a plan already, we would transfer its tasks to a strip board. Then we would be ready to shorten it. We will illustrate the process of transferring the plan to a strip board in the next section, where we do it to our worked example.

Worked Example

You'll be relieved to hear that the project planning and scoping session, which has been running in our worked example thus far, is over. You may recall that one of its outputs was the Gantt chart last seen in Figure 8.1. What we must do now is to move the jobs in the Gantt Chart to our strip board. This may seem like a terrifying task—tedious, time-consuming, and error-prone. Tedious, maybe. I could (and do) argue that a major part of your job as project manager is to figure out who's going to do what on what day. In building the strip board, you're just doing a lot of this all at once. Time-consuming? My experience is that you can move about 250 jobs from a Gantt chart to a strip board in somewhere between half a day and a day. Error-prone? Perhaps, but how much more error-prone is it to determine who will do what when on the fly during the project?

At all events, this is what you've got to do. My contention is that the payback will make it worthwhile a hundred times over. And anyway, you can't say I didn't warn you earlier in the book!

Okay, let's start. The first job in our Gantt chart is the job that we completed yesterday on day 1 of the project. We write it into the strip board as shown in Figure 10.3.

It shows that you as project manager, Charlie, Engineer #2, and some Marketing people attended yesterday's planning and scoping. (We have omitted some of the other attendees so as not to clutter up the strip board.) We now read the next item from the Gantt Chart and place it onto day 2 of the project.

Next is the job to review the competitive info with Marketing. This is a meeting between Charlie and the 3 Marketing people. It's half a day each, that is, 2 person-days and we were allowing a 5-day (elapsed) window in which the task could take place. We make the worst-case assumption that it takes place on the fifth day and the strip board shows this. Identify users? Charlie does this the other half of the day that he gathers the competitive info.

Charlie spends the next 2 days preparing the user questionnaires and the Administrative Assistant distributes these at the end of the second day. People are given 5 days to complete these questionnaires. Then the Administrative Assistant chases them up. The next day, Charlie analyzes the questionnaires. Finally, Charlie spends the next 9 days writing the Requirements document.

The review cycle for the Requirements document kicks off with the document being circulated by the Administrative Assistant. Again, the 5-day window is given to the five reviewers and we assume that they will take full advantage of the five days, not finishing until the fifth one. The review meeting, the changes to the document arising from the review, and the recirculation of the document cover the next 3 days. The second review and signoff take another day as shown with work by Charlie, the requirements reviewers, and the Administrative Assistant. That does it for the requirements document.

We move on to the System/Acceptance Test plan. Once the Requirements are signed off, let's assume that Tester #1 comes on board. And a week later let's assume his buddy, Tester #2 shows up. There are six types of tests, each estimated to take 3 days work each. The boys split the work between them and schedule it over the next 9 days. (Notice that for my own convenience here, I'm assuming people are available full-time. If, based on their Dance Cards, we had established that this was

Day #	Date	Charlie	Engineer #2	Engineer #3	Engineer #4	Technical author	Marketing people (3)	Admin. assistant	Reqs. reviewers (5)	Test and design reviewers (2)	Tester #1	Tester #2	Users	Project management
1	11-Jan-00	3 Proj	3 Project planning and scoping				3 Project planning and scoping meeting							3 Project planning and scoping meeting
2	12-Jan-00	6 Gatt												
3	13-Jan-00	9 Prepare user questionnaires												
4	14-Jan-00	9 Prepare user questionnaires					10 Distribute user questionnaires							
5	17-Jan-00													
6	18-Jan-00	7 Review with Marketing					7 Review with Marketing							
7	19-Jan-00													
8	20-Jan-00													
9	21-Jan-00						11 Retrieve questionnaires							
10	24-Jan-00	12 Analyse information												
11	25-Jan-00	13 Write requirements document												
12	26-Jan-00	13 Write requirements document												
13	27-Jan-00	13 Write requirements document												
14	28-Jan-00	13 Write requirements document												
15	31-Jan-00	13 Write requirements document												
16	1-Feb-00	13 Write requirements document												
17	2-Feb-00	13 Write requirements document												
18	3-Feb-00	13 Write requirements document												
19	4-Feb-00	13 Write requirements document												
20	7-Feb-00						15 Circulate document							
21	8-Feb-00													
22	9-Feb-00													
23	10-Feb-00													
24	11-Feb-00							16 Individual review [1/2 day each]						
25	14-Feb-00	17,18,19 Review meeting / changes to document (inc. cir					17 Review meeting [1/2 day]							
26	15-Feb-00	17,18,19 Review meeting / changes to document (inc. circulate again)												
27	16-Feb-00	17,18,19 Review meeting / changes to document (inc. circulate again)												
28	17-Feb-00	20-22 Second review / Signoff / Reqs complete [					18-20 S	18-20 Second review / Signoff / Reqs complete [1/4 day]						
29	18-Feb-00	58 Pro	58 Pro	58 Prototype		58 Prototype				24 Research into Test Plan				
30	21-Feb-00	58 Pro	58 Pro	58 Prototype		58 Prototype				24 Research into Test Plan				
31	22-Feb-00	58 Pro	58 Pro	58 Prototype		58 Prototype				24 Research into Test Plan				
32	23-Feb-00	58 Pro	58 Pro	58 Prototype		58 Prototype				24 Research into Test Plan				
33	24-Feb-00	58 Pro	58 Pro	58 Prototype		58 Prototype				24 Research into Test Plan				
34	25-Feb-00	58 Pro	58 Pro	58 Prototype		58 Prototype				25 Wri	37 Write Performance Tests			
35	28-Feb-00	58 Pro	58 Pro	58 Prototype		58 Prototype				25 Wri	37 Write Performance Tests			
36	29-Feb-00	58 Pro	58 Pro	58 Prototype		58 Prototype				25 Wri	37 Write Performance Tests			
37	1-Mar-00	58 Pro	58 Pro	58 Prototype		58 Prototype				29 Wri	41 Write Stress Tests			
38	2-Mar-00	58 Pro	58 Pro	58 Prototype		58 Prototype				29 Wri	41 Write Stress Tests			
39	3-Mar-00	58 Pro	58 Pro	58 Prototype		58 Prototype				29 Wri	41 Write Stress Tests			
40	6-Mar-00	58 Pro	58 Pro	58 Prototype		58 Prototype				33 Wri	45 Write Installation Tests			
41	7-Mar-00	58 Pro	58 Pro	58 Prototype		58 Prototype		61 Individ		33 Wri	45 Write Installation Tests			
42	8-Mar-00	58 Pro	58 Pro	58 Prototype		58 Prototype				33 Wri	45 Write Installation Tests			
43	9-Mar-00	58 Pro	58 Pro	58 Prototype		58 Proto	50 Circulate all Tests							
44	10-Mar-00	58 Pro	58 Pro	58 Prototype		58 Prototype								
45	13-Mar-00	58 Pro	58 Pro	58 Prototype		58 Prototype								
46	14-Mar-00	58 Pro	58 Pro	58 Prototype		58 Prototype								
47	15-Mar-00	51 Indi	51 Indi	51 Individual review						51 Individual review				

Figure 10.3   Strip board with jobs added from Gantt chart.

Day #	Date	Charlie	Engineer #2	Engineer #3	Engineer #4	Technical author	Marketing people (3)	Admin. assistant	Reqs. reviewers (5)	Test and design reviewers (2)	Tester #1	Tester #2	Users	Project management
48	16-Mar-00	52 Rev	52 Rev	52 Review meeting						52 Revie	52 Rev	52 Review meeting		
49	17-Mar-00	58 Pro	58 Pro	58 Prototype			58 Prototype				53 Cha	53 Changes to document		
50	20-Mar-00	58 Pro	58 Pro	58 Prototype			58 Prototype				53 Cha	53 Changes to document		
51	21-Mar-00	58 Pro	58 Pro	58 Prototype			58 Prototype				53, 54	53, 54 Changes to document and circulate again		
52	22-Mar-00	58 Pro	58 Pro	58 Prototype			58 Prototype			55-57 Se	55-57	55-57 Second review / sign / Test Plan complete		
53	23-Mar-00	60 Pric	73 Sett	86 Rep	99 Ford	209 Research tech. writing requirements								
54	24-Mar-00	60 Pric	73 Sett	86 Rep	99 Ford	209 Research tech. writing requir				65-67 Second review / signoff / HLD complete [1/4 day each]				
55	27-Mar-00	60 Pric	73 Sett	86 Rep	99 Ford	209 Research tech. writing requirements								
56	28-Mar-00	60 Pric	73 Sett	86 Rep	99 Ford	209 Research tech. writing requirements								
57	29-Mar-00	60 Pric	73 Sett	86 Rep	99 Ford	209 Research tech. writing requirements								
58	30-Mar-00	60 Pric	73 Sett	86 Rep	99 Ford	210 Set up environment and tools								
59	31-Mar-00	60 Pric	73 Sett	86 Rep	99 Ford	210 Set up environment and tools								
60	3-Apr-00	60 Pric	73 Sett	86 Rep	99 Ford	210 Set up environment and tools								
61	4-Apr-00	151 w	170 Se	138 Tu	99 Ford	210 Set up environment and tools								
62	5-Apr-00	151 w	170 Se	138 Tu	99 Ford	210 Set up environment and tools								
63	6-Apr-00	151 w	170 Se	138 Tu	99 Ford	211 Define style sheet & produce proto								
64	7-Apr-00	151 w	170 Se	138 Tu	99 Ford	211 Define style sheet & produce proto								
65	10-Apr-00	151 w	170 Se	138 Tu	99 Ford	211 Define style sheet & produce proto								
66	11-Apr-00	151 w	170 Se	138 Tu	99 Ford	211 Define style sheet & produce proto								
67	12-Apr-00	151 w	170 Se	138 Tu	99 Ford	211 Define style sheet & produce proto								
68	13-Apr-00	151 w	170 Se	138 Tu	99 Ford	212 Write documentation / Help text								
69	14-Apr-00	151 w	170 Se	138 Tu	112 Eu	212 Write documentation / Help text								
70	17-Apr-00	151 w	170 Se	138 Tu	112 Eu	212 Write documentation / Help text								
71	18-Apr-00	151 w	170 Se	138 Tu	112 Eu	212 Write documentation / Help text								
72	19-Apr-00	151 w	170 Se	138 Tu	112 Eu	212 Write documentation / Help text								
73	20-Apr-00	151 w	170 Se	138 Tu	112 Eu	212 Write documentation / Help text								
74	21-Apr-00	151 w	170 Se	138 Tu	112 Eu	212 Write documentation / Help text								
75	24-Apr-00	151 w	170 Se	138 Tu	112 Eu	212 Write documentation / Help text								
76	25-Apr-00	151 w	170 Se	138 Tu	112 Eu	212 Write documentation / Help text								
77	26-Apr-00	151 w	170 Se	138 Tu	112 Eu	212 Write documentation / Help text								
78	27-Apr-00	151 w	170 Se	189 Or	112 Eu	212 Write documentation / Help text								
79	28-Apr-00	151 w	170 Se	189 Or	112 Eu	212 Write documentation / Help text								
80	1-May-00	151 w	170 Se	189 Or	112 Eu	212 Write documentation / Help text								
81	2-May-00	151 w	170 Se	189 Or	112 Eu	212 Write documentation / Help text								
82	3-May-00	151 w	170 Se	189 Or	112 Eu	212 Write documentation / Help text								
83	4-May-00	151 w	170 Se	189 Or	112 Eu	212 Write documentation / Help text								
84	5-May-00	151 w	170 Se	189 Or	112 Eu	212 Write documentation / Help text								
85	8-May-00	151 w	170 Se	189 Or	125 3rd	212 Write documentation / Help text								
86	9-May-00	151 w	170 Se	189 Or	125 3rd	212 Write documentation / Help text								
87	10-May-00	151 w	170 Se	189 Or	125 3rd	212 Write documentation / Help text								
88	11-May-00	151 w	170 Se	189 Or	125 3rd	212 Write documentation / Help text								
89	12-May-00	151 w	170 Se	189 Or	125 3rd	212 Write documentation / Help text								
90	15-May-00	151 w	170 Se	189 Or	125 3rd	212 Write documentation / Help text								
91	16-May-00	151 w	170 Se	189 Or	125 3rd	212 Write documentation / Help text								
92	17-May-00	151 w	170 Se	189 Or	125 3rd	212 Write documentation / Help text								
93	18-May-00			189 Or	125 3rd	212 Write documentation / Help text								
94	19-May-00			189 Or	125 3rd	212 Write documentation / Help text								

Figure 10.3   (continued)

Day #	Date	Charlie	Engineer #2	Engineer #3	Engineer #4	Technical author	Marketing people (3)	Admin. assistant	Reqs. reviewers (5)	Test and design reviewers (2)	Tester #1	Tester #2	Users	Project management
95	22-May-00			189 Or	125 3rd	212 Write documentation / Help text								
96	23-May-00			189 Or	125 3rd	212 Write documentation / Help text								
97	24-May-00			189 Or	125 3rd	212 Write documentation / Help text								
98	25-May-00			189 Or	125 3rd	212 Write documentation / Help text								
99	26-May-00			189 Or	125 3rd	212 Write documentation / Help text								
100	29-May-00			189 Or	125 3rd	212 Write documentation / Help text								
101	30-May-00			189 Online help		212 Write documentation / Help text								
102	31-May-00			189 Online help		212 Write documentation / Help text								
103	1-Jun-00			189 Online help		212 Write documentation / Help text								
104	2-Jun-00			189 Online help		212 Write documentation / Help text								
105	5-Jun-00			189 Online help		212 Write documentation / Help text								
106	6-Jun-00			189 Online help		212 Write documentation / Help text								
107	7-Jun-00			189 Online help		212 Write documentation / Help text								
108	8-Jun-00			189 Online help		212 Write documentation / Help text								
109	9-Jun-00			189 Online help		212 Write documentation / Help text								
110	12-Jun-00					212 Write documentation / Help text					225 Te	225 Test #1 - follow script & report errors		
111	13-Jun-00					212 Write documentation / Help text					225 Te	225 Test #1 - follow script & report errors		
112	14-Jun-00					212 Write documentation / Help text					225 Te	225 Test #1 - follow script & report errors		
113	15-Jun-00					212 Write documentation / Help text					225 Te	225 Test #1 - follow script & report errors		
114	16-Jun-00					212 Write documentation / Help text					225 Te	225 Test #1 - follow script & report errors		
115	19-Jun-00					212 Write documentation / Help text					225 Te	225 Test #1 - follow script & report errors		
116	20-Jun-00					212 Write documentation / Help text					225 Te	225 Test #1 - follow script & report errors		
117	21-Jun-00					212 Write documentation / Help text					225 Te	225 Test #1 - follow script & report errors		
118	22-Jun-00					212 Write documentation / Help text					225 Te	225 Test #1 - follow script & report errors		
119	23-Jun-00					212 Write documentation / Help text					225 Te	225 Test #1 - follow script & report errors		
120	26-Jun-00					212 Write documentation / Help text					225 Te	225 Test #1 - follow script & report errors		
121	27-Jun-00					217 Edit documentation / Help text					225 Te	225 Test #1 - follow script & report errors		
122	28-Jun-00	226 Te	226 Te	226 Te	226 Te	217 Edit documentation / Help text								
123	29-Jun-00	226 Te	226 Te	226 Te	226 Te	217 Edit documentation / Help text								
124	30-Jun-00	226 Te	226 Te	226 Te	226 Te	217 Edit documentation / Help text								
125	3-Jul-00	226 Te	226 Te	226 Te	226 Te	217 Edit documentation / Help text								
126	4-Jul-00	226 Te	226 Te	226 Te	226 Te	217 Edit documentation / Help text								
127	5-Jul-00	226 Te	226 Te	226 Te	226 Te	217 Edit documentation / Help text								
128	6-Jul-00					217 Edit documentation / Help text					228 Te	228 Test #2 - follow script & report errors		
129	7-Jul-00					217 Edit documentation / Help text					228 Te	228 Test #2 - follow script & report errors		
130	10-Jul-00					217 Edit documentation / Help text					228 Te	228 Test #2 - follow script & report errors		
131	11-Jul-00					217 Edit documentation / Help text					228 Te	228 Test #2 - follow script & report errors		
132	12-Jul-00	229 Te	229 Te	229 Te	229 Te	217 Edit documentation / Help text								
133	13-Jul-00	229 Te	229 Te	229 Te	229 Te	217 Edit documentation / Help text								
134	14-Jul-00	229 Te	229 Te	229 Te	229 Te	217 Edit documentation / Help text								
135	17-Jul-00					217 Edit documentation / Help text					231 Te	231 Test #3 - follow script & report errors		
136	18-Jul-00					217 Edit documentation / Help text					231 Te	231 Test #3 - follow script & report errors		
137	19-Jul-00	232 Te	232 Te	232 Te	232 Te	217 Edit documentation / Help text								
138	20-Jul-00					217 Edit documentation / Help text					233 Finalise test documentation			
139	21-Jul-00					217 Edit documentation / Help text								
140	24-Jul-00					217 Edit documentation / Help text								
141	25-Jul-00					217 Edit documentation / Help text								

Figure 10.3 (continued)

Day #	Date	Cast (Jobs)	Charlie	Engineer #2	Engineer #3	Engineer #4	Technical author	Marketing people (3)	Admin. assistant	Reqs. reviewers (5)	Test and design reviewers (2)	Tester #1	Tester #2	Users	Project management
142	26-Jul-00						221 Final integration of Online Help								
143	27-Jul-00						221 Final integration of Online Help								
144	28-Jul-00						221 Final integration of Online Help								
145	31-Jul-00						221 Final integration of Online Help								
146	1-Aug-00						221 Final integration of Online Help								
147	2-Aug-00						222 Final pre-production of manuals								
148	3-Aug-00						222 Final pre-production of manuals								
149	4-Aug-00						222 Final pre-production of manuals								
150	7-Aug-00						222 Final pre-production of manuals								
151	8-Aug-00						222 Final pre-production of manuals								
152	9-Aug-00		235 En	235 En	235 En	235 En	235 End of project review				235 En	235 End of project review		
153	10-Aug-00	237 Contingency												
154	11-Aug-00	237 Contingency												
155	14-Aug-00	237 Contingency												
156	15-Aug-00	237 Contingency												
157	16-Aug-00	237 Contingency												
158	17-Aug-00	237 Contingency												
159	18-Aug-00	237 Contingency												
160	21-Aug-00	237 Contingency												
161	22-Aug-00	237 Contingency												
162	23-Aug-00	237 Contingency												
163	24-Aug-00	237 Contingency												
164	25-Aug-00	237 Contingency												
165	28-Aug-00	237 Contingency												
166	29-Aug-00	237 Contingency												
167	30-Aug-00													
168	31-Aug-00													
169	1-Sep-00													
170	4-Sep-00													
171	5-Sep-00													
172	6-Sep-00													
173	7-Sep-00													
174	8-Sep-00													
175	11-Sep-00													
176	12-Sep-00													
177	13-Sep-00													
178	14-Sep-00													
179	15-Sep-00													
180	18-Sep-00													
181	19-Sep-00													
182	20-Sep-00													
183	21-Sep-00													
184	22-Sep-00													
185	25-Sep-00													
186	26-Sep-00													
187	27-Sep-00													
188	28-Sep-00													

Figure 10.3 (continued)

not so, then their availability, as indicated by their Dance Cards, would tell us the duration of each task and hence, how many lines on the strip board to cover.) Then we enter into a review cycle as before. By this stage, Engineer #3 has come on the scene and so he can be involved in the review. We proceed as before with the Requirements document. One thing that perhaps is becoming clear by now is the lengthening of the project due to review cycles. This will be one of the first things we will target in the next chapter.

Next comes the prototype. Again, in the interests of clarity I will lump in the prototype as 22 elapsed days, and soaking up Charlie, the other two engineers and the Marketing people. The prototype can start as soon as the Requirements document is finished.

Now we move on to the coding blocks and we can move a bit quicker. Charlie spends 4 days on Pricing. Engineers #2 and #3 are allotted to their bits. Engineer #4 shows up and he gets assigned work. We insert all of the Coding blocks into the strip board. Next comes the User Documentation and Help system. We had made this dependent on the Prototype. Execute System Test is dependent on Code being finished. The End of Project Review is again given one of our 5-day windows. We add on 14 days contingency completing Figure 10.3.

Note that we still have 60 days project management to spread out over the life of the project. However, we don't yet know how long the project will be. If it were to last the duration shown in Figure 10.3, that is, 166 days, then the project management effort would be 60/166, or about a third of a day every day, or 1½–2 days per week. However, we need to shorten the project—which we will do in Chapter 11— to establish what the final daily or weekly project management load will be.

Just before we finish, notice that the elapsed time indicated by the strip board is greater than that indicated by the Gantt chart in Figure 8.1, upon which the strip board is based. The strip board indicates 166 days, the Gantt chart 154 days. This is because there are over allocations of peoples' time in the Gantt chart, which we haven't yet resolved. (We referred to this earlier.) If we resolved these then the two durations would come out the same. However, rather than resolve them in the Gantt chart, we are going to do it using the strip board in the next chapter.

Reference

1.   Tolkien, J.R.R., *The Lord of the Rings*, London: Allen & Unwin, 1968.

Shorten the Plan

► This chapter describes how to use the strip board developed in the previous chapter to establish the shortest possible time in which the project can be done.

► The worked example is updated.

Introduction

Here we are going to use the strip board developed in the previous chapter to shorten the plan for our project. We perhaps tend to think that if we had unlimited resources or budget, we could do amazing things with our project duration. In reality this is generally not the case. To shorten your project there are essentially only four things you can do, and not all of these will necessarily have an effect. The four things are:

1. *Reduce functionality*. For example, referring again to Figure 10.3, if we were to reduce in some way the amount of documentation that was being produced, then clearly this would have the effect of shortening the project. An important variation on "reduce functionality" is the "work smarter" idea, where you drop out a piece of the project and replace it with a different piece of project. For example, instead of having a "write design" sequence of jobs in our project, we decided a while back to put in a "develop prototype" sequence. Our hope and intention in doing this was that it would buy us a better quality product (i.e., closer to the customer requirements) in a shorter space of time.

2. *Shorten the elapsed time for individual tasks*. There are tasks where we have allowed an elapsed time to pass while a review gets done,

117

for example. If we could reduce this elapsed time, we might also shorten the project. A variation on this one is to overlap particular jobs so that one begins while another is still in progress, rather than having the start of one dependent on the end of another. While there are obvious risks with this approach, there can be occasions when it's both valuable and valid.

3. *Add more people.* Instead of reducing the documentation to be done, we could add another technical author. This might shorten the project.

4. *Reduce quality.* Of course, we don't compromise on quality! (But for those readers that do, reducing testing time, for instance, is a tried and trusted way of shortening projects. It's not recommended, we hasten to add, but that doesn't mean that people don't do it.)

In the next section, we will see which of these four things can be applied to the worked example. They are applied in no particular order—we just look for promising opportunities to apply them.

Worked Example

Shorten Elapsed Time

Let's begin by shortening some elapsed times. Looking at Figure 10.3, we can see that there are a few places where we have allowed an elapsed time so that people can review something or other. This occurs with the user questionnaires during the requirements gathering, the review of the requirements document, and the review of the System Test document.

If we could—by arrangement with the relevant people—shorten the time given to them to review something, then we could achieve some shortening. What we have to do here essentially, is to book the time at which those people will do the review and return the reviewed item to you. I hope you can see that there's nothing particularly onerous about this. All we're doing is giving them lots of advance warning that their services are going to be required on a particular day(s).

I think you might agree that this could actually have some positive effects. They put the thing in their diary. You stress to them the value in their doing this—"if you do this, Bozo, it will shave 3 days off project X." You point out that they can't let you down, that this entry in their diary must become as immovable as their foreign vacation. "Can you see"—you show them the strip board—"that if you let me down here, then the project will lengthen again?" They nod. "So can we make a deal that this can't change for anything? I've booked it far ahead, so nothing can override it."

If you were still not confident enough, you could try a couple of other things. Do their Dance Card with them, as they expect it to be around that time. This will unearth whether (a) they've already agreed to something that is impossible, or (b) things could be tight around that time and one request from their boss would be enough to throw it out, or (c) there's a fair amount of leeway and you needn't be too worried. If it's an (a) or (b) type situation, get stuck in even more. Ask what they're going to do if things go haywire and they can't deliver. Are they prepared to sign off anyway, that is, can the default be that if they don't do the review within the agreed time, then they are regarded as agreeing with what's in the document? (That'll scare 'em.) Or, if they don't deliver, is it then the default that only the other reviewers opinions count? (That'll scare 'em even more.) Your objective in all of this is to walk away with an ironclad agreement so that whether they review it or not, your project isn't held up. You are trying to ensure that there is no thread dangling here, which could come back to haunt you later.

Of course, none of this is an exact science. The risk with the approach I've just described is that they agree to a default type scenario, the default scenario happens and what gets delivered isn't what people wanted. Then nobody wins. So it might be that even if you had your ironclad agreement, you might still have to back off calling it in, if you knew that that person's input could have a dramatic effect on the eventual outcome of the project.

So we look at the three areas we had identified as potential targets earlier and we decide to do the following:

- The user questionnaires will now be circulated one day and—by agreement with everybody involved—collected, fully complete at the end of the next day (4 days saved).

- The requirements document will be circulated one day, individually reviewed the morning of the next day, and reviewed at a meeting the afternoon of that day. Again, this is by common agreement (5 days saved).

- The third opportunity to shorten the project is in the review of the System Test document. We notice—if we hadn't already—the big gap between the preparation of the tests and their execution. Perhaps this doesn't make a great deal of sense in terms of our utilization of the testers. Rather than bringing them onto the project, taking them off and bringing them back again, we should just bring them on, have them do all their stuff and then go off. We're about to act on this when we remember why we had it that way in the first place. Getting the tests written early is a good way of debugging the design. Okay. We decide to stay with our original idea. So shortening the review cycle won't particularly help our project—because it's the engineers who are on the critical path—but maybe it'd help somebody else. We decide to leave this issue for the moment and go talk to the testers about whether this would buy them anything useful.

The result of the two actions we have taken is shown in Figure 11.1. The project has reduced from 166 elapsed days to 157 elapsed days.

Add More People

Looking at our strip board, it is obvious that it is the technical writing that is causing the project to extend so far. If we could get our hands on another writer, we could improve that fairly dramatically. So we go out into the highways and byways, we call up central casting, we do all of the usual shenanigans, call in old favors or leave hostages to fortune for the future, but let's assume it's no dice, no more writers are available.

We ponder our strip board again. Can we get the writer earlier? Let's see if he can start three weeks earlier so that by the time his preparatory work is done, the prototype will be pretty far advanced and the writer will have stuff to work from. This time, we hit lucky and we get the writer a full five weeks ahead of time. The result is shown in Figure 11.2. The project is shortened by a further 13 days.

Looking at Figure 11.2, we wonder where to go next. There seem to be a couple of tempting opportunities—indicated by large amounts of white space—where the coding ends. However, the duration of the technical writing is still the thing that is causing the project to extend. It crosses our mind again that maybe we could somehow reduce the amount of technical writing being done. However, the "we don't compromise on quality" alarm bell goes off in our heads at this point. Cutting—whatever that might mean—the amount of documentation is skirting dangerously close to messing with the quality of the delivered

Day #	Date	Charlie	Engineer #2	Engineer #3	Engineer #4	Technical author	Marketing people (3)	Admin. assistant	Reqs. reviewers (5)	Test and design reviewers (2)	Tester #1	Tester #2	Users	Project management
1	11-Jan-00	3 Proj	3 Project planning and scoping				3 Project planning and scoping meeting							3 Project planning and sc
2	12-Jan-00	6 Gath												
3	13-Jan-00	9 Prepare user questionnaires												
4	14-Jan-00	9 Prepare user questionnaires					10 Distribute user questionnaires							
5	17-Jan-00	7 Review with Marketing				7 Review	11 Retrieve questionnaires							
6	18-Jan-00	12 Analyse information												
7	19-Jan-00	13 Write requirements document												
8	20-Jan-00	13 Write requirements document												
9	21-Jan-00	13 Write requirements document												
10	24-Jan-00	13 Write requirements document												
11	25-Jan-00	13 Write requirements document												
12	26-Jan-00	13 Write requirements document												
13	27-Jan-00	13 Write requirements document												
14	28-Jan-00	13 Write requirements document												
15	31-Jan-00	13 Write requirements document					15 Circulate document							
16	1-Feb-00	17,18,19 Review meeting / changes to document (inc. c							16, 17 Individual review [1/2 day each] & review meeting [1/2 day]					
17	2-Feb-00	18,19 Changes to document (inc. circulate again)												
18	3-Feb-00	17,18,19 Review meeting / changes to document (inc. circulate again)												
19	4-Feb-00	20-22 Second review / Signoff / Reqs complete							18-20 S	18-20 Second review / Signoff / Reqs complete [1/4 day]				
20	7-Feb-00	58 Pro	58 Prot	58 Prototype		58 Prototype					24 Research into Test Plan			
21	8-Feb-00	58 Pro	58 Prot	58 Prototype		58 Prototype					24 Research into Test Plan			
22	9-Feb-00	58 Pro	58 Prot	58 Prototype		58 Prototype					24 Research into Test Plan			
23	10-Feb-00	58 Pro	58 Prot	58 Prototype		58 Prototype					24 Research into Test Plan			
24	11-Feb-00	58 Pro	58 Prot	58 Prototype		58 Prototype					24 Research into Test Plan			
25	14-Feb-00	58 Pro	58 Prot	58 Prototype		58 Prototype					25 Writ	37 Write Performance Tests		
26	15-Feb-00	58 Pro	58 Prot	58 Prototype		58 Prototype					25 Writ	37 Write Performance Tests		
27	16-Feb-00	58 Pro	58 Prot	58 Prototype		58 Prototype					25 Writ	37 Write Performance Tests		
28	17-Feb-00	58 Pro	58 Prot	58 Prototype		58 Prototype					29 Writ	41 Write Stress Tests		
29	18-Feb-00	58 Pro	58 Prot	58 Prototype		58 Prototype					29 Writ	41 Write Stress Tests		
30	21-Feb-00	58 Pro	58 Prot	58 Prototype		58 Prototype					29 Writ	41 Write Stress Tests		
31	22-Feb-00	58 Pro	58 Prot	58 Prototype		58 Prototype					33 Writ	45 Write Installation Tests		
32	23-Feb-00	58 Pro	58 Prot	58 Prototype		58 Prototype				61 Individ	33 Writ	45 Write Installation Tests		
33	24-Feb-00	58 Pro	58 Prot	58 Prototype		58 Prototype					33 Writ	45 Write Installation Tests		
34	25-Feb-00	58 Pro	58 Prot	58 Prototype		58 Proto	50 Circulate all Tests							
35	28-Feb-00	58 Pro	58 Prot	58 Prototype		58 Prototype								
36	29-Feb-00	58 Pro	58 Prot	58 Prototype		58 Prototype								

Figure 11.1   Duration reduced by 9 days.

Day #	Date	Charlie	Engineer #2	Engineer #3	Engineer #4	Technical author	Marketing people (3)	Admin. assistant	Reqs. reviewers (5)	Test and design reviewers (2)	Tester #1	Tester #2	Users	Project management
37	1-Mar-00	58 Pro	58 Prot	58 Prototype			58 Prototype							
38	2-Mar-00	51 Indi	51 Indiv	51 Individual review						51 Individual review				
39	3-Mar-00	52 Rev	52 Rev	52 Review meeting						52 Revie	52 Rev	52 Review meeting		
40	6-Mar-00	58 Pro	58 Prot	58 Prototype			58 Prototype				53 Cha	53 Changes to document		
41	7-Mar-00	58 Pro	58 Prot	58 Prototype			58 Prototype				53 Cha	53 Changes to document		
42	8-Mar-00	58 Pro	58 Prot	58 Prototype			58 Prototype				53, 54	53, 54 Changes to document and circul		
43	9-Mar-00	58 Pro	58 Prot	58 Prototype			58 Prototype			55–57 Se	55–57	55–57 Second review / sign / Test Plan c		
44	10-Mar-00	60 Pric	73 Sett	86 Rep	99 Fore	209 Research tech. writing requirements								
45	13-Mar-00	60 Pric	73 Sett	86 Rep	99 Fore	209 Research tech. writing require				65–67 Second review / signoff / HLD complete [1/4 day ea				
46	14-Mar-00	60 Pric	73 Sett	86 Rep	99 Fore	209 Research tech. writing requirements								
47	15-Mar-00	60 Pric	73 Sett	86 Rep	99 Fore	209 Research tech. writing requirements								
48	16-Mar-00	60 Pric	73 Sett	86 Rep	99 Fore	209 Research tech. writing requirements								
49	17-Mar-00	60 Pric	73 Sett	86 Rep	99 Fore	210 Set up environment and tools								
50	20-Mar-00	60 Pric	73 Sett	86 Rep	99 Fore	210 Set up environment and tools								
51	21-Mar-00	60 Pric	73 Sett	86 Rep	99 Fore	210 Set up environment and tools								
52	22-Mar-00	151 W	170 Se	138 Tu	99 Fore	210 Set up environment and tools								
53	23-Mar-00	151 W	170 Se	138 Tu	99 Fore	210 Set up environment and tools								
54	24-Mar-00	151 W	170 Se	138 Tu	99 Fore	211 Define style sheet & produce proto								
55	27-Mar-00	151 W	170 Se	138 Tu	99 Fore	211 Define style sheet & produce proto								
56	28-Mar-00	151 W	170 Se	138 Tu	99 Fore	211 Define style sheet & produce proto								
57	29-Mar-00	151 W	170 Se	138 Tu	99 Fore	211 Define style sheet & produce proto								
58	30-Mar-00	151 W	170 Se	138 Tu	99 Fore	211 Define style sheet & produce proto								
59	31-Mar-00	151 W	170 Se	138 Tu	99 Fore	212 Write documentation / Help text								
60	3-Apr-00	151 W	170 Se	138 Tu	112 Eu	212 Write documentation / Help text								
61	4-Apr-00	151 W	170 Se	138 Tu	112 Eu	212 Write documentation / Help text								
62	5-Apr-00	151 W	170 Se	138 Tu	112 Eu	212 Write documentation / Help text								
63	6-Apr-00	151 W	170 Se	138 Tu	112 Eu	212 Write documentation / Help text								
64	7-Apr-00	151 W	170 Se	138 Tu	112 Eu	212 Write documentation / Help text								
65	10-Apr-00	151 W	170 Se	138 Tu	112 Eu	212 Write documentation / Help text								
66	11-Apr-00	151 W	170 Se	138 Tu	112 Eu	212 Write documentation / Help text								
67	12-Apr-00	151 W	170 Se	138 Tu	112 Eu	212 Write documentation / Help text								
68	13-Apr-00	151 W	170 Se	138 Tu	112 Eu	212 Write documentation / Help text								
69	14-Apr-00	151 W	170 Se	189 Or	112 Eu	212 Write documentation / Help text								
70	17-Apr-00	151 W	170 Se	189 Or	112 Eu	212 Write documentation / Help text								
71	18-Apr-00	151 W	170 Se	189 Or	112 Eu	212 Write documentation / Help text								
72	19-Apr-00	151 W	170 Se	189 Or	112 Eu	212 Write documentation / Help text								
73	20-Apr-00	151 W	170 Se	189 Or	112 Eu	212 Write documentation / Help text								
74	21-Apr-00	151 W	170 Se	189 Or	112 Eu	212 Write documentation / Help text								

Figure 11.1   (continued)

Day #	Date	Charlie	Engineer #2	Engineer #3	Engineer #4	Technical author	Marketing people (3)	Admin. assistant	Reqs. reviewers (5)	Test and design reviewers (2)	Tester #1	Tester #2	Users	Project management
75	24-Apr-00	151 W	170 Se	189 Or	112 Eu	212 Write documentation / Help text								
76	25-Apr-00	151 W	170 Se	189 Or	125 3rd	212 Write documentation / Help text								
77	26-Apr-00	151 W	170 Se	189 Or	125 3rd	212 Write documentation / Help text								
78	27-Apr-00	151 W	170 Se	189 Or	125 3rd	212 Write documentation / Help text								
79	28-Apr-00	151 W	170 Se	189 Or	125 3rd	212 Write documentation / Help text								
80	1-May-00	151 W	170 Se	189 Or	125 3rd	212 Write documentation / Help text								
81	2-May-00	151 W	170 Se	189 Or	125 3rd	212 Write documentation / Help text								
82	3-May-00	151 W	170 Se	189 Or	125 3rd	212 Write documentation / Help text								
83	4-May-00	151 W	170 Se	189 Or	125 3rd	212 Write documentation / Help text								
84	5-May-00			189 Or	125 3rd	212 Write documentation / Help text								
85	8-May-00			189 Or	125 3rd	212 Write documentation / Help text								
86	9-May-00			189 Or	125 3rd	212 Write documentation / Help text								
87	10-May-00			189 Or	125 3rd	212 Write documentation / Help text								
88	11-May-00			189 Or	125 3rd	212 Write documentation / Help text								
89	12-May-00			189 Or	125 3rd	212 Write documentation / Help text								
90	15-May-00			189 Or	125 3rd	212 Write documentation / Help text								
91	16-May-00			189 Or	125 3rd	212 Write documentation / Help text								
92	17-May-00			189 Online help		212 Write documentation / Help text								
93	18-May-00			189 Online help		212 Write documentation / Help text								
94	19-May-00			189 Online help		212 Write documentation / Help text								
95	22-May-00			189 Online help		212 Write documentation / Help text								
96	23-May-00			189 Online help		212 Write documentation / Help text								
97	24-May-00			189 Online help		212 Write documentation / Help text								
98	25-May-00			189 Online help		212 Write documentation / Help text								
99	26-May-00			189 Online help		212 Write documentation / Help text								
100	29-May-00			189 Online help		212 Write documentation / Help text								
101	30-May-00					212 Write documentation / Help text					225 Te	225 Test #1 – follow script & report errors		
102	31-May-00					212 Write documentation / Help text					225 Te	225 Test #1 – follow script & report errors		
103	1-Jun-00					212 Write documentation / Help text					225 Te	225 Test #1 – follow script & report errors		
104	2-Jun-00					212 Write documentation / Help text					225 Te	225 Test #1 – follow script & report errors		
105	5-Jun-00					212 Write documentation / Help text					225 Te	225 Test #1 – follow script & report errors		
106	6-Jun-00					212 Write documentation / Help text					225 Te	225 Test #1 – follow script & report errors		
107	7-Jun-00					212 Write documentation / Help text					225 Te	225 Test #1 – follow script & report errors		
108	8-Jun-00					212 Write documentation / Help text					225 Te	225 Test #1 – follow script & report errors		
109	9-Jun-00					212 Write documentation / Help text					225 Te	225 Test #1 – follow script & report errors		
110	12-Jun-00					212 Write documentation / Help text					225 Te	225 Test #1 – follow script & report errors		
111	13-Jun-00					212 Write documentation / Help text					225 Te	225 Test #1 – follow script & report errors		
112	14-Jun-00					217 Edit documentation / Help text					225 Te	225 Test #1 – follow script & report errors		

Figure 11.1   (continued)

Day #	Date	Cast (Jobs) Charlie	Engineer #2	Engineer #3	Engineer #4	Technical author	Marketing people (3)	Admin. assistant	Reqs. reviewers (5)	Test and design reviewers (2)	Tester #1	Tester #2	Users	Project management
113	15-Jun-00	226 Te	226 Te	226 Te	226 Te	217 Edit documentation / Help text								
114	16-Jun-00	226 Te	226 Te	226 Te	226 Te	217 Edit documentation / Help text								
115	19-Jun-00	226 Te	226 Te	226 Te	226 Te	217 Edit documentation / Help text								
116	20-Jun-00	226 Te	226 Te	226 Te	226 Te	217 Edit documentation / Help text								
117	21-Jun-00	226 Te	226 Te	226 Te	226 Te	217 Edit documentation / Help text								
118	22-Jun-00	226 Te	226 Te	226 Te	226 Te	217 Edit documentation / Help text								
119	23-Jun-00					217 Edit documentation / Help text					228 Te	228 Test #2 – follow script & report errors		
120	26-Jun-00					217 Edit documentation / Help text					228 Te	228 Test #2 – follow script & report errors		
121	27-Jun-00					217 Edit documentation / Help text					228 Te	228 Test #2 – follow script & report errors		
122	28-Jun-00					217 Edit documentation / Help text					228 Te	228 Test #2 – follow script & report errors		
123	29-Jun-00	229 Te	229 Te	229 Te	229 Te	217 Edit documentation / Help text								
124	30-Jun-00	229 Te	229 Te	229 Te	229 Te	217 Edit documentation / Help text								
125	3-Jul-00	229 Te	229 Te	229 Te	229 Te	217 Edit documentation / Help text								
126	4-Jul-00					217 Edit documentation / Help text					231 Te	231 Test #3 – follow script & report errors		
127	5-Jul-00					217 Edit documentation / Help text					231 Te	231 Test #3 – follow script & report errors		
128	6-Jul-00	232 Te	232 Te	232 Te	232 Te	217 Edit documentation / Help text								
129	7-Jul-00					217 Edit documentation / Help text				233 Finalise test documentation				
130	10-Jul-00					217 Edit documentation / Help text								
131	11-Jul-00					217 Edit documentation / Help text								
132	12-Jul-00					217 Edit documentation / Help text								
133	13-Jul-00					221 Final integration of Online Help								
134	14-Jul-00					221 Final integration of Online Help								
135	17-Jul-00					221 Final integration of Online Help								
136	18-Jul-00					221 Final integration of Online Help								
137	19-Jul-00					221 Final integration of Online Help								
138	20-Jul-00					222 Final pre-production of manuals								
139	21-Jul-00					222 Final pre-production of manuals								
140	24-Jul-00					222 Final pre-production of manuals								
141	25-Jul-00					222 Final pre-production of manuals								
142	26-Jul-00					222 Final pre-production of manuals								
143	27-Jul-00	235 En	235 En	235 En	235 En	235 End of project review					235 En	235 End of project review		
144	28-Jul-00	237 Contingency												
145	31-Jul-00	237 Contingency												
146	1-Aug-00	237 Contingency												
147	2-Aug-00	237 Contingency												
148	3-Aug-00	237 Contingency												
149	4-Aug-00	237 Contingency												
150	7-Aug-00	237 Contingency												

Figure 11.1 (continued)

Day #	Date	Cast (Jobs)	Charlie	Engineer #2	Engineer #3	Engineer #4	Technical author	Marketing people (3)	Admin. assistant	Reqs. reviewers (5)	Test and design reviewers (2)	Tester #1	Tester #2	Users	Project management
151	8-Aug-00	237 Contingency													
152	9-Aug-00	237 Contingency													
153	10-Aug-00	237 Contingency													
154	11-Aug-00	237 Contingency													
155	14-Aug-00	237 Contingency													
156	15-Aug-00	237 Contingency													
157	16-Aug-00	237 Contingency													

Figure 11.1   (continued)

Day #	Date	Cast (Jobs)												
		Charlie	Engineer #2	Engineer #3	Engineer #4	Technical author	Marketing people (3)	Admin. assistant	Reqs. reviewers (5)	Test and design reviewers (2)	Tester #1	Tester #2	Users	Project management
1	11-Jan-00	3 Proj	3 Project planning and scoping				3 Project planning and scoping meeting							3 Project planning and so
2	12-Jan-00	6 Gath												
3	13-Jan-00	9 Prepare user questionnaires												
4	14-Jan-00	9 Prepare user questionnaires					10 Distribute user questionnaires							
5	17-Jan-00	7 Review with Marketing					7 Review	11 Retrieve questionnaires						
6	18-Jan-00	12 Analyse information												
7	19-Jan-00	13 Write requirements document												
8	20-Jan-00	13 Write requirements document												
9	21-Jan-00	13 Write requirements document												
10	24-Jan-00	13 Write requirements document												
11	25-Jan-00	13 Write requirements document												
12	26-Jan-00	13 Write requirements document												
13	27-Jan-00	13 Write requirements document												
14	28-Jan-00	13 Write requirements document												
15	31-Jan-00	13 Write requirements document					15 Circulate document							
16	1-Feb-00	17,18,19 Review meeting / changes to document (inc. c						16, 17 Individual review [1/2 day each] & review meeting [1/2 day]						
17	2-Feb-00	18,19 Changes to document (inc. circulate again)												
18	3-Feb-00	17,18,19 Review meeting / changes to document (inc. circulate again)												
19	4-Feb-00	20–22 Second review / Signoff / Reqs complete			18–20 S	18–20 Second review / Signoff / Reqs complete [1/4 day]								
20	7-Feb-00	58 Pro	58 Prot	58 Prototype		209 Research tech. writing requirements				24 Research into Test Plan				
21	8-Feb-00	58 Pro	58 Prot	58 Prototype		209 Research tech. writing requirements				24 Research into Test Plan				
22	9-Feb-00	58 Pro	58 Prot	58 Prototype		209 Research tech. writing requirements				24 Research into Test Plan				
23	10-Feb-00	58 Pro	58 Prot	58 Prototype		209 Research tech. writing requirements				24 Research into Test Plan				
24	11-Feb-00	58 Pro	58 Prot	58 Prototype		209 Research tech. writing requirements				24 Research into Test Plan				
25	14-Feb-00	58 Pro	58 Prot	58 Prototype		210 Set up environment and tools				25 Writ	37 Write Performance Tests			
26	15-Feb-00	58 Pro	58 Prot	58 Prototype		210 Set up environment and tools				25 Writ	37 Write Performance Tests			
27	16-Feb-00	58 Pro	58 Prot	58 Prototype		210 Set up environment and tools				25 Writ	37 Write Performance Tests			
28	17-Feb-00	58 Pro	58 Prot	58 Prototype		210 Set up environment and tools				29 Writ	41 Write Stress Tests			
29	18-Feb-00	58 Pro	58 Prot	58 Prototype		210 Set up environment and tools				29 Writ	41 Write Stress Tests			
30	21-Feb-00	58 Pro	58 Prot	58 Prototype		211 Define style sheet & produce proto				29 Writ	41 Write Stress Tests			
31	22-Feb-00	58 Pro	58 Prot	58 Prototype		211 Define style sheet & produce proto				33 Writ	45 Write Installation Tests			
32	23-Feb-00	58 Pro	58 Prot	58 Prototype		211 Define style sheet & produce			61 Individ	33 Writ	45 Write Installation Tests			
33	24-Feb-00	58 Pro	58 Prot	58 Prototype		211 Define style sheet & produce proto				33 Writ	45 Write Installation Tests			
34	25-Feb-00	58 Pro	58 Prot	58 Prototype		211 Define style	50 Circulate all Tests							
35	28-Feb-00	58 Pro	58 Prot	58 Prototype		212 Write documentation / Help text								
36	29-Feb-00	58 Pro	58 Prot	58 Prototype		212 Write documentation / Help text								
37	1-Mar-00	58 Pro	58 Prot	58 Prototype		212 Write documentation / Help text								
38	2-Mar-00	51 Indi	51 Indiv	51 Individual re		212 Write documentation / Help te	51 Individual review							

Figure 11.2   Duration reduced further by 13 days.

How to Run Successful Projects in Web Time

Day #	Date	Charlie	Engineer #2	Engineer #3	Engineer #4	Technical author	Marketing people (3)	Admin. assistant	Reqs. reviewers (5)	Test and design reviewers (2)	Tester #1	Tester #2	Users	Project management
39	3-Mar-00	52 Rev	52 Rev	52 Review mee		212 Write documentation / Help te				52 Revie	52 Rev			52 Review meeting
40	6-Mar-00	58 Pro	58 Prot	58 Prototype		212 Write documentation / Help text						53 Cha		53 Changes to document
41	7-Mar-00	58 Pro	58 Prot	58 Prototype		212 Write documentation / Help text						53 Cha		53 Changes to document
42	8-Mar-00	58 Pro	58 Prot	58 Prototype		212 Write documentation / Help text					53, 54			53, 54 Changes to document and circul
43	9-Mar-00	58 Pro	58 Prot	58 Prototype		212 Write documentation / Help te				55–57 Se	55–57			55–57 Second review / sign / Test Plan c
44	10-Mar-00	60 Pric	73 Sett	86 Rep	99 Fore	212 Write documentation / Help text								
45	13-Mar-00	60 Pric	73 Sett	86 Rep	99 Fore	212 Write documentation / Help te				65–67 Second review / signoff / HLD complete [1/4 day ea				
46	14-Mar-00	60 Pric	73 Sett	86 Rep	99 Fore	212 Write documentation / Help text								
47	15-Mar-00	60 Pric	73 Sett	86 Rep	99 Fore	212 Write documentation / Help text								
48	16-Mar-00	60 Pric	73 Sett	86 Rep	99 Fore	212 Write documentation / Help text								
49	17-Mar-00	60 Pric	73 Sett	86 Rep	99 Fore	212 Write documentation / Help text								
50	20-Mar-00	60 Pric	73 Sett	86 Rep	99 Fore	212 Write documentation / Help text								
51	21-Mar-00	60 Pric	73 Sett	86 Rep	99 Fore	212 Write documentation / Help text								
52	22-Mar-00	151 W	170 Se	138 Tu	99 Fore	212 Write documentation / Help text								
53	23-Mar-00	151 W	170 Se	138 Tu	99 Fore	212 Write documentation / Help text								
54	24-Mar-00	151 W	170 Se	138 Tu	99 Fore	212 Write documentation / Help text								
55	27-Mar-00	151 W	170 Se	138 Tu	99 Fore	212 Write documentation / Help text								
56	28-Mar-00	151 W	170 Se	138 Tu	99 Fore	212 Write documentation / Help text								
57	29-Mar-00	151 W	170 Se	138 Tu	99 Fore	212 Write documentation / Help text								
58	30-Mar-00	151 W	170 Se	138 Tu	99 Fore	212 Write documentation / Help text								
59	31-Mar-00	151 W	170 Se	138 Tu	99 Fore	212 Write documentation / Help text								
60	3-Apr-00	151 W	170 Se	138 Tu	112 Eu	212 Write documentation / Help text								
61	4-Apr-00	151 W	170 Se	138 Tu	112 Eu	212 Write documentation / Help text								
62	5-Apr-00	151 W	170 Se	138 Tu	112 Eu	212 Write documentation / Help text								
63	6-Apr-00	151 W	170 Se	138 Tu	112 Eu	212 Write documentation / Help text								
64	7-Apr-00	151 W	170 Se	138 Tu	112 Eu	212 Write documentation / Help text								
65	10-Apr-00	151 W	170 Se	138 Tu	112 Eu	212 Write documentation / Help text								
66	11-Apr-00	151 W	170 Se	138 Tu	112 Eu	212 Write documentation / Help text								
67	12-Apr-00	151 W	170 Se	138 Tu	112 Eu	212 Write documentation / Help text								
68	13-Apr-00	151 W	170 Se	138 Tu	112 Eu	212 Write documentation / Help text								
69	14-Apr-00	151 W	170 Se	189 Or	112 Eu	212 Write documentation / Help text								
70	17-Apr-00	151 W	170 Se	189 Or	112 Eu	212 Write documentation / Help text								
71	18-Apr-00	151 W	170 Se	189 Or	112 Eu	212 Write documentation / Help text								
72	19-Apr-00	151 W	170 Se	189 Or	112 Eu	212 Write documentation / Help text								
73	20-Apr-00	151 W	170 Se	189 Or	112 Eu	212 Write documentation / Help text								
74	21-Apr-00	151 W	170 Se	189 Or	112 Eu	212 Write documentation / Help text								
75	24-Apr-00	151 W	170 Se	189 Or	112 Eu	212 Write documentation / Help text								
76	25-Apr-00	151 W	170 Se	189 Or	125 3rd	212 Write documentation / Help text								

Figure 11.2   (continued)

Day #	Date	Charlie	Engineer #2	Engineer #3	Engineer #4	Technical author	Marketing people (3)	Admin. assistant	Reqs. reviewers (5)	Test and design reviewers (2)	Tester #1	Tester #2	Users	Project management
77	26-Apr-00	151 W	170 Se	189 Or	125 3rd	212 Write documentation / Help text								
78	27-Apr-00	151 W	170 Se	189 Or	125 3rd	212 Write documentation / Help text								
79	28-Apr-00	151 W	170 Se	189 Or	125 3rd	212 Write documentation / Help text								
80	1-May-00	151 W	170 Se	189 Or	125 3rd	212 Write documentation / Help text								
81	2-May-00	151 W	170 Se	189 Or	125 3rd	212 Write documentation / Help text								
82	3-May-00	151 W	170 Se	189 Or	125 3rd	212 Write documentation / Help text								
83	4-May-00	151 W	170 Se	189 Or	125 3rd	212 Write documentation / Help text								
84	5-May-00			189 Or	125 3rd	212 Write documentation / Help text								
85	8-May-00			189 Or	125 3rd	212 Write documentation / Help text								
86	9-May-00			189 Or	125 3rd	212 Write documentation / Help text								
87	10-May-00			189 Or	125 3rd	212 Write documentation / Help text								
88	11-May-00			189 Or	125 3rd	217 Edit documentation / Help text								
89	12-May-00			189 Or	125 3rd	217 Edit documentation / Help text								
90	15-May-00			189 Or	125 3rd	217 Edit documentation / Help text								
91	16-May-00			189 Or	125 3rd	217 Edit documentation / Help text								
92	17-May-00			189 Online help		217 Edit documentation / Help text								
93	18-May-00			189 Online help		217 Edit documentation / Help text								
94	19-May-00			189 Online help		217 Edit documentation / Help text								
95	22-May-00			189 Online help		217 Edit documentation / Help text								
96	23-May-00			189 Online help		217 Edit documentation / Help text								
97	24-May-00			189 Online help		217 Edit documentation / Help text								
98	25-May-00			189 Online help		217 Edit documentation / Help text								
99	26-May-00			189 Online help		217 Edit documentation / Help text								
100	29-May-00			189 Online help		217 Edit documentation / Help text								
101	30-May-00					217 Edit documentation / Help text					225 Te	225 Test #1 – follow script & report errors		
102	31-May-00					217 Edit documentation / Help text					225 Te	225 Test #1 – follow script & report errors		
103	1-Jun-00					217 Edit documentation / Help text					225 Te	225 Test #1 – follow script & report errors		
104	2-Jun-00					217 Edit documentation / Help text					225 Te	225 Test #1 – follow script & report errors		
105	5-Jun-00					217 Edit documentation / Help text					225 Te	225 Test #1 – follow script & report errors		
106	6-Jun-00					217 Edit documentation / Help text					225 Te	225 Test #1 – follow script & report errors		
107	7-Jun-00					217 Edit documentation / Help text					225 Te	225 Test #1 – follow script & report errors		
108	8-Jun-00					217 Edit documentation / Help text					225 Te	225 Test #1 – follow script & report errors		
109	9-Jun-00					221 Final integration of Online Help					225 Te	225 Test #1 – follow script & report errors		
110	12-Jun-00					221 Final integration of Online Help					225 Te	225 Test #1 – follow script & report errors		
111	13-Jun-00					221 Final integration of Online Help					225 Te	225 Test #1 – follow script & report errors		
112	14-Jun-00					221 Final integration of Online Help					225 Te	225 Test #1 – follow script & report errors		
113	15-Jun-00	226 Te	226 Te	226 Te	226 Te	221 Final integration of Online Help								
114	16-Jun-00	226 Te	226 Te	226 Te	226 Te	222 Final pre-production of manuals								

Figure 11.2   (continued)

How to Run Successful Projects in Web Time

Day #	Date	Cast (Jobs) Charlie	Engineer #2	Engineer #3	Engineer #4	Technical author	Marketing people (3)	Admin. assistant	Reqs. reviewers (5)	Test and design reviewers (2)	Tester #1	Tester #2	Users	Project management
115	19-Jun-00	226 Te	226 Te	226 Te	226 Te	222 Final pre-production of manuals								
116	20-Jun-00	226 Te	226 Te	226 Te	226 Te	222 Final pre-production of manuals								
117	21-Jun-00	226 Te	226 Te	226 Te	226 Te	222 Final pre-production of manuals								
118	22-Jun-00	226 Te	226 Te	226 Te	226 Te	222 Final pre-production of manuals								
119	23-Jun-00										228 Te	228 Test #2 – follow script & report errors		
120	26-Jun-00										228 Te	228 Test #2 – follow script & report errors		
121	27-Jun-00										228 Te	228 Test #2 – follow script & report errors		
122	28-Jun-00										228 Te	228 Test #2 – follow script & report errors		
123	29-Jun-00	229 Te	229 Te	229 Te	229 Test #2 – make corrections									
124	30-Jun-00	229 Te	229 Te	229 Te	229 Test #2 – make corrections									
125	3-Jul-00	229 Te	229 Te	229 Te	229 Test #2 – make corrections									
126	4-Jul-00										231 Te	231 Test #3 – follow script & report errors		
127	5-Jul-00										231 Te	231 Test #3 – follow script & report errors		
128	6-Jul-00	232 Te	232 Te	232 Te	232 Test #3 – make corrections									
129	7-Jul-00									233 Finalise test documentation				
130	10-Jul-00	235 En	235 En	235 En	235 En	235 End of project review				235 En	235 End of project review			
131	11-Jul-00	237 Contingency												
132	12-Jul-00	237 Contingency												
133	13-Jul-00	237 Contingency												
134	14-Jul-00	237 Contingency												
135	17-Jul-00	237 Contingency												
136	18-Jul-00	237 Contingency												
137	19-Jul-00	237 Contingency												
138	20-Jul-00	237 Contingency												
139	21-Jul-00	237 Contingency												
140	24-Jul-00	237 Contingency												
141	25-Jul-00	237 Contingency												
142	26-Jul-00	237 Contingency												
143	27-Jul-00	237 Contingency												
144	28-Jul-00	237 Contingency												

Figure 11.2   (continued)

documentation, something we definitely don't want to do. We leave it for the present.

Again, in Figure 11.2, we notice that there might be potential to overlap, to a certain extent, the system testing and correcting the software activities. However, again for the present, we don't tamper with this.

We wonder whether we should be looking at trying to reduce estimates for individual tasks, for example, the coding tasks, but we decide against it. Our rationale for this is that, at this stage, if we were to do this, we would really only be playing computer games. Clearly we can change any estimate we like. But we have no basis for doing so, other than our desire to make the project shorter. This is a rather silly circular argument. We would like to make the project shorter, so we shorten the estimates and, hey presto, the project is shorter. Forget it! If we shorten individual task estimates, we have to have some basis for doing so. The next time such a basis will arise for us will be when we see some actuals coming in to compare against our estimates. If, for example, coding actuals start coming in 50% shorter than we had estimated, then that would be some basis for shortening the remaining coding estimates. Without such a basis, however, we would just be engaging in a great game of self-delusion.

Two things need to be added to the strip board. First is the project management effort. The 60 days is now going to be spread over 144 elapsed days. This represents about 40% of your time. So, you can think of it in terms of about 2 days per week on your Dance Card, or up to half a day every day in terms of how you might be spending your time. We add in the project management effort as shown in Figure 11.3.

The final thing is the issue of public holidays and annual leave. Public holidays are easy—just count them up. If the worked example were taking place in my country, there would be five in the period covered by this project—St Patrick's Day (March 17), Good Friday, Easter Monday, May 1 and June 5. While we can insert these into the relevant parts of the strip board, it's maybe just as easy to show them in a block at the end. This is what I have done here.

Annual leave? It obviously varies from country to country. A good working assumption is that everyone is going to take two weeks over the period June through August. It might be, looking at the plan, you decide it would be nice if nobody took their vacation until the project was over. You consider this for a while. Like many things in project management, it's a two-edged sword. On the one hand, it'll certainly shorten the

Day #	Date	Charlie	Engineer #2	Engineer #3	Engineer #4	Technical author	Marketing people (3)	Admin. assistant	Reqs. reviewers (5)	Test and design reviewers (2)	Tester #1	Tester #2	Users	Project management
1	11-Jan-00	3 Proj	3 Project planning and scopin		3 Project planning and scoping meeting									3 Project planning and scoping meeting
2	12-Jan-00	6 Gath												236 Project management [up to 1/2 day]
3	13-Jan-00	9 Prepare user questionnaires												236 Project management [up to 1/2 day]
4	14-Jan-00	9 Prepare user questionnaires					10 Distribute user questionnaires							236 Project management [up to 1/2 day]
5	17-Jan-00	7 Review with Marketing					7 Review	11 Retrieve questionnaires						236 Project management [up to 1/2 day]
6	18-Jan-00	12 Analyse information												236 Project management [up to 1/2 day]
7	19-Jan-00	13 Write requirements document												236 Project management [up to 1/2 day]
8	20-Jan-00	13 Write requirements document												236 Project management [up to 1/2 day]
9	21-Jan-00	13 Write requirements document												236 Project management [up to 1/2 day]
10	24-Jan-00	13 Write requirements document												236 Project management [up to 1/2 day]
11	25-Jan-00	13 Write requirements document												236 Project management [up to 1/2 day]
12	26-Jan-00	13 Write requirements document												236 Project management [up to 1/2 day]
13	27-Jan-00	13 Write requirements document												236 Project management [up to 1/2 day]
14	28-Jan-00	13 Write requirements document												236 Project management [up to 1/2 day]
15	31-Jan-00	13 Write requirements document					15 Circulate document							236 Project management [up to 1/2 day]
16	1-Feb-00	17,18,19 Review meeting / changes to document (inc. cir					16, 17 Individual review [1/2 day each] &							236 Project management [up to 1/2 day]
17	2-Feb-00	18,19 Changes to document (inc. circulate again)												236 Project management [up to 1/2 day]
18	3-Feb-00	17,18,19 Review meeting / changes to document (inc. circulate again)												236 Project management [up to 1/2 day]
19	4-Feb-00	20-22 Second review / Signoff / Reqs complete [					18-20 S	18-20 Second review / Signoff / Reqs cc						236 Project management [up to 1/2 day]
20	7-Feb-00	58 Pro	58 Pro	58 Prototype		209 Research tech. writing requirements				24 Research into Te				236 Project management [up to 1/2 day]
21	8-Feb-00	58 Pro	58 Pro	58 Prototype		209 Research tech. writing requirements				24 Research into Te				236 Project management [up to 1/2 day]
22	9-Feb-00	58 Pro	58 Pro	58 Prototype		209 Research tech. writing requirements				24 Research into Te				236 Project management [up to 1/2 day]
23	10-Feb-00	58 Pro	58 Pro	58 Prototype		209 Research tech. writing requirements				24 Research into Te				236 Project management [up to 1/2 day]
24	11-Feb-00	58 Pro	58 Pro	58 Prototype		209 Research tech. writing requirements				24 Research into Te				236 Project management [up to 1/2 day]
25	14-Feb-00	58 Pro	58 Pro	58 Prototype		210 Set up environment and tools				25 Wri	37 Write Perf			236 Project management [up to 1/2 day]
26	15-Feb-00	58 Pro	58 Pro	58 Prototype		210 Set up environment and tools				25 Wri	37 Write Perf			236 Project management [up to 1/2 day]
27	16-Feb-00	58 Pro	58 Pro	58 Prototype		210 Set up environment and tools				25 Wri	37 Write Perf			236 Project management [up to 1/2 day]
28	17-Feb-00	58 Pro	58 Pro	58 Prototype		210 Set up environment and tools				29 Wri	41 Write Stre			236 Project management [up to 1/2 day]
29	18-Feb-00	58 Pro	58 Pro	58 Prototype		210 Set up environment and tools				29 Wri	41 Write Stre			236 Project management [up to 1/2 day]
30	21-Feb-00	58 Pro	58 Pro	58 Prototype		211 Define style sheet & produce proto				29 Wri	41 Write Stre			236 Project management [up to 1/2 day]
31	22-Feb-00	58 Pro	58 Pro	58 Prototype		211 Define style sheet & produce proto				33 Wri	45 Write Insta			236 Project management [up to 1/2 day]
32	23-Feb-00	58 Pro	58 Pro	58 Prototype		211 Define style sheet & produce	61 Individ			33 Wri	45 Write Insta			236 Project management [up to 1/2 day]
33	24-Feb-00	58 Pro	58 Pro	58 Prototype		211 Define style sheet & produce proto				33 Wri	45 Write Insta			236 Project management [up to 1/2 day]
34	25-Feb-00	58 Pro	58 Pro	58 Prototype		211 Define style	50 Circulate all Tests							236 Project management [up to 1/2 day]
35	28-Feb-00	58 Pro	58 Pro	58 Prototype		212 Write documentation / Help text								236 Project management [up to 1/2 day]
36	29-Feb-00	58 Pro	58 Pro	58 Prototype		212 Write documentation / Help text								236 Project management [up to 1/2 day]
37	1-Mar-00	58 Pro	58 Pro	58 Prototype		212 Write documentation / Help text								236 Project management [up to 1/2 day]
38	2-Mar-00	51 Indi	51 Indi	51 Individual re		212 Write documentation / Help te				51 Individual review				236 Project management [up to 1/2 day]
39	3-Mar-00	52 Rev	52 Rev	52 Review mee		212 Write documentation / Help te				52 Revie	52 Rev	52 Review me		236 Project management [up to 1/2 day]
40	6-Mar-00	58 Pro	58 Pro	58 Prototype		212 Write documentation / Help text				53 Cha	53 Changes t			236 Project management [up to 1/2 day]
41	7-Mar-00	58 Pro	58 Pro	58 Prototype		212 Write documentation / Help text				53 Cha	53 Changes t			236 Project management [up to 1/2 day]
42	8-Mar-00	58 Pro	58 Pro	58 Prototype		212 Write documentation / Help text				53, 54	53, 54 Chang			236 Project management [up to 1/2 day]
43	9-Mar-00	58 Pro	58 Pro	58 Prototype		212 Write documentation / Help te	55-57 Se			55-57	55-57 Secon			236 Project management [up to 1/2 day]
44	10-Mar-00	60 Pric	73 Sett	86 Rep	99 Forc	212 Write documentation / Help text								236 Project management [up to 1/2 day]
45	13-Mar-00	60 Pric	73 Sett	86 Rep	99 Forc	212 Write documentation / Help te	65-67 Second review / signoff /							236 Project management [up to 1/2 day]
46	14-Mar-00	60 Pric	73 Sett	86 Rep	99 Forc	212 Write documentation / Help text								236 Project management [up to 1/2 day]
47	15-Mar-00	60 Pric	73 Sett	86 Rep	99 Forc	212 Write documentation / Help text								236 Project management [up to 1/2 day]

Figure 11.3 Strip board with project management shown.

Day #	Date	Charlie	Engineer #2	Engineer #3	Engineer #4	Technical author	Marketing people (3)	Admin. assistant	Reqs. reviewers (5)	Test and design reviewers (2)	Tester #1	Tester #2	Users	Project management
48	16-Mar-00	60 Pric	73 Sett	86 Rep	99 Forc	212 Write documentation / Help text								236 Project management [up to 1/2 day]
49	17-Mar-00	60 Pric	73 Sett	86 Rep	99 Forc	212 Write documentation / Help text								236 Project management [up to 1/2 day]
50	20-Mar-00	60 Pric	73 Sett	86 Rep	99 Forc	212 Write documentation / Help text								236 Project management [up to 1/2 day]
51	21-Mar-00	60 Pric	73 Sett	86 Rep	99 Forc	212 Write documentation / Help text								236 Project management [up to 1/2 day]
52	22-Mar-00	151 W	170 Se	138 Tu	99 Forc	212 Write documentation / Help text								236 Project management [up to 1/2 day]
53	23-Mar-00	151 W	170 Se	138 Tu	99 Forc	212 Write documentation / Help text								236 Project management [up to 1/2 day]
54	24-Mar-00	151 W	170 Se	138 Tu	99 Forc	212 Write documentation / Help text								236 Project management [up to 1/2 day]
55	27-Mar-00	151 W	170 Se	138 Tu	99 Forc	212 Write documentation / Help text								236 Project management [up to 1/2 day]
56	28-Mar-00	151 W	170 Se	138 Tu	99 Forc	212 Write documentation / Help text								236 Project management [up to 1/2 day]
57	29-Mar-00	151 W	170 Se	138 Tu	99 Forc	212 Write documentation / Help text								236 Project management [up to 1/2 day]
58	30-Mar-00	151 W	170 Se	138 Tu	99 Forc	212 Write documentation / Help text								236 Project management [up to 1/2 day]
59	31-Mar-00	151 W	170 Se	138 Tu	99 Forc	212 Write documentation / Help text								236 Project management [up to 1/2 day]
60	3-Apr-00	151 W	170 Se	138 Tu	112 Eu	212 Write documentation / Help text								236 Project management [up to 1/2 day]
61	4-Apr-00	151 W	170 Se	138 Tu	112 Eu	212 Write documentation / Help text								236 Project management [up to 1/2 day]
62	5-Apr-00	151 W	170 Se	138 Tu	112 Eu	212 Write documentation / Help text								236 Project management [up to 1/2 day]
63	6-Apr-00	151 W	170 Se	138 Tu	112 Eu	212 Write documentation / Help text								236 Project management [up to 1/2 day]
64	7-Apr-00	151 W	170 Se	138 Tu	112 Eu	212 Write documentation / Help text								236 Project management [up to 1/2 day]
65	10-Apr-00	151 W	170 Se	138 Tu	112 Eu	212 Write documentation / Help text								236 Project management [up to 1/2 day]
66	11-Apr-00	151 W	170 Se	138 Tu	112 Eu	212 Write documentation / Help text								236 Project management [up to 1/2 day]
67	12-Apr-00	151 W	170 Se	138 Tu	112 Eu	212 Write documentation / Help text								236 Project management [up to 1/2 day]
68	13-Apr-00	151 W	170 Se	138 Tu	112 Eu	212 Write documentation / Help text								236 Project management [up to 1/2 day]
69	14-Apr-00	151 W	170 Se	189 Or	112 Eu	212 Write documentation / Help text								236 Project management [up to 1/2 day]
70	17-Apr-00	151 W	170 Se	189 Or	112 Eu	212 Write documentation / Help text								236 Project management [up to 1/2 day]
71	18-Apr-00	151 W	170 Se	189 Or	112 Eu	212 Write documentation / Help text								236 Project management [up to 1/2 day]
72	19-Apr-00	151 W	170 Se	189 Or	112 Eu	212 Write documentation / Help text								236 Project management [up to 1/2 day]
73	20-Apr-00	151 W	170 Se	189 Or	112 Eu	212 Write documentation / Help text								236 Project management [up to 1/2 day]
74	21-Apr-00	151 W	170 Se	189 Or	112 Eu	212 Write documentation / Help text								236 Project management [up to 1/2 day]
75	24-Apr-00	151 W	170 Se	189 Or	112 Eu	212 Write documentation / Help text								236 Project management [up to 1/2 day]
76	25-Apr-00	151 W	170 Se	189 Or	125 3rc	212 Write documentation / Help text								236 Project management [up to 1/2 day]
77	26-Apr-00	151 W	170 Se	189 Or	125 3rc	212 Write documentation / Help text								236 Project management [up to 1/2 day]
78	27-Apr-00	151 W	170 Se	189 Or	125 3rc	212 Write documentation / Help text								236 Project management [up to 1/2 day]
79	28-Apr-00	151 W	170 Se	189 Or	125 3rc	212 Write documentation / Help text								236 Project management [up to 1/2 day]
80	1-May-00	151 W	170 Se	189 Or	125 3rc	212 Write documentation / Help text								236 Project management [up to 1/2 day]
81	2-May-00	151 W	170 Se	189 Or	125 3rc	212 Write documentation / Help text								236 Project management [up to 1/2 day]
82	3-May-00	151 W	170 Se	189 Or	125 3rc	212 Write documentation / Help text								236 Project management [up to 1/2 day]
83	4-May-00	151 W	170 Se	189 Or	125 3rc	212 Write documentation / Help text								236 Project management [up to 1/2 day]
84	5-May-00			189 Or	125 3rc	212 Write documentation / Help text								236 Project management [up to 1/2 day]
85	8-May-00			189 Or	125 3rc	212 Write documentation / Help text								236 Project management [up to 1/2 day]
86	9-May-00			189 Or	125 3rc	212 Write documentation / Help text								236 Project management [up to 1/2 day]
87	10-May-00			189 Or	125 3rc	212 Write documentation / Help text								236 Project management [up to 1/2 day]
88	11-May-00			189 Or	125 3rc	217 Edit documentation / Help text								236 Project management [up to 1/2 day]
89	12-May-00			189 Or	125 3rc	217 Edit documentation / Help text								236 Project management [up to 1/2 day]
90	15-May-00			189 Or	125 3rc	217 Edit documentation / Help text								236 Project management [up to 1/2 day]
91	16-May-00			189 Or	125 3rc	217 Edit documentation / Help text								236 Project management [up to 1/2 day]
92	17-May-00			189 Online help		217 Edit documentation / Help text								236 Project management [up to 1/2 day]
93	18-May-00			189 Online help		217 Edit documentation / Help text								236 Project management [up to 1/2 day]
94	19-May-00			189 Online help		217 Edit documentation / Help text								236 Project management [up to 1/2 day]

Figure 11.3   (continued)

Day #	Date	Charlie	Engineer #2	Engineer #3	Engineer #4	Technical author	Marketing people (3)	Admin. assistant	Reqs. reviewers (5)	Test and design reviewers (2)	Tester #1	Tester #2	Users	Project management
95	22-May-00				189 Online help	217 Edit documentation / Help text								236 Project management [up to 1/2 day]
96	23-May-00				189 Online help	217 Edit documentation / Help text								236 Project management [up to 1/2 day]
97	24-May-00				189 Online help	217 Edit documentation / Help text								236 Project management [up to 1/2 day]
98	25-May-00				189 Online help	217 Edit documentation / Help text								236 Project management [up to 1/2 day]
99	26-May-00				189 Online help	217 Edit documentation / Help text								236 Project management [up to 1/2 day]
100	29-May-00				189 Online help	217 Edit documentation / Help text								236 Project management [up to 1/2 day]
101	30-May-00					217 Edit documentation / Help text					225 Te	225 Test #1 -		236 Project management [up to 1/2 day]
102	31-May-00					217 Edit documentation / Help text					225 Te	225 Test #1 -		236 Project management [up to 1/2 day]
103	1-Jun-00					217 Edit documentation / Help text					225 Te	225 Test #1 -		236 Project management [up to 1/2 day]
104	2-Jun-00					217 Edit documentation / Help text					225 Te	225 Test #1 -		236 Project management [up to 1/2 day]
105	5-Jun-00					217 Edit documentation / Help text					225 Te	225 Test #1 -		236 Project management [up to 1/2 day]
106	6-Jun-00					217 Edit documentation / Help text					225 Te	225 Test #1 -		236 Project management [up to 1/2 day]
107	7-Jun-00					217 Edit documentation / Help text					225 Te	225 Test #1 -		236 Project management [up to 1/2 day]
108	8-Jun-00					217 Edit documentation / Help text					225 Te	225 Test #1 -		236 Project management [up to 1/2 day]
109	9-Jun-00					221 Final integration of Online Help					225 Te	225 Test #1 -		236 Project management [up to 1/2 day]
110	12-Jun-00					221 Final integration of Online Help					225 Te	225 Test #1 -		236 Project management [up to 1/2 day]
111	13-Jun-00					221 Final integration of Online Help					225 Te	225 Test #1 -		236 Project management [up to 1/2 day]
112	14-Jun-00					221 Final integration of Online Help					225 Te	225 Test #1 -		236 Project management [up to 1/2 day]
113	15-Jun-00	226 Te	226 Te	226 Te	226 Te	221 Final integration of Online Help								236 Project management [up to 1/2 day]
114	16-Jun-00	226 Te	226 Te	226 Te	226 Te	222 Final pre-production of manuals								236 Project management [up to 1/2 day]
115	19-Jun-00	226 Te	226 Te	226 Te	226 Te	222 Final pre-production of manuals								236 Project management [up to 1/2 day]
116	20-Jun-00	226 Te	226 Te	226 Te	226 Te	222 Final pre-production of manuals								236 Project management [up to 1/2 day]
117	21-Jun-00	226 Te	226 Te	226 Te	226 Te	222 Final pre-production of manuals								236 Project management [up to 1/2 day]
118	22-Jun-00	226 Te	226 Te	226 Te	226 Te	222 Final pre-production of manuals								236 Project management [up to 1/2 day]
119	23-Jun-00										228 Te	228 Test #2 -		236 Project management [up to 1/2 day]
120	26-Jun-00										228 Te	228 Test #2 -		236 Project management [up to 1/2 day]
121	27-Jun-00										228 Te	228 Test #2 -		236 Project management [up to 1/2 day]
122	28-Jun-00										228 Te	228 Test #2 -		236 Project management [up to 1/2 day]
123	29-Jun-00	229 Te	229 Te	229 Te	229 Test #2 - make corrections									236 Project management [up to 1/2 day]
124	30-Jun-00	229 Te	229 Te	229 Te	229 Test #2 - make corrections									236 Project management [up to 1/2 day]
125	3-Jul-00	229 Te	229 Te	229 Te	229 Test #2 - make corrections									236 Project management [up to 1/2 day]
126	4-Jul-00										231 Te	231 Test #3 -		236 Project management [up to 1/2 day]
127	5-Jul-00										231 Te	231 Test #3 -		236 Project management [up to 1/2 day]
128	6-Jul-00	232 Te	232 Te	232 Te	232 Test #3 - make corrections									236 Project management [up to 1/2 day]
129	7-Jul-00										233 Finalise test doc			236 Project management [up to 1/2 day]
130	10-Jul-00	235 En	235 En	235 En	235 En	235 End of project review					235 En	235 End of pr		236 Project management [up to 1/2 day]
131	11-Jul-00	237 Contingency												236 Project management [up to 1/2 day]
132	12-Jul-00	237 Contingency												236 Project management [up to 1/2 day]
133	13-Jul-00	237 Contingency												236 Project management [up to 1/2 day]
134	14-Jul-00	237 Contingency												236 Project management [up to 1/2 day]
135	17-Jul-00	237 Contingency												236 Project management [up to 1/2 day]
136	18-Jul-00	237 Contingency												236 Project management [up to 1/2 day]
137	19-Jul-00	237 Contingency												236 Project management [up to 1/2 day]
138	20-Jul-00	237 Contingency												236 Project management [up to 1/2 day]
139	21-Jul-00	237 Contingency												236 Project management [up to 1/2 day]
140	24-Jul-00	237 Contingency												236 Project management [up to 1/2 day]
141	25-Jul-00	237 Contingency												236 Project management [up to 1/2 day]

Figure 11.3   (continued)

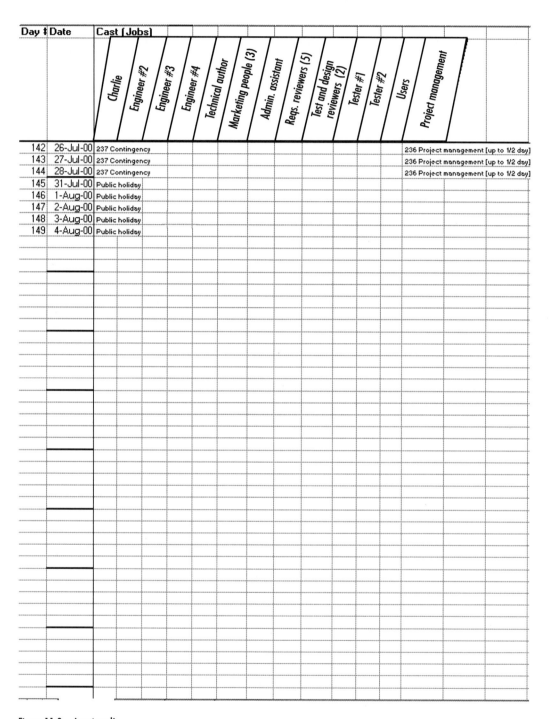

Day #	Date	Cast [Jobs]	Charlie	Engineer #2	Engineer #3	Engineer #4	Technical author	Marketing people (3)	Admin. assistant	Reqs. reviewers (5)	Test and design reviewers (2)	Tester #1	Tester #2	Users	Project management	
142	26-Jul-00	237 Contingency													236 Project management [up to 1/2 day]	
143	27-Jul-00	237 Contingency													236 Project management [up to 1/2 day]	
144	28-Jul-00	237 Contingency													236 Project management [up to 1/2 day]	
145	31-Jul-00	Public holiday														
146	1-Aug-00	Public holiday														
147	2-Aug-00	Public holiday														
148	3-Aug-00	Public holiday														
149	4-Aug-00	Public holiday														

Figure 11.3   (continued)

How to Run Successful Projects in Web Time

project if nobody takes time out to go on vacation. However, it wouldn't be a great idea just to send out an edict to this effect. I think this is very much something you would discuss and agree with the team. If they thought it was a good idea, then you would go with it. If not, it might be better not to try and drive it through against their wishes. After all, if they're not with you, what chance do you have then? Let's assume though, for the simplicity of our example if nothing else, that the team has agreed to leave their vacations until after the project is over.

Epilogue

You may be thinking that at the end of all this song and dance, we haven't accomplished a great deal. We peeled about 4 weeks off the project, but was it worth all the work of producing a strip board? I will argue that it was. First, this is a considerable saving, whose dollar value we can calculate using the techniques in Chapter 3. The even better news, however, is that we're not finished yet. We will see, in the two chapters which follow, that the whole process of executing the plan becomes a continuous search for ways to shorten the project. Again, the strip board is the tool we will use to do that.

12 Sell the Plan

> ➤ This chapter describes how to sell the plan, firstly to the team members, then having done that, to the powers-that-be, bosses and customers.
>
> ➤ The worked example is used to illustrate the various points raised.

Introduction

In my experience, one of the areas that project managers in general are not good at, is what might loosely be termed "communications." More precisely, it's about keeping the stakeholders involved at all stages with regard to how the project is unrolling. It's about managing the stakeholders' expectations.

This activity, important on conventional projects, is crucial on shortened projects. It's crucial because days lost due to misunderstandings, or people being confused about something, or people being grumpy about something, days lost for whatever reason, can never be recovered. The more you can ensure that this doesn't happen by keeping everyone in tune, the better your chances will be that you will either achieve your shortened plan or improve on it still further.

The place to start is at the beginning, when you kick off the project. There are two constituencies that need to be addressed and they need to be addressed in somewhat different ways. They are the team and the powers-that-be (i.e., your management and customer).

The Team

There are two points you want to get across to the team. First, you want to explain the big picture and everybody's part in it. Then you want to

137

get them thinking in terms of sweeping for opportunities to shorten the project.

To do the first of these, you do the following:

1. Get the team together. Get them to bring their diaries / calendars.

2. Issue everybody with a copy of the plan including the strip board.

3. Talk them through the overall picture—what's being delivered, when it's being delivered, the effort or budget involved, how quality is being ensured, who the team is, the key assumptions upon which the plan is based, and any outstanding issues which have yet to be resolved.

4. Give them a brief summary of how the strip board was generated i.e., about the shortenings you managed to find when you were doing the things described in Chapter 11.

5. Now, take them through the strip board line by line. Ask them to note in their diaries when events that are of particular significance to them occur.

6. Next, address the whole business of where the contingency is in the plan.

7. Take them through the risk analysis.

8. Answer questions as you go, and if some questions throw up issues, then do your best to resolve them while the group is all together. (There may be some issues that are only of interest to a smaller group of people, and then these can be taken offline provided there is a commitment to come back to you with an answer by a certain time.)

Now, you want to get them thinking in terms of further shortening the project. Here are the points you want to make:

1. Let's make every day count.

2. Let's all keep an eagle eye out for changes to the scope of the project.

3. If you find yourself waiting for somebody else, raise a flag so that we can go do something about it.

4. Keep Dance Cards up to date so that, at worst, you'll know if you have overallocated yourself, at best, you may actually avoid overallocating yourself altogether.

5. If you can start a job early, do so.

6. If you can finish a job early without compromising quality, do so.

The Powers-That-Be

In the old way of running projects, this was always one of the most difficult parts of the whole business. It generally involved a misfortunate project manager, with a wholly inadequate team, trying to stand up to repeated assaults on his plan by people who didn't like what it showed. ("What's 'old' about that?" I hear you ask. "That's exactly how all my projects start out.")

My advice to project managers faced with these situations has always been to stand over your estimates and not back down. How to go about doing this is discussed extensively in my previous two books [1, 2].

In the case of a shortened project, this whole business is made a good deal easier. First you can show the efforts you have gone through to shorten the project. Then you can show, on a day by day basis, how everybody is gainfully employed, chipping away at the project until eventually, it is all complete. As you build up this picture in their heads, they will go through the same thought processes you have gone through. They will understand the same tradeoffs you have had to make, and the same constraints you have had to live with. At the conclusion of your presentation, they still may not like the result. But the chances of them then trying to get you to commit to something that is impossible are severely reduced. To put it another way, a strip board presentation of the plan is almost impossible to argue against. Whereas, too often people seem to think that Gantt Charts, especially if they have been generated by computer, have just been "rigged" to show whatever their author wants them to show. And if they have been rigged to show one thing, they can just as easily be rigged to show something different.

All the advice of my previous books about standing over your plan still applies. But I think you'll find that a strip board plan makes that process even easier and more straightforward.

The presentation you do to the powers-that-be can use much of the same format that you used for the team. You tell them the big picture, you take them through the strip board and then you say that you'll be looking for further opportunities to shorten the project as described above.

Let's look at all of this in action in our worked example.

Worked Example — Pitching to the Team

You may be familiar with movies like *The Dam Busters* [3] or *Memphis Belle* [4]. If you are, you'll know the scene where the bomber crews pile into the Ops Room for the mission briefing. Your pitch to the team won't be unlike this.

Ideally you will have been able to get everyone along for the couple of hours that this will take. If not, then you'll have to do a second, or maybe even several of these briefings until everyone has been covered. In addition, if new people join the team as the project proceeds, you will have to do briefings for them. One briefing is best, though. As well as being the most effective use of your time, it minimizes the chances of something falling between the cracks, and being missed or forgotten.[1]

Let's assume then that you're organizing the briefing. In building the invitee list, you realize there are some inaccuracies in your strip board. The "Requirements reviewers" you thought you needed are, in fact, the Marketing people. Thus you can delete the Requirements reviewers from the cast and move the couple of jobs they were down to do, to the Marketing people. Equally the only "Test & Design reviewers" you've ended up with are the engineering people. So those cast members get knocked out as well. Finally, the "Users" go. Marketing is now taking the view that the users who buy the product at Comdex will constitute the first pool of test users.

---

1   It's quite likely that not all of the people who will eventually come to work on the project are available for the "sell the plan" meeting. As a result, videotaping the meeting so that it is available as an orientation film to newcomers is a convenient, cheap, and very valuable aid to bringing people up to speed. If you liked this notion, you could also extend it to project post-mortems (too late to help your project, but a help to those who will run projects after you) and even design reviews, provided they were focussed and didn't just end up wasting miles of videotape.

A second tool—and I am grateful to Chuck Howell for both suggestions—is to set up a news group, accessible via a Web interface. (There are lots of free and cheap software packages available to do this.) It's much less intrusive than e-mail, which we all get too much of anyway. One can review it when interested or search for specific issues. The news group content is also a useful by-product at the end of the project and can be made part of the post-mortem material that is made available to other projects, particularly if they are working in a similar technology, application, or product area.

These three realizations reflect the fact that often, when doing your preliminary planning, you make assumptions that may not turn out to be particularly valid. As the project begins to get rolling these things come to light, and then you must update the plan accordingly. Bearing this in mind, you realize—looking at your strip board—that if day 1 of the project was the day of the planning and scoping, then a few days are going to elapse before the project really gets going. To make the plan reflect this, you revise day 1 of your project to be the project kickoff/ team briefing meeting.

With this out of the way, let's assume that you've managed to get everyone along to your briefing. Let's assume too that the team briefing will take place in the morning, and then the one for the powers-that-be will take place in the afternoon. (This is always a good order to do things in, in that the one for the team can act, amongst other things, as a re-hearsal for the one for the higher-ups.) And so ... action!

You watch them as they file in—your motley crew. Charlie, the other three engineers—Engineer #2, Engineer #3, Engineer #4, the Technical Author, the three Marketing people—Marketing #1, Marketing #2, Marketing #3, the Admin. Assistant and the two testers—Tester #1, Tester #2. You've got a PowerPoint presentation, plus a handout that consists of copies of the slides, plus the strip board shown in Figure 12.1.

You've also brought along your trusty Scribe who was with you at the project planning and scoping session. The Scribe will update any part of the plan, but particularly the strip board, based on the discussions that occur here today. You begin.

"The aim of this project is to release to Beta Test a version of the Killer Product version 1.0. The Killer Product will have these features and we have sized them as shown on the slide." (see Figure 12.2).

"We estimate there are 610 person-days in this project, that is, about 3 person-years. As you know, we have developed a shortened version of the plan, and that's the version we'll be talking through in a few moments. That version of the plan shows that if the kickoff is today, and we start tomorrow, 12 January, then we will bring the project in on or before 4 August."

A general guffaw runs round the room. The organization hasn't exactly been renowned for delivering on its commitments. You ignore it and carry on.

"To ensure we deliver (a) the right product and (b) a good product, we're doing the following:

Day #	Date	Charlie	Engineer #2	Engineer #3	Engineer #4	Technical author	Marketing people (3)	Admin. assistant	Reqs. reviewers (5)	Test and design reviewers (2)	Tester #1	Tester #2	Users	Project management
1	11-Jan-00	3 Proj	3 Project planning and scopin				3 Project planning and scoping meeting							3 Project planning and scoping meeting
2	12-Jan-00	6 Gath												236 Project management [up to 1/2 day]
3	13-Jan-00	9 Prepare user questionnaires												236 Project management [up to 1/2 day]
4	14-Jan-00	9 Prepare user questionnaires						10 Distribute user questionnaires						236 Project management [up to 1/2 day]
5	17-Jan-00	7 Review with Marketing					7 Review	11 Retrieve questionnaires						236 Project management [up to 1/2 day]
6	18-Jan-00	12 Analyse information												236 Project management [up to 1/2 day]
7	19-Jan-00	13 Write requirements document												236 Project management [up to 1/2 day]
8	20-Jan-00	13 Write requirements document												236 Project management [up to 1/2 day]
9	21-Jan-00	13 Write requirements document												236 Project management [up to 1/2 day]
10	24-Jan-00	13 Write requirements document												236 Project management [up to 1/2 day]
11	25-Jan-00	13 Write requirements document												236 Project management [up to 1/2 day]
12	26-Jan-00	13 Write requirements document												236 Project management [up to 1/2 day]
13	27-Jan-00	13 Write requirements document												236 Project management [up to 1/2 day]
14	28-Jan-00	13 Write requirements document												236 Project management [up to 1/2 day]
15	31-Jan-00	13 Write requirements document						15 Circulate document						236 Project management [up to 1/2 day]
16	1-Feb-00	17,18,19 Review meeting/ changes to document (inc. cir					16, 17 Individual review [1/2 day each] &							236 Project management [up to 1/2 day]
17	2-Feb-00	18,19 Changes to document (inc. circulate again)												236 Project management [up to 1/2 day]
18	3-Feb-00	17,18,19 Review meeting/ changes to document(inc. circulate again)												236 Project management [up to 1/2 day]
19	4-Feb-00	20-22 Second review/ Signoff/ Reqs complete [					18-20 S	18-20 Second review/ Signoff/ Reqs cc						236 Project management [up to 1/2 day]
20	7-Feb-00	58 Pro	58 Pro	58 Prototype		209 Research tech. writing requirements					24 Research into Te:			236 Project management [up to 1/2 day]
21	8-Feb-00	58 Pro	58 Pro	58 Prototype		209 Research tech. writing requirements					24 Research into Te:			236 Project management [up to 1/2 day]
22	9-Feb-00	58 Pro	58 Pro	58 Prototype		209 Research tech. writing requirements					24 Research into Te:			236 Project management [up to 1/2 day]
23	10-Feb-00	58 Pro	58 Pro	58 Prototype		209 Research tech. writing requirements					24 Research into Te:			236 Project management [up to 1/2 day]
24	11-Feb-00	58 Pro	58 Pro	58 Prototype		209 Research tech. writing requirements					24 Research into Te:			236 Project management [up to 1/2 day]
25	14-Feb-00	58 Pro	58 Pro	58 Prototype		210 Set up environment and tools					25 Wri	37 Write Perf		236 Project management [up to 1/2 day]
26	15-Feb-00	58 Pro	58 Pro	58 Prototype		210 Set up environment and tools					25 Wri	37 Write Perf		236 Project management [up to 1/2 day]
27	16-Feb-00	58 Pro	58 Pro	58 Prototype		210 Set up environment and tools					25 Wri	37 Write Perf		236 Project management [up to 1/2 day]
28	17-Feb-00	58 Pro	58 Pro	58 Prototype		210 Set up environment and tools					29 Wri	41 Write Stre		236 Project management [up to 1/2 day]
29	18-Feb-00	58 Pro	58 Pro	58 Prototype		210 Set up environment and tools					29 Wri	41 Write Stre		236 Project management [up to 1/2 day]
30	21-Feb-00	58 Pro	58 Pro	58 Prototype		211 Define style sheet & produce proto					29 Wri	41 Write Stre		236 Project management [up to 1/2 day]
31	22-Feb-00	58 Pro	58 Pro	58 Prototype		211 Define style sheet & produce proto					33 Wri	45 Write Insta		236 Project management [up to 1/2 day]
32	23-Feb-00	58 Pro	58 Pro	58 Prototype		211 Define style sheet & produce			61 Individ		33 Wri	45 Write Insta		236 Project management [up to 1/2 day]
33	24-Feb-00	58 Pro	58 Pro	58 Prototype		211 Define style sheet & produce proto					33 Wri	45 Write Insta		236 Project management [up to 1/2 day]
34	25-Feb-00	58 Pro	58 Pro	58 Prototype		211 Define style	50 Circulate all Tests							236 Project management [up to 1/2 day]
35	28-Feb-00	58 Pro	58 Pro	58 Prototype		212 Write documentation/ Help text								236 Project management [up to 1/2 day]
36	29-Feb-00	58 Pro	58 Pro	58 Prototype		212 Write documentation/ Help text								236 Project management [up to 1/2 day]
37	1-Mar-00	58 Pro	58 Pro	58 Prototype		212 Write documentation/ Help text								236 Project management [up to 1/2 day]
38	2-Mar-00	51 Indi	51 Indi	51 Individual re		212 Write documentation/ Help te				51 Individual review				236 Project management [up to 1/2 day]
39	3-Mar-00	52 Rev	52 Rev	52 Review mee		212 Write documentation/ Help te				52 Revie	52 Rev	52 Review me		236 Project management [up to 1/2 day]
40	6-Mar-00	58 Pro	58 Pro	58 Prototype		212 Write documentation/ Help text					53 Cha	53 Changes t		236 Project management [up to 1/2 day]
41	7-Mar-00	58 Pro	58 Pro	58 Prototype		212 Write documentation/ Help text					53 Cha	53 Changes t		236 Project management [up to 1/2 day]
42	8-Mar-00	58 Pro	58 Pro	58 Prototype		212 Write documentation/ Help text					53, 54	53, 54 Chang		236 Project management [up to 1/2 day]
43	9-Mar-00	58 Pro	58 Pro	58 Prototype		212 Write documentation/ Help te				55-57 Se	55-57	55-57 Secon		236 Project management [up to 1/2 day]
44	10-Mar-00	60 Pric	73 Sett	86 Rep	99 Ford	212 Write documentation/ Help te								236 Project management [up to 1/2 day]
45	13-Mar-00	60 Pric	73 Sett	86 Rep	99 Ford	212 Write documentation/ Help te				65-67 Second review/ signoff/				236 Project management [up to 1/2 day]
46	14-Mar-00	60 Pric	73 Sett	86 Rep	99 Ford	212 Write documentation/ Help text								236 Project management [up to 1/2 day]
47	15-Mar-00	60 Pric	73 Sett	86 Rep	99 Ford	212 Write documentation/ Help text								236 Project management [up to 1/2 day]

Figure 12.1   Original strip board.

How to Run Successful Projects in Web Time

Day #	Date	Charlie	Engineer #2	Engineer #3	Engineer #4	Technical author	Marketing people (3)	Admin. assistant	Reqs. reviewers (5)	Test and design reviewers (2)	Tester #1	Tester #2	Users	Project management
48	16-Mar-00	60 Pri	73 Set	86 Rep	99 Ford	212 Write documentation/Help text								236 Project management [up to 1/2 day]
49	17-Mar-00	60 Pri	73 Set	86 Rep	99 Ford	212 Write documentation/Help text								236 Project management [up to 1/2 day]
50	20-Mar-00	60 Pri	73 Set	86 Rep	99 Ford	212 Write documentation/Help text								236 Project management [up to 1/2 day]
51	21-Mar-00	60 Pri	73 Set	86 Rep	99 Ford	212 Write documentation/Help text								236 Project management [up to 1/2 day]
52	22-Mar-00	151 W	170 Se	138 Tu	99 Ford	212 Write documentation/Help text								236 Project management [up to 1/2 day]
53	23-Mar-00	151 W	170 Se	138 Tu	99 Ford	212 Write documentation/Help text								236 Project management [up to 1/2 day]
54	24-Mar-00	151 W	170 Se	138 Tu	99 Ford	212 Write documentation/Help text								236 Project management [up to 1/2 day]
55	27-Mar-00	151 W	170 Se	138 Tu	99 Ford	212 Write documentation/Help text								236 Project management [up to 1/2 day]
56	28-Mar-00	151 W	170 Se	138 Tu	99 Ford	212 Write documentation/Help text								236 Project management [up to 1/2 day]
57	29-Mar-00	151 W	170 Se	138 Tu	99 Ford	212 Write documentation/Help text								236 Project management [up to 1/2 day]
58	30-Mar-00	151 W	170 Se	138 Tu	99 Ford	212 Write documentation/Help text								236 Project management [up to 1/2 day]
59	31-Mar-00	151 W	170 Se	138 Tu	99 Ford	212 Write documentation/Help text								236 Project management [up to 1/2 day]
60	3-Apr-00	151 W	170 Se	138 Tu	112 Eu	212 Write documentation/Help text								236 Project management [up to 1/2 day]
61	4-Apr-00	151 W	170 Se	138 Tu	112 Eu	212 Write documentation/Help text								236 Project management [up to 1/2 day]
62	5-Apr-00	151 W	170 Se	138 Tu	112 Eu	212 Write documentation/Help text								236 Project management [up to 1/2 day]
63	6-Apr-00	151 W	170 Se	138 Tu	112 Eu	212 Write documentation/Help text								236 Project management [up to 1/2 day]
64	7-Apr-00	151 W	170 Se	138 Tu	112 Eu	212 Write documentation/Help text								236 Project management [up to 1/2 day]
65	10-Apr-00	151 W	170 Se	138 Tu	112 Eu	212 Write documentation/Help text								236 Project management [up to 1/2 day]
66	11-Apr-00	151 W	170 Se	138 Tu	112 Eu	212 Write documentation/Help text								236 Project management [up to 1/2 day]
67	12-Apr-00	151 W	170 Se	138 Tu	112 Eu	212 Write documentation/Help text								236 Project management [up to 1/2 day]
68	13-Apr-00	151 W	170 Se	138 Tu	112 Eu	212 Write documentation/Help text								236 Project management [up to 1/2 day]
69	14-Apr-00	151 W	170 Se	189 Or	112 Eu	212 Write documentation/Help text								236 Project management [up to 1/2 day]
70	17-Apr-00	151 W	170 Se	189 Or	112 Eu	212 Write documentation/Help text								236 Project management [up to 1/2 day]
71	18-Apr-00	151 W	170 Se	189 Or	112 Eu	212 Write documentation/Help text								236 Project management [up to 1/2 day]
72	19-Apr-00	151 W	170 Se	189 Or	112 Eu	212 Write documentation/Help text								236 Project management [up to 1/2 day]
73	20-Apr-00	151 W	170 Se	189 Or	112 Eu	212 Write documentation/Help text								236 Project management [up to 1/2 day]
74	21-Apr-00	151 W	170 Se	189 Or	112 Eu	212 Write documentation/Help text								236 Project management [up to 1/2 day]
75	24-Apr-00	151 W	170 Se	189 Or	112 Eu	212 Write documentation/Help text								236 Project management [up to 1/2 day]
76	25-Apr-00	151 W	170 Se	189 Or	125 3r	212 Write documentation/Help text								236 Project management [up to 1/2 day]
77	26-Apr-00	151 W	170 Se	189 Or	125 3r	212 Write documentation/Help text								236 Project management [up to 1/2 day]
78	27-Apr-00	151 W	170 Se	189 Or	125 3r	212 Write documentation/Help text								236 Project management [up to 1/2 day]
79	28-Apr-00	151 W	170 Se	189 Or	125 3r	212 Write documentation/Help text								236 Project management [up to 1/2 day]
80	1-May-00	151 W	170 Se	189 Or	125 3r	212 Write documentation/Help text								236 Project management [up to 1/2 day]
81	2-May-00	151 W	170 Se	189 Or	125 3r	212 Write documentation/Help text								236 Project management [up to 1/2 day]
82	3-May-00	151 W	170 Se	189 Or	125 3r	212 Write documentation/Help text								236 Project management [up to 1/2 day]
83	4-May-00	151 W	170 Se	189 Or	125 3r	212 Write documentation/Help text								236 Project management [up to 1/2 day]
84	5-May-00			189 Or	125 3r	212 Write documentation/Help text								236 Project management [up to 1/2 day]
85	8-May-00			189 Or	125 3r	212 Write documentation/Help text								236 Project management [up to 1/2 day]
86	9-May-00			189 Or	125 3r	212 Write documentation/Help text								236 Project management [up to 1/2 day]
87	10-May-00			189 Or	125 3r	212 Write documentation/Help text								236 Project management [up to 1/2 day]
88	11-May-00			189 Or	125 3r	217 Edit documentation/Help text								236 Project management [up to 1/2 day]
89	12-May-00			189 Or	125 3r	217 Edit documentation/Help text								236 Project management [up to 1/2 day]
90	15-May-00			189 Or	125 3r	217 Edit documentation/Help text								236 Project management [up to 1/2 day]
91	16-May-00			189 Or	125 3r	217 Edit documentation/Help text								236 Project management [up to 1/2 day]
92	17-May-00			189 Online help		217 Edit documentation/Help text								236 Project management [up to 1/2 day]
93	18-May-00			189 Online help		217 Edit documentation/Help text								236 Project management [up to 1/2 day]
94	19-May-00			189 Online help		217 Edit documentation/Help text								236 Project management [up to 1/2 day]

Figure 12.1   (continued)

Day #	Date	Charlie	Engineer #2	Engineer #3	Engineer #4	Technical author	Marketing people (3)	Admin. assistant	Reqs. reviewers (5)	Test and design reviewers (2)	Tester #1	Tester #2	Users	Project management
95	22-May-00			189 Online hel		217 Edit documentation / Help text								236 Project management [up to 1/2 day]
96	23-May-00			189 Online hel		217 Edit documentation / Help text								236 Project management [up to 1/2 day]
97	24-May-00			189 Online hel		217 Edit documentation / Help text								236 Project management [up to 1/2 day]
98	25-May-00			189 Online hel		217 Edit documentation / Help text								236 Project management [up to 1/2 day]
99	26-May-00			189 Online hel		217 Edit documentation / Help text								236 Project management [up to 1/2 day]
100	29-May-00			189 Online hel		217 Edit documentation / Help text								236 Project management [up to 1/2 day]
101	30-May-00					217 Edit documentation / Help text					225 Te	225 Test #1 -		236 Project management [up to 1/2 day]
102	31-May-00					217 Edit documentation / Help text					225 Te	225 Test #1 -		236 Project management [up to 1/2 day]
103	1-Jun-00					217 Edit documentation / Help text					225 Te	225 Test #1 -		236 Project management [up to 1/2 day]
104	2-Jun-00					217 Edit documentation / Help text					225 Te	225 Test #1 -		236 Project management [up to 1/2 day]
105	5-Jun-00					217 Edit documentation / Help text					225 Te	225 Test #1 -		236 Project management [up to 1/2 day]
106	6-Jun-00					217 Edit documentation / Help text					225 Te	225 Test #1 -		236 Project management [up to 1/2 day]
107	7-Jun-00					217 Edit documentation / Help text					225 Te	225 Test #1 -		236 Project management [up to 1/2 day]
108	8-Jun-00					217 Edit documentation / Help text					225 Te	225 Test #1 -		236 Project management [up to 1/2 day]
109	9-Jun-00					221 Final integration of Online Help					225 Te	225 Test #1 -		236 Project management [up to 1/2 day]
110	12-Jun-00					221 Final integration of Online Help					225 Te	225 Test #1 -		236 Project management [up to 1/2 day]
111	13-Jun-00					221 Final integration of Online Help					225 Te	225 Test #1 -		236 Project management [up to 1/2 day]
112	14-Jun-00					221 Final integration of Online Help					225 Te	225 Test #1 -		236 Project management [up to 1/2 day]
113	15-Jun-00	226 Te	226 Te	226 Te	226 Te	221 Final integration of Online Help								236 Project management [up to 1/2 day]
114	16-Jun-00	226 Te	226 Te	226 Te	226 Te	222 Final pre-production of manuals								236 Project management [up to 1/2 day]
115	19-Jun-00	226 Te	226 Te	226 Te	226 Te	222 Final pre-production of manuals								236 Project management [up to 1/2 day]
116	20-Jun-00	226 Te	226 Te	226 Te	226 Te	222 Final pre-production of manuals								236 Project management [up to 1/2 day]
117	21-Jun-00	226 Te	226 Te	226 Te	226 Te	222 Final pre-production of manuals								236 Project management [up to 1/2 day]
118	22-Jun-00	226 Te	226 Te	226 Te	226 Te	222 Final pre-production of manuals								236 Project management [up to 1/2 day]
119	23-Jun-00										228 Te	228 Test #2 -		236 Project management [up to 1/2 day]
120	26-Jun-00										228 Te	228 Test #2 -		236 Project management [up to 1/2 day]
121	27-Jun-00										228 Te	228 Test #2 -		236 Project management [up to 1/2 day]
122	28-Jun-00										228 Te	228 Test #2 -		236 Project management [up to 1/2 day]
123	29-Jun-00	229 Te	229 Te	229 Te	229 Test #2 - make corrections									236 Project management [up to 1/2 day]
124	30-Jun-00	229 Te	229 Te	229 Te	229 Test #2 - make corrections									236 Project management [up to 1/2 day]
125	3-Jul-00	229 Te	229 Te	229 Te	229 Test #2 - make corrections									236 Project management [up to 1/2 day]
126	4-Jul-00										231 Te	231 Test #3 -		236 Project management [up to 1/2 day]
127	5-Jul-00										231 Te	231 Test #3 -		236 Project management [up to 1/2 day]
128	6-Jul-00	232 Te	232 Te	232 Te	232 Test #3 - make corrections									236 Project management [up to 1/2 day]
129	7-Jul-00										233 Finalise test doc			236 Project management [up to 1/2 day]
130	10-Jul-00	235 En	235 En	235 En	235 En	235 End of project review					235 En	235 End of pr		236 Project management [up to 1/2 day]
131	11-Jul-00	237 Contingency												236 Project management [up to 1/2 day]
132	12-Jul-00	237 Contingency												236 Project management [up to 1/2 day]
133	13-Jul-00	237 Contingency												236 Project management [up to 1/2 day]
134	14-Jul-00	237 Contingency												236 Project management [up to 1/2 day]
135	17-Jul-00	237 Contingency												236 Project management [up to 1/2 day]
136	18-Jul-00	237 Contingency												236 Project management [up to 1/2 day]
137	19-Jul-00	237 Contingency												236 Project management [up to 1/2 day]
138	20-Jul-00	237 Contingency												236 Project management [up to 1/2 day]
139	21-Jul-00	237 Contingency												236 Project management [up to 1/2 day]
140	24-Jul-00	237 Contingency												236 Project management [up to 1/2 day]
141	25-Jul-00	237 Contingency												236 Project management [up to 1/2 day]

Figure 12.1   (continued)

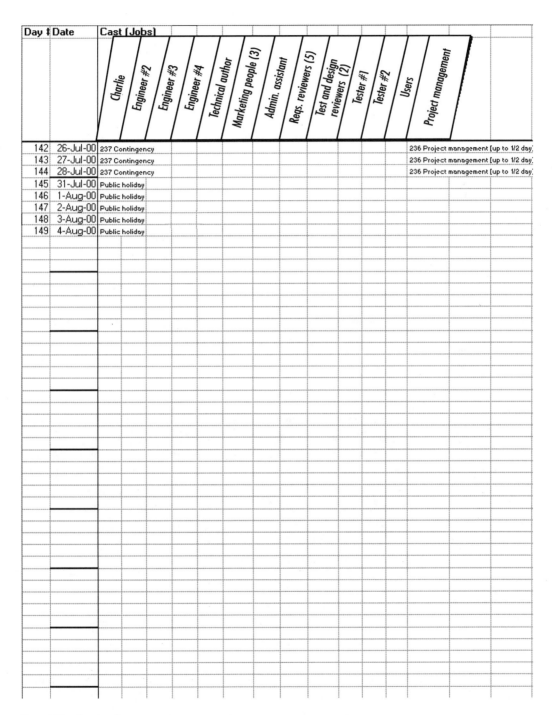

Day #	Date	Cast (Jobs)	Charlie	Engineer #2	Engineer #3	Engineer #4	Technical author	Marketing people (3)	Admin. assistant	Reqs. reviewers (5)	Test and design reviewers (2)	Tester #1	Tester #2	Users	Project management
142	26-Jul-00	237 Contingency													236 Project management [up to 1/2 day]
143	27-Jul-00	237 Contingency													236 Project management [up to 1/2 day]
144	28-Jul-00	237 Contingency													236 Project management [up to 1/2 day]
145	31-Jul-00	Public holiday													
146	1-Aug-00	Public holiday													
147	2-Aug-00	Public holiday													
148	3-Aug-00	Public holiday													
149	4-Aug-00	Public holiday													

Figure 12.1   (continued)

Figure 12.2
Features list.

1. Pricing (S)
2. Foreign exchange (M)
3. Euro support (M)
4. 3rd party payments (M)
5. Settlement (S)
6. Reporting (S)
7. Web interface (L)
8. Security (L)
9. Tutorial (M)
10. Online help (L).

1.   We're building a requirements document which Marketing will input to and review.

2.   We're building a prototype and a team of engineers and marketeers will work on this to get it right.

3.   And finally, our buddies from the QA department"—you nod in the direction of Testers #1 and #2—"will be providing us with a comprehensive system test. Our intention is that we will ship when our testing can uncover no more bugs of severity 1 (showstoppers) or 2 (inhibits a piece of functionality but a workaround exists)."

"I heard a rumor that this product had to go to some Comdex show or other," Engineer #3 asks. "This true?"

"Sales want to demo the prototype at a Comdex show. We can make that deadline, no problem. Then they wanted to be able to ship Beta units within 30 days of Comdex. That's not gonna happen. The prototype is available 9 March. The product doesn't go into Beta until 4 August."

There are whistles of astonishment around the room.

"Have you told them yet?"

"Gonna tell them this afternoon."

"Good luck," somebody says ominously.

You carry on. You feel a bit deflated.

"The team is as you see here. Since you were involved in the estimating you know how the plan was put together and what the main assumptions are. I'll remind you of them anyway as we go through the plan. The only major outstanding issue at the moment is that Sales won't be happy with this schedule. I'll try to resolve that this afternoon."

"If you still have a job," somebody mutters.

You pretend you didn't hear. Instead you bring their attention to the strip board. You explain how it works. You acknowledge that maybe they haven't seen plans laid out like this before, but you hope that they see its benefit—that it makes it crystal clear who is doing what every day. "I'd like to take you through the plan day by day," you say. "Please make notes in your diaries and calendars about the bits that are relevant to you."

And so it begins. You feel something of your old bravado returning. As Obi-Wan Kenobi would say, the force is with you, albeit a fairly weakened version of it.

"Assuming I don't get fired this afternoon, assuming they give us the approval to proceed, then this project kicks off tomorrow, Wednesday 12 January. What will happen tomorrow is that Charlie will begin trawling the Web looking at competitive products."

"I've already started," announces Charlie. You smile inwardly. One of the advantages of people knowing precisely what they have to do is that sometimes they go do it! You continue. "We had talked one time about having a panel of users work on the requirements with us. However, Marketing feel they know as much about this as the users. And anyway, we're going to bring in some users to see the prototype. So what we're going to do instead is identify a number of different types of users, and Marketing will represent their interests."

Notice that even as you're explaining these things, the plan is changing. The plan initially said that Charlie would identify the users. But Marketing also needs to be involved in that. Your Scribe updates the strip board accordingly. You describe it in words:

"So tomorrow Charlie will finish getting the info on competitive products in the morning. Then in the afternoon, he will work with Marketing to identify user types." You mention that this idea of using user types or "personas", as Alan Cooper [5] calls them, is a good piece of best practice. One or two of the team that know you the best exchange a meaningful look. You press on.

"On Thursday and Friday, Charlie will prepare the user type questionnaires and these must go out to Marketing before close of business on Friday." You remind the Admin. Assistant, whose name the author now decides make Anna, that this is her job. She nods. Anna is the best Admin. Assistant in the world —you know it'll happen. "And that does it for this week. Apart from Charlie, the Marketing people and Anna, most of you are untouched by this."

"Next week on Monday Charlie will review the competitive info with Marketing—he'll already have sent it to them"—you look questioningly at Anna, even as the word "them" comes out sounding like a question rather than a statement. She nods and scribbles something down in her diary. "Anna will also retrieve the user questionnaires from Marketing at the end of Monday."

"We're not going to be able to do those questionnaires on Monday," Marketing #1 pipes up. "Monday is a really busy day for us."

You're tempted to say "but we had a deal", but you know it'll only sound like you're whining. Instead you say "OK, but that's gonna cause the project to run late. Just tell me how much time you're gonna need and I'll add that on to the end date for my presentation this afternoon." It's a fairly blunt and brutal approach, but you don't really have time for niceties. They take the hint. Marketing #1 says grumpily "OK, I suppose we'll do them over the weekend." "Let them work the weekend for a change," one of the engineers hisses to another. "It won't take that long," says Charlie. "These are going to be easy questionnaires. One of you guys for half a day would get it done." You notice that Charlie has really bought in to the "who does what when" method of estimating.

You recap. "Monday, Charlie and the Marketing people review the competitive info, one of you Marketing guys also works with Charlie to do the questionnaires. Let's save Anna some work and say that Charlie goes home that evening with the questionnaires in his briefcase." "I'll check just to make sure," says Anna. "Tuesday Charlie spends analyzing all of this input—the competitive info, Marketing's input and the user questionnaires. Then he starts writing the Requirements document. He spends the rest of the week doing that, as well as all of the following week and Monday of week 4."

"Once the Requirements document is complete, there's a review cycle that goes like this. Anna gets the Requirements document on Monday evening and circulates it to the guilty parties. Tuesday morning the Marketing people have set aside time for an individual review of the document and Tuesday afternoon Charlie's having a review meeting with them. Rest of Tuesday, Wednesday, and Thursday, Charlie works on changes to the Requirements document and Thursday evening, Anna makes sure it goes out to everybody again. Friday is a second review and signoff, which Anna will make sure happens." (It occurs to you that Anna is the real project manager here, not you! You make a mental note to ask her some time if she's interested in a career change. She'd be good at it, you reckon.)

"Week 5. Now the fun really starts. Engineers #2 and #3 sign on, as does Ted, the Tech. Author, and Tester #1. Charlie and the engineers work on the prototype." You put another slide up (Table 12.1). This one shows the detailed plan for the prototype.

Table 12.1   Prototype Plan. (All estimates in person-days).

Job/Iteration	1	2	3	4	5	6	7	8	Totals
1. Build/revise prototype	5	3	2	2	2	1	1	1	17
2. Review with Marketing	1	1	0.5	0.5	0.5	0.5	0.5	0.5	5
Total per iteration	6	4	2.5	2.5	2.5	1.5	1.5	1.5	22

"As far as Charlie, the two engineers and the Marketing people are concerned, this is how the next 22 days will pass. You can see from this precisely when you're going to be needed." Even if they *can* see it, you talk them through it, iteration by iteration, alternately pointing out which dates the engineering people are working and (crucially) which dates the Marketing people (and the users they intend to bring in) are needed to give their blessing. The Marketing people moan about "this isn't the only project in the company," but you ignore them. You note again contentedly, that there are tiny morsels of contingency buried in the prototype schedule—for those 5 days when Marketing are reviewing, Engineering don't stop, so you're actually getting 22 Engineering days rather than 17. You also suddenly realize that there's been a big foul-up in your strip board. You've counted all three engineers for 22 days. What to do about this?

At least two possibilities present themselves:

- The first is that you could let Charlie do the prototype and not bring the other two engineers on for another few weeks. They would then be free to work on other projects. However, you have them now—it would be a pity to lose them.

- The other possibility is to get the prototype done quicker with more people working on it. Sure three people working on it might be too many, but an extra body might not hurt. However, you realize, looking at the strip board, that a shortened prototype won't necessarily buy you anything since the critical path is over with the technical writing.

You decide to leave the business of the prototype for a minute while you consider again the technical writing. The technical writer absolutely can't start any earlier. You've already explored this avenue without success. But this whole notion of "not doing so much technical writing" has continued to nag at you. You consider it one more time.

The original estimates for the writing were based on 10 features in the product and 5 days work per feature to produce the associated documentation. But you remember that the features aren't all the same size. Supposing you made the assumption that Large features were indeed going to take 5 person-days, but Mediums might be 4 person-days and Smalls might be 3 person-days? Then the amount of work in the technical writing would be

- 3 × Small features (3 person-days) = 9 person-days;

- 4 × Medium features (4 person-days) = 16 person-days;

- 3 × Large features (5 person-days) = 15 person-days,

giving a total of 40 person-days. You run it by Ted, the Technical Author. It doesn't sound unreasonable, he agrees. "You can do a lot of writing in 3 days," is his comment. You modify the strip board accordingly.

And now you see that shortening the prototype is indeed going to help. You decide you'll put all three engineers on it and revise the estimates as follows:

Table 12.2 Original Estimate. (All estimates in person-days.)

Job/Iteration	1	2	3	4	5	6	7	8	Totals
1. Build/revise prototype	5	3	2	2	2	1	1	1	17
2. Review with Marketing	1	1	0.5	0.5	0.5	0.5	0.5	0.5	5
Total per iteration	6	4	2.5	2.5	2.5	1.5	1.5	1.5	22

Table 12.3 Revised Estimate. (All estimates in person-days.)

Job/Iteration	1	2	3	4	5	6	7	8	Totals
1. Build/revise prototype using 3 engineers	2	2	1	1	1	1	0.5	0.5	9
2. Review with Marketing	1	1	0.5	0.5	0.5	0.5	0.5	0.5	5
Total per iteration	3	3	1.5	1.5	1.5	1.5	1	1	14

Your Scribe's strip board now looks like the one in Figure 12.3.

Week #	Day #	Date	Cast (Jobs)									
			Charlie	Engineer #2	Engineer #3	Engineer #4	Technical author	Marketing people (3)	Anna	Tester #1	Tester #2	Project management
1	1	11-Jan-00	Projec	Project	Project	Project	Project	Project F	Project	Projec	Projec	Project kickoff
	2	12-Jan-00	6 Gath									236 Project management [up to 1/2 day]
	3	13-Jan-00	9 Prepare user questionnaires									236 Project management [up to 1/2 day]
	4	14-Jan-00	9 Prepare user questionnaires						10 Distribute user ques			236 Project management [up to 1/2 day]
2	5	17-Jan-00	7 Review with Marketing					7 Review	11 Retrieve questionn			236 Project management [up to 1/2 day]
	6	18-Jan-00	12 Analyse information									236 Project management [up to 1/2 day]
	7	19-Jan-00	13 Write requirements document									236 Project management [up to 1/2 day]
	8	20-Jan-00	13 Write requirements document									236 Project management [up to 1/2 day]
	9	21-Jan-00	13 Write requirements document									236 Project management [up to 1/2 day]
3	10	24-Jan-00	13 Write requirements document									236 Project management [up to 1/2 day]
	11	25-Jan-00	13 Write requirements document									236 Project management [up to 1/2 day]
	12	26-Jan-00	13 Write requirements document									236 Project management [up to 1/2 day]
	13	27-Jan-00	13 Write requirements document									236 Project management [up to 1/2 day]
	14	28-Jan-00	13 Write requirements document									236 Project management [up to 1/2 day]
4	15	31-Jan-00	13 Write requirements document					15 Circulate document				236 Project management [up to 1/2 day]
	16	1-Feb-00	17,18 Review meeting / changes to doc					16, 17 Individual review [1/2 day]				236 Project management [up to 1/2 day]
	17	2-Feb-00	18 Changes to document									236 Project management [up to 1/2 day]
	18	3-Feb-00	18,19 Changes to document (inc. circulate again)									236 Project management [up to 1/2 day]
	19	4-Feb-00	20-22 Second review / Signoff / Reqs c				20-22 Se		20-22 Second review /			236 Project management [up to 1/2 day]
5	20	7-Feb-00	58 Pro	58 Prot	58 Prototype		209 Research tech. writir		24 Research i			236 Project management [up to 1/2 day]
	21	8-Feb-00	58 Pro	58 Prot	58 Prototype		209 Research tech. writir		24 Research i			236 Project management [up to 1/2 day]
	22	9-Feb-00	58 Pro	58 Prot	58 Prototype		209 Research tech. writir		24 Research i			236 Project management [up to 1/2 day]
	23	10-Feb-00	58 Pro	58 Prot	58 Prototype		209 Research tech. writir		24 Research i			236 Project management [up to 1/2 day]
	24	11-Feb-00	58 Pro	58 Prot	58 Prototype		209 Research tech. writir		24 Research i			236 Project management [up to 1/2 day]
	25	14-Feb-00	58 Pro	58 Prot	58 Prototype		210 Set up environment a		25 Wri	37 Wri		236 Project management [up to 1/2 day]
	26	15-Feb-00	58 Pro	58 Prot	58 Prototype		210 Set up environment a		25 Wri	37 Wri		236 Project management [up to 1/2 day]
	27	16-Feb-00	58 Pro	58 Prot	58 Prototype		210 Set up environment a		25 Wri	37 Wri		236 Project management [up to 1/2 day]
	28	17-Feb-00	58 Pro	58 Prot	58 Prototype		210 Set up environment a		29 Wri	41 Wri		236 Project management [up to 1/2 day]
	29	18-Feb-00	58 Pro	58 Prot	58 Prototype		210 Set up environment a		29 Wri	41 Wri		236 Project management [up to 1/2 day]
	30	21-Feb-00	58 Pro	58 Prot	58 Prototype		211 Define style sheet &		29 Wri	41 Wri		236 Project management [up to 1/2 day]
	31	22-Feb-00	58 Pro	58 Prot	58 Prototype		211 Define style sheet &		33 Wri	45 Wri		236 Project management [up to 1/2 day]
	32	23-Feb-00	58, 60,	58 Prot	58 Prototype		211 Define style sheet &		33 Wri	45 Wri		236 Project management [up to 1/2 day]
	33	24-Feb-00	58 Pro	58 Prot	58 Prototype		211 Define style sheet &		33 Wri	45 Wri		236 Project management [up to 1/2 day]
	34	25-Feb-00	58 Pro	58 Prot	58 Prototype		211 Define style	50 Circulate all Tests				236 Project management [up to 1/2 day]
	35	28-Feb-00	60 Pric	73 Sett	86 Rep	99 Ford	212 Write documentation / Help text					236 Project management [up to 1/2 day]
	36	29-Feb-00	60, 65	73 Sett	86 Rep	99 Ford	212 Write documentation / Help text					236 Project management [up to 1/2 day]
	37	1-Mar-00	60 Pric	73 Sett	86 Rep	99 Ford	212 Write documentation / Help text					236 Project management [up to 1/2 day]
	38	2-Mar-00	51 Indi	51 Indi	51 Individual re		212 Write documentation / Help text					236 Project management [up to 1/2 day]
	39	3-Mar-00	52 Rev	52 Rev	52 Review mee		212 Write documentation		52 Rev	52 Rev		236 Project management [up to 1/2 day]
	40	6-Mar-00	60 Pric	73 Sett	86 Rep	99 Ford	212 Write documentation		53 Cha	53 Cha		236 Project management [up to 1/2 day]
	41	7-Mar-00	60 Pric	73 Sett	86 Rep	99 Ford	212 Write documentation		53 Cha	53 Cha		236 Project management [up to 1/2 day]
	42	8-Mar-00	60 Pric	73 Sett	86 Rep	99 Ford	212 Write documentation		53, 54	53, 54		236 Project management [up to 1/2 day]
	43	9-Mar-00	55-57, 58 Second review / sign				212 Write documentation		55-57	55-57		236 Project management [up to 1/2 day]
	44	10-Mar-00	60 Pric	73 Sett	86 Rep	99 Ford	212 Write documentation / Help text					236 Project management [up to 1/2 day]
	45	13-Mar-00	60 Pric	73 Sett	86 Rep	99 Ford	212 Write documentation / Help text					236 Project management [up to 1/2 day]
	46	14-Mar-00	151 W	170 Se	138 Tu	99 Ford	212 Write documentation / Help text					236 Project management [up to 1/2 day]
	47	15-Mar-00	151 W	170 Se	138 Tu	99 Ford	212 Write documentation / Help text					236 Project management [up to 1/2 day]
	48	16-Mar-00	151 W	170 Se	138 Tu	99 Ford	212 Write documentation / Help text					236 Project management [up to 1/2 day]
	49	17-Mar-00	151 W	170 Se	138 Tu	99 Ford	212 Write documentation / Help text					236 Project management [up to 1/2 day]

Figure 12.3   Strip board with revised estimates for prototype.

Week #	Day #	Date	Charlie	Engineer #2	Engineer #3	Engineer #4	Technical author	Marketing people (3)	Anna	Tester #1	Tester #2	Project management
	50	20-Mar-00	151 W	170 Se	138 Tu	99 Ford	212 Write documentation / Help text					236 Project management [up to 1/2 day]
	51	21-Mar-00	151 W	170 Se	138 Tu	99 Ford	212 Write documentation / Help text					236 Project management [up to 1/2 day]
	52	22-Mar-00	151 W	170 Se	138 Tu	99 Ford	212 Write documentation / Help text					236 Project management [up to 1/2 day]
	53	23-Mar-00	151 W	170 Se	138 Tu	99 Ford	212 Write documentation / Help text					236 Project management [up to 1/2 day]
	54	24-Mar-00	151 W	170 Se	138 Tu	112 Eu	212 Write documentation / Help text					236 Project management [up to 1/2 day]
	55	27-Mar-00	151 W	170 Se	138 Tu	112 Eu	212 Write documentation / Help text					236 Project management [up to 1/2 day]
	56	28-Mar-00	151 W	170 Se	138 Tu	112 Eu	212 Write documentation / Help text					236 Project management [up to 1/2 day]
	57	29-Mar-00	151 W	170 Se	138 Tu	112 Eu	212 Write documentation / Help text					236 Project management [up to 1/2 day]
	58	30-Mar-00	151 W	170 Se	138 Tu	112 Eu	212 Write documentation / Help text					236 Project management [up to 1/2 day]
	59	31-Mar-00	151 W	170 Se	138 Tu	112 Eu	212 Write documentation / Help text					236 Project management [up to 1/2 day]
	60	3-Apr-00	151 W	170 Se	138 Tu	112 Eu	212 Write documentation / Help text					236 Project management [up to 1/2 day]
	61	4-Apr-00	151 W	170 Se	138 Tu	112 Eu	212 Write documentation / Help text					236 Project management [up to 1/2 day]
	62	5-Apr-00	151 W	170 Se	138 Tu	112 Eu	212 Write documentation / Help text					236 Project management [up to 1/2 day]
	63	6-Apr-00	151 W	170 Se	189 Or	112 Eu	212 Write documentation / Help text					236 Project management [up to 1/2 day]
	64	7-Apr-00	151 W	170 Se	189 Or	112 Eu	212 Write documentation / Help text					236 Project management [up to 1/2 day]
	65	10-Apr-00	151 W	170 Se	189 Or	112 Eu	212 Write documentation / Help text					236 Project management [up to 1/2 day]
	66	11-Apr-00	151 W	170 Se	189 Or	112 Eu	212 Write documentation / Help text					236 Project management [up to 1/2 day]
	67	12-Apr-00	151 W	170 Se	189 Or	112 Eu	212 Write documentation / Help text					236 Project management [up to 1/2 day]
	68	13-Apr-00	151 W	170 Se	189 Or	112 Eu	212 Write documentation / Help text					236 Project management [up to 1/2 day]
	69	14-Apr-00	151 W	170 Se	189 Or	112 Eu	212 Write documentation / Help text					236 Project management [up to 1/2 day]
	70	17-Apr-00	151 W	170 Se	189 Or	125 3rd	212 Write documentation / Help text					236 Project management [up to 1/2 day]
	71	18-Apr-00	151 W	170 Se	189 Or	125 3rd	212 Write documentation / Help text					236 Project management [up to 1/2 day]
	72	19-Apr-00	151 W	170 Se	189 Or	125 3rd	212 Write documentation / Help text					236 Project management [up to 1/2 day]
	73	20-Apr-00	151 W	170 Se	189 Or	125 3rd	212 Write documentation / Help text					236 Project management [up to 1/2 day]
	74	21-Apr-00	151 W	170 Se	189 Or	125 3rd	212 Write documentation / Help text					236 Project management [up to 1/2 day]
	75	24-Apr-00	151 W	170 Se	189 Or	125 3rd	217 Edit documentation / Help text					236 Project management [up to 1/2 day]
	76	25-Apr-00	151 W	170 Se	189 Or	125 3rd	217 Edit documentation / Help text					236 Project management [up to 1/2 day]
	77	26-Apr-00	151 W	170 Se	189 Or	125 3rd	217 Edit documentation / Help text					236 Project management [up to 1/2 day]
	78	27-Apr-00			189 Or	125 3rd	217 Edit documentation / Help text					236 Project management [up to 1/2 day]
	79	28-Apr-00			189 Or	125 3rd	217 Edit documentation / Help text					236 Project management [up to 1/2 day]
	80	1-May-00			189 Or	125 3rd	217 Edit documentation / Help text					236 Project management [up to 1/2 day]
	81	2-May-00			189 Or	125 3rd	217 Edit documentation / Help text					236 Project management [up to 1/2 day]
	82	3-May-00			189 Or	125 3rd	217 Edit documentation / Help text					236 Project management [up to 1/2 day]
	83	4-May-00			189 Or	125 3rd	217 Edit documentation / Help text					236 Project management [up to 1/2 day]
	84	5-May-00			189 Or	125 3rd	217 Edit documentation / Help text					236 Project management [up to 1/2 day]
	85	8-May-00			189 Or	125 3rd	217 Edit documentation / Help text					236 Project management [up to 1/2 day]
	86	9-May-00			189 Online help		217 Edit documentation / Help text					236 Project management [up to 1/2 day]
	87	10-May-00			189 Online help		217 Edit documentation / Help text					236 Project management [up to 1/2 day]
	88	11-May-00			189 Online help		217 Edit documentation / Help text					236 Project management [up to 1/2 day]
	89	12-May-00			189 Online help		217 Edit documentation / Help text					236 Project management [up to 1/2 day]
	90	15-May-00			189 Online help		217 Edit documentation / Help text					236 Project management [up to 1/2 day]
	91	16-May-00			189 Online help		217 Edit documentation / Help text					236 Project management [up to 1/2 day]
	92	17-May-00			189 Online help		217 Edit documentation / Help text					236 Project management [up to 1/2 day]
	93	18-May-00			189 Online help		217 Edit documentation / Help text					236 Project management [up to 1/2 day]
	94	19-May-00			189 Online help		217 Edit documentation / Help text					236 Project management [up to 1/2 day]
	95	22-May-00					217 Edit documentation /			225 Te	225 Te	236 Project management [up to 1/2 day]
	96	23-May-00					221 Final integration of C			225 Te	225 Te	236 Project management [up to 1/2 day]
	97	24-May-00					221 Final integration of C			225 Te	225 Te	236 Project management [up to 1/2 day]
	98	25-May-00					221 Final integration of C			225 Te	225 Te	236 Project management [up to 1/2 day]

Figure 12.3   (continued)

How to Run Successful Projects in Web Time

Week #	Day #	Date	Charlie	Engineer #2	Engineer #3	Engineer #4	Technical author	Marketing people (3)	Anna	Tester #1	Tester #2	Project management
99	26-May-00						221 Final integration of C			225 Te	225 Te	236 Project management [up to 1/2 day]
100	29-May-00						221 Final integration of C			225 Te	225 Te	236 Project management [up to 1/2 day]
101	30-May-00						222 Final pre-production			225 Te	225 Te	236 Project management [up to 1/2 day]
102	31-May-00						222 Final pre-production			225 Te	225 Te	236 Project management [up to 1/2 day]
103	1-Jun-00						222 Final pre-production			225 Te	225 Te	236 Project management [up to 1/2 day]
104	2-Jun-00						222 Final pre-production			225 Te	225 Te	236 Project management [up to 1/2 day]
105	5-Jun-00						222 Final pre-production			225 Te	225 Te	236 Project management [up to 1/2 day]
106	6-Jun-00									225 Te	225 Te	236 Project management [up to 1/2 day]
113	7-Jun-00	226 Te	226 Te	226 Te	226 Test #1 - make corrections						236 Project management [up to 1/2 day]
114	8-Jun-00	226 Te	226 Te	226 Te	226 Test #1 - make corrections						236 Project management [up to 1/2 day]
115	9-Jun-00	226 Te	226 Te	226 Te	226 Test #1 - make corrections						236 Project management [up to 1/2 day]
116	12-Jun-00	226 Te	226 Te	226 Te	226 Test #1 - make corrections						236 Project management [up to 1/2 day]
117	13-Jun-00	226 Te	226 Te	226 Te	226 Test #1 - make corrections						236 Project management [up to 1/2 day]
118	14-Jun-00	226 Te	226 Te	226 Te	226 Test #1 - make corrections						236 Project management [up to 1/2 day]
119	15-Jun-00									228 Te	228 Te	236 Project management [up to 1/2 day]
120	16-Jun-00									228 Te	228 Te	236 Project management [up to 1/2 day]
121	19-Jun-00									228 Te	228 Te	236 Project management [up to 1/2 day]
122	20-Jun-00									228 Te	228 Te	236 Project management [up to 1/2 day]
123	21-Jun-00	229 Te	229 Te	229 Te	229 Test #2 - make corrections						236 Project management [up to 1/2 day]
124	22-Jun-00	229 Te	229 Te	229 Te	229 Test #2 - make corrections						236 Project management [up to 1/2 day]
125	23-Jun-00	229 Te	229 Te	229 Te	229 Test #2 - make corrections						236 Project management [up to 1/2 day]
126	26-Jun-00									231 Te	231 Te	236 Project management [up to 1/2 day]
127	27-Jun-00									231 Te	231 Te	236 Project management [up to 1/2 day]
128	28-Jun-00	232 Te	232 Te	232 Te	232 Test #3 - make corrections						236 Project management [up to 1/2 day]
129	29-Jun-00									233 Finalise t		236 Project management [up to 1/2 day]
130	30-Jun-00	235 Er	235 En	235 En	235 En	235 End of project review		235 Er	235 Er		236 Project management [up to 1/2 day]
131	3-Jul-00	237 Contingency									236 Project management [up to 1/2 day]
132	4-Jul-00	237 Contingency									236 Project management [up to 1/2 day]
133	5-Jul-00	237 Contingency									236 Project management [up to 1/2 day]
134	6-Jul-00	237 Contingency									236 Project management [up to 1/2 day]
135	7-Jul-00	237 Contingency									236 Project management [up to 1/2 day]
136	10-Jul-00	237 Contingency									236 Project management [up to 1/2 day]
137	11-Jul-00	237 Contingency									236 Project management [up to 1/2 day]
138	12-Jul-00	237 Contingency									236 Project management [up to 1/2 day]
139	13-Jul-00	237 Contingency									236 Project management [up to 1/2 day]
140	14-Jul-00	237 Contingency									236 Project management [up to 1/2 day]
141	17-Jul-00	237 Contingency									236 Project management [up to 1/2 day]
142	18-Jul-00	237 Contingency									236 Project management [up to 1/2 day]
143	19-Jul-00	237 Contingency									236 Project management [up to 1/2 day]
144	20-Jul-00	237 Contingency									236 Project management [up to 1/2 day]
145	21-Jul-00	Public holiday									
146	24-Jul-00	Public holiday									
147	25-Jul-00	Public holiday									
148	26-Jul-00	Public holiday									
149	27-Jul-00	Public holiday									
		28-Jul-00										
		31-Jul-00										
		1-Aug-00										
		2-Aug-00										

Figure 12.3 (continued)

You continue your unfolding of the project, picking up again from week 5. "Week 5, the engineers and Marketing work the detailed plan for the prototype, Ted begins his authoring and the Tester #1 begins his work. Both Ted and Tester #1 gotta finish their research by the end of week 5."

"Weeks 6 and 7 we can take together. Tester #2 comes on board beginning of week 6. The prototype completes at the end of week 7. Also by the end of week 7, Ted is finished all his set up type work, and the tests are complete and should have been circulated for review by Anna."

"Week 8, coding begins. Engineer #4 joins. You three engineers have to review these guys' System Test Plan." You ask the Testers "Any advantage if these guys review your tests earlier that week?" They shake their heads. "Doesn't matter. We can work on other stuff for other projects while we're waiting." "OK, so coding begins on Pricing, Settlement, Reporting, and Foreign exchange. You each put 4 days in on those. On Friday of that week you engineers take a day out to review the tests. Ted is working away, presumably beginning to write some of the text related to Pricing, Settlement, Reporting, and Foreign exchange." Ted nods.

"Week 9, you testers make your changes to the System Test Plan arising out of the review, and you get sign off. Anna does whatever legwork is required to achieve that. Then you testers can go about your business until we're ready for you again. You engineers continue coding and Ted continues writing."

Ted says "I'll be working off a detailed schedule which shows what chapters get written what days." Ted's solid as a rock. You knew he would but it's still good to get the reassurance. The author is also happy not to have to include Ted's schedule in the strip board in the interests of clarity.

"Monday of week 10, Pricing, Settlement, and Forecasting finish, while Foreign exchange continues. On Tuesday, you three guys start Web Interface, Security, and Tutorial respectively. Ted carries on writing." (In glancing at the strip board, you're reminded of the project management task that appears there every day. It occurs to you that in this meeting you are actually doing a lot of that project management *now*. It's a fairly wild idea when you think about it. Here it is, 11 January and you're telling the team precisely what they will be doing on particular days in March. If it carries on like this, you won't need to do any of that daily project management!)

"Week 11. You three guys carry on. Engineer #4 finishes Foreign exchange on Thursday and starts Euro support on Friday. Ted writes." Ted smiles.

"Week 12, everybody just keeps doing what they're doing."

"Week 13, everybody just keeps doing what they're doing, except for Engineer #3 who finishes the Tutorial on Wednesday and starts the Online Help on Thursday."

"Week 14, business as usual, except on Friday of that week, courtesy of Engineer #4, Euro support completes."

"Week 15, business as usual, with Engineer #4 starting 3rd party payments. Ted finishes his writing."

"Wednesday of week 16, Charlie and Engineer #2 finish up. Online Help (Engineer #3) and 3rd party payments (Engineer #4) continue. Ted begins editing the stuff he has written. He may need to draw a bit on you engineers, but I hope you'll be able to live with that." The engineers nod. Some of them have worked with Ted before. They know that a good technical author can make a lot of this review and editing process as painless as possible for engineers. Figure 12.4 is the result.

A block of white space has come into view on the strip board. We know that any such white space will be pounced on at this afternoon's meeting, because white space equals people not working. We're going to have to do something about it. And we would do something anyway, because white space also equals a potential opportunity to shorten the project. The bit of Online Help that sticks out after May 9, we give to Engineer #2 to complete. This enables testing to start sooner and the result is Figure 12.5.

You're still not finished with week 16. You recap. "Charlie finishes the Web interface on Wednesday. Engineer #2 finishes Security on Wednesday and turns to Online Help on Thursday. Engineer #3 is already working on Online Help while Engineer #4 does 3rd party payments. Ted edits."

There's still too much white space on the plan. In addition, Charlie points out that as soon as he finishes Coding, he'd be ready to start bug fixing, if the Testers had some bugs to report. A quick check establishes that you can get the Testers a week and a bit earlier, at the beginning of week 17. You go for it. Charlie announces that he'll take his vacation at the beginning of May. It fills the white space. Everybody's happy.

"Week 17. Charlie's on vacation. The three engineers are coding, Ted is editing and the Testers have started testing."

Week #	Day #	Date	Charlie	Engineer #2	Engineer #3	Engineer #4	Technical author	Marketing people (3)	Anna	Tester #1	Tester #2	Project management
1	1	11-Jan-00	Projec	Project	Project	Project	Project	Project k	Project	Projec	Projec	Project kickoff
	2	12-Jan-00	6 Gatl									236 Project management [up to 1/2 day]
	3	13-Jan-00	9 Prepare user questionnaires									236 Project management [up to 1/2 day]
	4	14-Jan-00	9 Prepare user questionnaires						10 Distribute user que:			236 Project management [up to 1/2 day]
2	5	17-Jan-00	7 Review with Marketing					7 Review	11 Retrieve questionn			236 Project management [up to 1/2 day]
	6	18-Jan-00	12 Analyse information									236 Project management [up to 1/2 day]
	7	19-Jan-00	13 Write requirements document									236 Project management [up to 1/2 day]
	8	20-Jan-00	13 Write requirements document									236 Project management [up to 1/2 day]
	9	21-Jan-00	13 Write requirements document									236 Project management [up to 1/2 day]
3	10	24-Jan-00	13 Write requirements document									236 Project management [up to 1/2 day]
	11	25-Jan-00	13 Write requirements document									236 Project management [up to 1/2 day]
	12	26-Jan-00	13 Write requirements document									236 Project management [up to 1/2 day]
	13	27-Jan-00	13 Write requirements document									236 Project management [up to 1/2 day]
	14	28-Jan-00	13 Write requirements document									236 Project management [up to 1/2 day]
4	15	31-Jan-00	13 Write requirements document					15 Circulate document				236 Project management [up to 1/2 day]
	16	1-Feb-00	17,18 Review meeting / changes to doc				16, 17 Individual review [1/2 day					236 Project management [up to 1/2 day]
	17	2-Feb-00	18 Changes to document									236 Project management [up to 1/2 day]
	18	3-Feb-00	18,19 Changes to document (inc. circulate again)									236 Project management [up to 1/2 day]
	19	4-Feb-00	20-22 Second review / Signoff / Reqs c		20-22 Se	20-22 Second review /						236 Project management [up to 1/2 day]
5	20	7-Feb-00	58 Pro	58 Prot	58 Prototype		209 Research tech. writi	24 Research i				236 Project management [up to 1/2 day]
	21	8-Feb-00	58 Pro	58 Prot	58 Prototype		209 Research tech. writi	24 Research i				236 Project management [up to 1/2 day]
	22	9-Feb-00	58 Pro	58 Prot	58 Prototype		209 Research tech. writi	24 Research i				236 Project management [up to 1/2 day]
	23	10-Feb-00	58 Pro	58 Prot	58 Prototype		209 Research tech. writi	24 Research i				236 Project management [up to 1/2 day]
	24	11-Feb-00	58 Pro	58 Prot	58 Prototype		209 Research tech. writi	24 Research i				236 Project management [up to 1/2 day]
6	25	14-Feb-00	58 Pro	58 Prot	58 Prototype		210 Set up environment :	25 Wri	37 Wri			236 Project management [up to 1/2 day]
	26	15-Feb-00	58 Pro	58 Prot	58 Prototype		210 Set up environment :	25 Wri	37 Wri			236 Project management [up to 1/2 day]
	27	16-Feb-00	58 Pro	58 Prot	58 Prototype		210 Set up environment :	25 Wri	37 Wri			236 Project management [up to 1/2 day]
	28	17-Feb-00	58 Pro	58 Prot	58 Prototype		210 Set up environment :	29 Wri	41 Wri			236 Project management [up to 1/2 day]
	29	18-Feb-00	58 Pro	58 Prot	58 Prototype		210 Set up environment :	29 Wri	41 Wri			236 Project management [up to 1/2 day]
7	30	21-Feb-00	58 Pro	58 Prot	58 Prototype		211 Define style sheet &	29 Wri	41 Wri			236 Project management [up to 1/2 day]
	31	22-Feb-00	58 Pro	58 Prot	58 Prototype		211 Define style sheet &	33 Wri	45 Wri			236 Project management [up to 1/2 day]
	32	23-Feb-00	58, 60,	58 Prot	58 Prototype		211 Define style sheet &	33 Wri	45 Wri			236 Project management [up to 1/2 day]
	33	24-Feb-00	58 Pro	58 Prot	58 Prototype		211 Define style sheet &	33 Wri	45 Wri			236 Project management [up to 1/2 day]
	34	25-Feb-00	58 Pro	58 Prot	58 Prototype		211 Define style	50 Circulate all Tests				236 Project management [up to 1/2 day]
8	35	28-Feb-00	60 Pric	73 Setl	86 Rep	99 Forc	212 Write documentation / Help text					236 Project management [up to 1/2 day]
	36	29-Feb-00	60 Pric	73 Setl	86 Rep	99 Forc	212 Write documentation / Help text					236 Project management [up to 1/2 day]
	37	1-Mar-00	60 Pric	73 Setl	86 Rep	99 Forc	212 Write documentation / Help text					236 Project management [up to 1/2 day]
	38	2-Mar-00	51 Indi	51 Indi	51 Indi	51 Indi	212 Write documentation / Help text					236 Project management [up to 1/2 day]
	39	3-Mar-00	52 Rev	52 Rev	52 Rev	52 Rev	212 Write documentation		52 Rev	52 Rev	236 Project management [up to 1/2 day]
9	40	6-Mar-00	60 Pric	73 Setl	86 Rep	99 Forc	212 Write documentation		53 Cha	53 Cha	236 Project management [up to 1/2 day]
	41	7-Mar-00	60 Pric	73 Setl	86 Rep	99 Forc	212 Write documentation		53 Cha	53 Cha	236 Project management [up to 1/2 day]
	42	8-Mar-00	60 Pric	73 Setl	86 Rep	99 Forc	212 Write documentation		53, 54	53, 54	236 Project management [up to 1/2 day]
	43	9-Mar-00	55-57,	55-57,	55-57,	55-57,	212 Write documentation		55-57	55-57	236 Project management [up to 1/2 day]
	44	10-Mar-00	60 Pric	73 Setl	86 Rep	99 Forc	212 Write documentation / Help text					236 Project management [up to 1/2 day]
10	45	13-Mar-00	60 Pric	73 Setl	86 Rep	99 Forc	212 Write documentation / Help text					236 Project management [up to 1/2 day]
	46	14-Mar-00	151 W	170 Se	138 Tu	99 Forc	212 Write documentation / Help text					236 Project management [up to 1/2 day]
	47	15-Mar-00	151 W	170 Se	138 Tu	99 Forc	212 Write documentation / Help text					236 Project management [up to 1/2 day]
	48	16-Mar-00	151 W	170 Se	138 Tu	99 Forc	212 Write documentation / Help text					236 Project management [up to 1/2 day]
	49	17-Mar-00	151 W	170 Se	138 Tu	99 Forc	212 Write documentation / Help text					236 Project management [up to 1/2 day]

Figure 12.4   Strip board updated to Week 16 Wednesday.

Week #	Day #	Date	Cast [Jobs]									
			Charlie	Engineer #2	Engineer #3	Engineer #4	Technical author	Marketing people (3)	Anna	Tester #1	Tester #2	Project management
11	50	20-Mar-00	151 W	170 Se	138 Tu	99 Ford	212 Write documentation		Help text			236 Project management [up to 1/2 day]
	51	21-Mar-00	151 W	170 Se	138 Tu	99 Ford	212 Write documentation		Help text			236 Project management [up to 1/2 day]
	52	22-Mar-00	151 W	170 Se	138 Tu	99 Ford	212 Write documentation		Help text			236 Project management [up to 1/2 day]
	53	23-Mar-00	151 W	170 Se	138 Tu	99 Ford	212 Write documentation		Help text			236 Project management [up to 1/2 day]
	54	24-Mar-00	151 W	170 Se	138 Tu	112 Eu	212 Write documentation		Help text			236 Project management [up to 1/2 day]
12	55	27-Mar-00	151 W	170 Se	138 Tu	112 Eu	212 Write documentation		Help text			236 Project management [up to 1/2 day]
	56	28-Mar-00	151 W	170 Se	138 Tu	112 Eu	212 Write documentation		Help text			236 Project management [up to 1/2 day]
	57	29-Mar-00	151 W	170 Se	138 Tu	112 Eu	212 Write documentation		Help text			236 Project management [up to 1/2 day]
	58	30-Mar-00	151 W	170 Se	138 Tu	112 Eu	212 Write documentation		Help text			236 Project management [up to 1/2 day]
	59	31-Mar-00	151 W	170 Se	138 Tu	112 Eu	212 Write documentation		Help text			236 Project management [up to 1/2 day]
13	60	3-Apr-00	151 W	170 Se	138 Tu	112 Eu	212 Write documentation		Help text			236 Project management [up to 1/2 day]
	61	4-Apr-00	151 W	170 Se	138 Tu	112 Eu	212 Write documentation		Help text			236 Project management [up to 1/2 day]
	62	5-Apr-00	151 W	170 Se	138 Tu	112 Eu	212 Write documentation		Help text			236 Project management [up to 1/2 day]
	63	6-Apr-00	151 W	170 Se	189 Or	112 Eu	212 Write documentation		Help text			236 Project management [up to 1/2 day]
	64	7-Apr-00	151 W	170 Se	189 Or	112 Eu	212 Write documentation		Help text			236 Project management [up to 1/2 day]
14	65	10-Apr-00	151 W	170 Se	189 Or	112 Eu	212 Write documentation		Help text			236 Project management [up to 1/2 day]
	66	11-Apr-00	151 W	170 Se	189 Or	112 Eu	212 Write documentation		Help text			236 Project management [up to 1/2 day]
	67	12-Apr-00	151 W	170 Se	189 Or	112 Eu	212 Write documentation		Help text			236 Project management [up to 1/2 day]
	68	13-Apr-00	151 W	170 Se	189 Or	112 Eu	212 Write documentation		Help text			236 Project management [up to 1/2 day]
	69	14-Apr-00	151 W	170 Se	189 Or	112 Eu	212 Write documentation		Help text			236 Project management [up to 1/2 day]
15	70	17-Apr-00	151 W	170 Se	189 Or	125 3rd	212 Write documentation		Help text			236 Project management [up to 1/2 day]
	71	18-Apr-00	151 W	170 Se	189 Or	125 3rd	212 Write documentation		Help text			236 Project management [up to 1/2 day]
	72	19-Apr-00	151 W	170 Se	189 Or	125 3rd	212 Write documentation		Help text			236 Project management [up to 1/2 day]
	73	20-Apr-00	151 W	170 Se	189 Or	125 3rd	212 Write documentation		Help text			236 Project management [up to 1/2 day]
	74	21-Apr-00	151 W	170 Se	189 Or	125 3rd	212 Write documentation		Help text			236 Project management [up to 1/2 day]
16	75	24-Apr-00	151 W	170 Se	189 Or	125 3rd	217 Edit documentation		Help text			236 Project management [up to 1/2 day]
	76	25-Apr-00	151 W	170 Se	189 Or	125 3rd	217 Edit documentation		Help text			236 Project management [up to 1/2 day]
	77	26-Apr-00	151 W	170 Se	189 Or	125 3rd	217 Edit documentation		Help text			236 Project management [up to 1/2 day]
	78	27-Apr-00			189 Or	125 3rd	217 Edit documentation		Help text			236 Project management [up to 1/2 day]
	79	28-Apr-00			189 Or	125 3rd	217 Edit documentation		Help text			236 Project management [up to 1/2 day]
17	80	1-May-00			189 Or	125 3rd	217 Edit documentation		Help text			236 Project management [up to 1/2 day]
	81	2-May-00			189 Or	125 3rd	217 Edit documentation		Help text			236 Project management [up to 1/2 day]
	82	3-May-00			189 Or	125 3rd	217 Edit documentation		Help text			236 Project management [up to 1/2 day]
	83	4-May-00			189 Or	125 3rd	217 Edit documentation		Help text			236 Project management [up to 1/2 day]
	84	5-May-00			189 Or	125 3rd	217 Edit documentation		Help text			236 Project management [up to 1/2 day]
	85	8-May-00			189 Or	125 3rd	217 Edit documentation		Help text			236 Project management [up to 1/2 day]
	86	9-May-00			189 Online help		217 Edit documentation		Help text			236 Project management [up to 1/2 day]
	87	10-May-00			189 Online help		217 Edit documentation		Help text			236 Project management [up to 1/2 day]
	88	11-May-00			189 Online help		217 Edit documentation		Help text			236 Project management [up to 1/2 day]
	89	12-May-00			189 Online help		217 Edit documentation		Help text			236 Project management [up to 1/2 day]
	90	15-May-00			189 Online help		217 Edit documentation		Help text			236 Project management [up to 1/2 day]
	91	16-May-00			189 Online help		217 Edit documentation		Help text			236 Project management [up to 1/2 day]
	92	17-May-00			189 Online help		217 Edit documentation		Help text			236 Project management [up to 1/2 day]
	93	18-May-00			189 Online help		217 Edit documentation		Help text			236 Project management [up to 1/2 day]
	94	19-May-00			189 Online help		217 Edit documentation		Help text			236 Project management [up to 1/2 day]
	95	22-May-00					217 Edit documentation			225 T	225 T	236 Project management [up to 1/2 day]
	96	23-May-00					221 Final integration of C			225 T	225 T	236 Project management [up to 1/2 day]
	97	24-May-00					221 Final integration of C			225 T	225 T	236 Project management [up to 1/2 day]
	98	25-May-00					221 Final integration of C			225 T	225 T	236 Project management [up to 1/2 day]

Figure 12.4   (continued)

How to Run Successful Projects in Web Time

Week #	Day #	Date	Charlie	Engineer #2	Engineer #3	Engineer #4	Technical author	Marketing people (3)	Anna	Tester #1	Tester #2	Project management
	99	26-May-00					221 Final integration of C			225 Te	225 Te	236 Project management [up to 1/2 day]
	100	29-May-00					221 Final integration of C			225 Te	225 Te	236 Project management [up to 1/2 day]
	101	30-May-00					222 Final pre-production			225 Te	225 Te	236 Project management [up to 1/2 day]
	102	31-May-00					222 Final pre-production			225 Te	225 Te	236 Project management [up to 1/2 day]
	103	1-Jun-00					222 Final pre-production			225 Te	225 Te	236 Project management [up to 1/2 day]
	104	2-Jun-00					222 Final pre-production			225 Te	225 Te	236 Project management [up to 1/2 day]
	105	5-Jun-00					222 Final pre-production			225 Te	225 Te	236 Project management [up to 1/2 day]
	106	6-Jun-00								225 Te	225 Te	236 Project management [up to 1/2 day]
	113	7-Jun-00	226 Te	226 Te	226 Te	226 Test #1 - make corrections						236 Project management [up to 1/2 day]
	114	8-Jun-00	226 Te	226 Te	226 Te	226 Test #1 - make corrections						236 Project management [up to 1/2 day]
	115	9-Jun-00	226 Te	226 Te	226 Te	226 Test #1 - make corrections						236 Project management [up to 1/2 day]
	116	12-Jun-00	226 Te	226 Te	226 Te	226 Test #1 - make corrections						236 Project management [up to 1/2 day]
	117	13-Jun-00	226 Te	226 Te	226 Te	226 Test #1 - make corrections						236 Project management [up to 1/2 day]
	118	14-Jun-00	226 Te	226 Te	226 Te	226 Test #1 - make corrections						236 Project management [up to 1/2 day]
	119	15-Jun-00								228 Te	228 Te	236 Project management [up to 1/2 day]
	120	16-Jun-00								228 Te	228 Te	236 Project management [up to 1/2 day]
	121	19-Jun-00								228 Te	228 Te	236 Project management [up to 1/2 day]
	122	20-Jun-00								228 Te	228 Te	236 Project management [up to 1/2 day]
	123	21-Jun-00	229 Te	229 Te	229 Te	229 Test #2 - make corrections						236 Project management [up to 1/2 day]
	124	22-Jun-00	229 Te	229 Te	229 Te	229 Test #2 - make corrections						236 Project management [up to 1/2 day]
	125	23-Jun-00	229 Te	229 Te	229 Te	229 Test #2 - make corrections						236 Project management [up to 1/2 day]
	126	26-Jun-00								231 Te	231 Te	236 Project management [up to 1/2 day]
	127	27-Jun-00								231 Te	231 Te	236 Project management [up to 1/2 day]
	128	28-Jun-00	232 Te	232 Te	232 Te	232 Test #3 - make corrections						236 Project management [up to 1/2 day]
	129	29-Jun-00							233 Finalise to			236 Project management [up to 1/2 day]
	130	30-Jun-00	235 En	235 En	235 En	235 En	235 End of project review		235 En	235 En	235 En	236 Project management [up to 1/2 day]
	131	3-Jul-00	237 Contingency									236 Project management [up to 1/2 day]
	132	4-Jul-00	237 Contingency									236 Project management [up to 1/2 day]
	133	5-Jul-00	237 Contingency									236 Project management [up to 1/2 day]
	134	6-Jul-00	237 Contingency									236 Project management [up to 1/2 day]
	135	7-Jul-00	237 Contingency									236 Project management [up to 1/2 day]
	136	10-Jul-00	237 Contingency									236 Project management [up to 1/2 day]
	137	11-Jul-00	237 Contingency									236 Project management [up to 1/2 day]
	138	12-Jul-00	237 Contingency									236 Project management [up to 1/2 day]
	139	13-Jul-00	237 Contingency									236 Project management [up to 1/2 day]
	140	14-Jul-00	237 Contingency									236 Project management [up to 1/2 day]
	141	17-Jul-00	237 Contingency									236 Project management [up to 1/2 day]
	142	18-Jul-00	237 Contingency									236 Project management [up to 1/2 day]
	143	19-Jul-00	237 Contingency									236 Project management [up to 1/2 day]
	144	20-Jul-00	237 Contingency									236 Project management [up to 1/2 day]
	145	21-Jul-00	Public holiday									
	146	24-Jul-00	Public holiday									
	147	25-Jul-00	Public holiday									
	148	26-Jul-00	Public holiday									
	149	27-Jul-00	Public holiday									
		28-Jul-00										
		31-Jul-00										
		1-Aug-00										
		2-Aug-00										

Figure 12.4   (continued)

How to Run Successful Projects in Web Time

Week #	Day #	Date	Charlie	Engineer #2	Engineer #3	Engineer #4	Technical author	Marketing people (3)	Anna	Tester #1	Tester #2	Project management
1	1	11-Jan-00	Projec	Project	Project	Project	Project	Project k	Project	Projec	Projec	Project kickoff
	2	12-Jan-00	6 Gath									236 Project management [up to 1/2 day]
	3	13-Jan-00	9 Prepare user questionnaires									236 Project management [up to 1/2 day]
	4	14-Jan-00	9 Prepare user questionnaires						10 Distribute user que:			236 Project management [up to 1/2 day]
2	5	17-Jan-00	7 Review with Marketing					7 Review	11 Retrieve questionn:			236 Project management [up to 1/2 day]
	6	18-Jan-00	12 Analyse information									236 Project management [up to 1/2 day]
	7	19-Jan-00	13 Write requirements document									236 Project management [up to 1/2 day]
	8	20-Jan-00	13 Write requirements document									236 Project management [up to 1/2 day]
	9	21-Jan-00	13 Write requirements document									236 Project management [up to 1/2 day]
3	10	24-Jan-00	13 Write requirements document									236 Project management [up to 1/2 day]
	11	25-Jan-00	13 Write requirements document									236 Project management [up to 1/2 day]
	12	26-Jan-00	13 Write requirements document									236 Project management [up to 1/2 day]
	13	27-Jan-00	13 Write requirements document									236 Project management [up to 1/2 day]
	14	28-Jan-00	13 Write requirements document									236 Project management [up to 1/2 day]
4	15	31-Jan-00	13 Write requirements document					15 Circulate document				236 Project management [up to 1/2 day]
	16	1-Feb-00	17,18 Review meeting / changes to doc					16, 17 Individual review [1/2 day				236 Project management [up to 1/2 day]
	17	2-Feb-00	18 Changes to document									236 Project management [up to 1/2 day]
	18	3-Feb-00	18,19 Changes to document (inc. circulate again)									236 Project management [up to 1/2 day]
	19	4-Feb-00	20-22 Second review / Signoff / Reqs c	20-22 Se	20-22 Second review /							236 Project management [up to 1/2 day]
5	20	7-Feb-00	58 Pro	58 Prot	58 Prototype		209 Research tech. writin	24 Research i				236 Project management [up to 1/2 day]
	21	8-Feb-00	58 Pro	58 Prot	58 Prototype		209 Research tech. writin	24 Research i				236 Project management [up to 1/2 day]
	22	9-Feb-00	58 Pro	58 Prot	58 Prototype		209 Research tech. writin	24 Research i				236 Project management [up to 1/2 day]
	23	10-Feb-00	58 Pro	58 Prot	58 Prototype		209 Research tech. writin	24 Research i				236 Project management [up to 1/2 day]
	24	11-Feb-00	58 Pro	58 Prot	58 Prototype		209 Research tech. writin	24 Research i				236 Project management [up to 1/2 day]
6	25	14-Feb-00	58 Pro	58 Prot	58 Prototype		210 Set up environment :	25 Wri	37 Wri			236 Project management [up to 1/2 day]
	26	15-Feb-00	58 Pro	58 Prot	58 Prototype		210 Set up environment :	25 Wri	37 Wri			236 Project management [up to 1/2 day]
	27	16-Feb-00	58 Pro	58 Prot	58 Prototype		210 Set up environment :	25 Wri	37 Wri			236 Project management [up to 1/2 day]
	28	17-Feb-00	58 Pro	58 Prot	58 Prototype		210 Set up environment :	29 Wri	41 Wri			236 Project management [up to 1/2 day]
	29	18-Feb-00	58 Pro	58 Prot	58 Prototype		210 Set up environment :	29 Wri	41 Wri			236 Project management [up to 1/2 day]
7	30	21-Feb-00	58 Pro	58 Prot	58 Prototype		211 Define style sheet &	29 Wri	41 Wri			236 Project management [up to 1/2 day]
	31	22-Feb-00	58 Pro	58 Prot	58 Prototype		211 Define style sheet &	33 Wri	45 Wri			236 Project management [up to 1/2 day]
	32	23-Feb-00	58, 60,	58 Prot	58 Prototype		211 Define style sheet &	33 Wri	45 Wri			236 Project management [up to 1/2 day]
	33	24-Feb-00	58 Pro	58 Prot	58 Prototype		211 Define style sheet &	33 Wri	45 Wri			236 Project management [up to 1/2 day]
	34	25-Feb-00	58 Pro	58 Prot	58 Prototype		211 Define style	50 Circulate all Tests				236 Project management [up to 1/2 day]
8	35	28-Feb-00	60 Pric	73 Sett	86 Rep	99 Ford	212 Write documentation / Help text					236 Project management [up to 1/2 day]
	36	29-Feb-00	60 Pric	73 Sett	86 Rep	99 Ford	212 Write documentation / Help text					236 Project management [up to 1/2 day]
	37	1-Mar-00	60 Pric	73 Sett	86 Rep	99 Ford	212 Write documentation / Help text					236 Project management [up to 1/2 day]
	38	2-Mar-00	51 Indi	51 Indi	51 Indi	51 Indi	212 Write documentation / Help text					236 Project management [up to 1/2 day]
	39	3-Mar-00	52 Rev	52 Rev	52 Rev	52 Rev	212 Write documentation			52 Rev	52 Rev	236 Project management [up to 1/2 day]
9	40	6-Mar-00	60 Pric	73 Sett	86 Rep	99 Ford	212 Write documentation			53 Cha	53 Cha	236 Project management [up to 1/2 day]
	41	7-Mar-00	60 Pric	73 Sett	86 Rep	99 Ford	212 Write documentation			53 Cha	53 Cha	236 Project management [up to 1/2 day]
	42	8-Mar-00	60 Pric	73 Sett	86 Rep	99 Ford	212 Write documentation			53, 54	53, 54	236 Project management [up to 1/2 day]
	43	9-Mar-00	55-57,	55-57,	55-57,	55-57,	212 Write documentation			55-57	55-57	236 Project management [up to 1/2 day]
	44	10-Mar-00	60 Pric	73 Sett	86 Rep	99 Ford	212 Write documentation / Help text					236 Project management [up to 1/2 day]
10	45	13-Mar-00	60 Pric	73 Sett	86 Rep	99 Ford	212 Write documentation / Help text					236 Project management [up to 1/2 day]
	46	14-Mar-00	151 W	170 Se	138 Tu	99 Ford	212 Write documentation / Help text					236 Project management [up to 1/2 day]
	47	15-Mar-00	151 W	170 Se	138 Tu	99 Ford	212 Write documentation / Help text					236 Project management [up to 1/2 day]
	48	16-Mar-00	151 W	170 Se	138 Tu	99 Ford	212 Write documentation / Help text					236 Project management [up to 1/2 day]
	49	17-Mar-00	151 W	170 Se	138 Tu	99 Ford	212 Write documentation / Help text					236 Project management [up to 1/2 day]

Figure 12.5   Strip board updated to Week 16 Friday.

Week #	Day #	Date	Charlie	Engineer #2	Engineer #3	Engineer #4	Technical author	Marketing people (3)	Anna	Tester #1	Tester #2	Project management
11	50	20-Mar-00	151 W	170 Se	138 Tu	99 Ford	212 Write documentation / Help text					236 Project management [up to 1/2 day]
	51	21-Mar-00	151 W	170 Se	138 Tu	99 Ford	212 Write documentation / Help text					236 Project management [up to 1/2 day]
	52	22-Mar-00	151 W	170 Se	138 Tu	99 Ford	212 Write documentation / Help text					236 Project management [up to 1/2 day]
	53	23-Mar-00	151 W	170 Se	138 Tu	99 Ford	212 Write documentation / Help text					236 Project management [up to 1/2 day]
	54	24-Mar-00	151 W	170 Se	138 Tu	112 Eu	212 Write documentation / Help text					236 Project management [up to 1/2 day]
12	55	27-Mar-00	151 W	170 Se	138 Tu	112 Eu	212 Write documentation / Help text					236 Project management [up to 1/2 day]
	56	28-Mar-00	151 W	170 Se	138 Tu	112 Eu	212 Write documentation / Help text					236 Project management [up to 1/2 day]
	57	29-Mar-00	151 W	170 Se	138 Tu	112 Eu	212 Write documentation / Help text					236 Project management [up to 1/2 day]
	58	30-Mar-00	151 W	170 Se	138 Tu	112 Eu	212 Write documentation / Help text					236 Project management [up to 1/2 day]
	59	31-Mar-00	151 W	170 Se	138 Tu	112 Eu	212 Write documentation / Help text					236 Project management [up to 1/2 day]
13	60	3-Apr-00	151 W	170 Se	138 Tu	112 Eu	212 Write documentation / Help text					236 Project management [up to 1/2 day]
	61	4-Apr-00	151 W	170 Se	138 Tu	112 Eu	212 Write documentation / Help text					236 Project management [up to 1/2 day]
	62	5-Apr-00	151 W	170 Se	138 Tu	112 Eu	212 Write documentation / Help text					236 Project management [up to 1/2 day]
	63	6-Apr-00	151 W	170 Se	189 Or	112 Eu	212 Write documentation / Help text					236 Project management [up to 1/2 day]
	64	7-Apr-00	151 W	170 Se	189 Or	112 Eu	212 Write documentation / Help text					236 Project management [up to 1/2 day]
14	65	10-Apr-00	151 W	170 Se	189 Or	112 Eu	212 Write documentation / Help text					236 Project management [up to 1/2 day]
	66	11-Apr-00	151 W	170 Se	189 Or	112 Eu	212 Write documentation / Help text					236 Project management [up to 1/2 day]
	67	12-Apr-00	151 W	170 Se	189 Or	112 Eu	212 Write documentation / Help text					236 Project management [up to 1/2 day]
	68	13-Apr-00	151 W	170 Se	189 Or	112 Eu	212 Write documentation / Help text					236 Project management [up to 1/2 day]
	69	14-Apr-00	151 W	170 Se	189 Or	112 Eu	212 Write documentation / Help text					236 Project management [up to 1/2 day]
15	70	17-Apr-00	151 W	170 Se	189 Or	125 3rd	212 Write documentation / Help text					236 Project management [up to 1/2 day]
	71	18-Apr-00	151 W	170 Se	189 Or	125 3rd	212 Write documentation / Help text					236 Project management [up to 1/2 day]
	72	19-Apr-00	151 W	170 Se	189 Or	125 3rd	212 Write documentation / Help text					236 Project management [up to 1/2 day]
	73	20-Apr-00	151 W	170 Se	189 Or	125 3rd	212 Write documentation / Help text					236 Project management [up to 1/2 day]
	74	21-Apr-00	151 W	170 Se	189 Or	125 3rd	212 Write documentation / Help text					236 Project management [up to 1/2 day]
16	75	24-Apr-00	151 W	170 Se	189 Or	125 3rd	217 Edit documentation / Help text					236 Project management [up to 1/2 day]
	76	25-Apr-00	151 W	170 Se	189 Or	125 3rd	217 Edit documentation / Help text					236 Project management [up to 1/2 day]
	77	26-Apr-00	151 W	170 Se	189 Or	125 3rd	217 Edit documentation / Help text					236 Project management [up to 1/2 day]
	78	27-Apr-00		189 Or	189 Or	125 3rd	217 Edit documentation / Help text					236 Project management [up to 1/2 day]
	79	28-Apr-00		189 Or	189 Or	125 3rd	217 Edit documentation / Help text					236 Project management [up to 1/2 day]
17	80	1-May-00	Vacati	189 Or	189 Or	125 3rd	217 Edit documentation /			225 Te	225 Te	236 Project management [up to 1/2 day]
	81	2-May-00	Vacati	189 Or	189 Or	125 3rd	217 Edit documentation /			225 Te	225 Te	236 Project management [up to 1/2 day]
	82	3-May-00	Vacati	189 Or	189 Or	125 3rd	217 Edit documentation /			225 Te	225 Te	236 Project management [up to 1/2 day]
	83	4-May-00	Vacati	189 Or	189 Or	125 3rd	217 Edit documentation /			225 Te	225 Te	236 Project management [up to 1/2 day]
	84	5-May-00	Vacati	189 Or	189 Or	125 3rd	217 Edit documentation /			225 Te	225 Te	236 Project management [up to 1/2 day]
18	85	8-May-00	Vacati	189 Or	189 Or	125 3rd	217 Edit documentation /			225 Te	225 Te	236 Project management [up to 1/2 day]
	86	9-May-00	Vacati	189 Online help			217 Edit documentation /			225 Te	225 Te	236 Project management [up to 1/2 day]
	87	10-May-00	Vacati	226 Te	226 Te	226 Te	217 Edit documentation /			225 Te	225 Te	236 Project management [up to 1/2 day]
	88	11-May-00	Vacati	226 Te	226 Te	226 Te	217 Edit documentation /			225 Te	225 Te	236 Project management [up to 1/2 day]
	89	12-May-00	Vacati	226 Te	226 Te	226 Te	217 Edit documentation /			225 Te	225 Te	236 Project management [up to 1/2 day]
19	90	15-May-00	226 Te	226 Te	226 Te	226 Te	217 Edit documentation /			225 Te	225 Te	236 Project management [up to 1/2 day]
	91	16-May-00	226 Te	226 Te	226 Te	226 Te	217 Edit documentation /			225 Te	225 Te	236 Project management [up to 1/2 day]
	92	17-May-00	226 Te	226 Te	226 Te	226 Te	217 Edit documentation /			228 Te	228 Te	236 Project management [up to 1/2 day]
	93	18-May-00					217 Edit documentation /			228 Te	228 Te	236 Project management [up to 1/2 day]
	94	19-May-00					217 Edit documentation /			228 Te	228 Te	236 Project management [up to 1/2 day]
20	95	22-May-00					217 Edit documentation /			228 Te	228 Te	236 Project management [up to 1/2 day]
	96	23-May-00	229 Te	229 Te	229 Te	229 Te	221 Final integration of Online Help					236 Project management [up to 1/2 day]
	97	24-May-00	229 Te	229 Te	229 Te	229 Te	221 Final integration of Online Help					236 Project management [up to 1/2 day]
	98	25-May-00	229 Te	229 Te	229 Te	229 Te	221 Final integration of Online Help					236 Project management [up to 1/2 day]

Figure 12.5   (continued)

Week #	Day #	Date	Charlie	Engineer #2	Engineer #3	Engineer #4	Technical author	Marketing people (3)	Anna	Tester #1	Tester #2	Project management
	99	26-May-00					221 Final integration of C		231 Te	231 Te		236 Project management [up to 1/2 day]
21	100	29-May-00					221 Final integration of C		231 Te	231 Te		236 Project management [up to 1/2 day]
	101	30-May-00	232 Te	232 Te	232 Te	232 Test #3 - make corrections						236 Project management [up to 1/2 day]
	102	31-May-00					222 Final pre-production		233 Finalise to			236 Project management [up to 1/2 day]
	103	1-Jun-00					222 Final pre-production of manuals					236 Project management [up to 1/2 day]
	104	2-Jun-00					222 Final pre-production of manuals					236 Project management [up to 1/2 day]
22	105	5-Jun-00	235 En	235 En	235 En	235 En	235 End of project review		235 Er	235 Er		236 Project management [up to 1/2 day]
	106	6-Jun-00	237 Contingency									236 Project management [up to 1/2 day]
	113	7-Jun-00	237 Contingency									236 Project management [up to 1/2 day]
	114	8-Jun-00	237 Contingency									236 Project management [up to 1/2 day]
	115	9-Jun-00	237 Contingency									236 Project management [up to 1/2 day]
23	116	12-Jun-00	237 Contingency									236 Project management [up to 1/2 day]
	117	13-Jun-00	237 Contingency									236 Project management [up to 1/2 day]
	118	14-Jun-00	237 Contingency									236 Project management [up to 1/2 day]
	119	15-Jun-00	237 Contingency									236 Project management [up to 1/2 day]
	120	16-Jun-00	237 Contingency									236 Project management [up to 1/2 day]
24	121	19-Jun-00	237 Contingency									236 Project management [up to 1/2 day]
	122	20-Jun-00	237 Contingency									236 Project management [up to 1/2 day]
	123	21-Jun-00	237 Contingency									236 Project management [up to 1/2 day]
	124	22-Jun-00	237 Contingency									236 Project management [up to 1/2 day]
	125	23-Jun-00	237 Contingency									236 Project management [up to 1/2 day]
25	126	26-Jun-00	Public holiday									236 Project management [up to 1/2 day]
	127	27-Jun-00	Public holiday									236 Project management [up to 1/2 day]
	128	28-Jun-00	Public holiday									236 Project management [up to 1/2 day]
	129	29-Jun-00	Public holiday									236 Project management [up to 1/2 day]
	130	30-Jun-00	Public holiday									236 Project management [up to 1/2 day]
	131	3-Jul-00										
	132	4-Jul-00										
	133	5-Jul-00										
	134	6-Jul-00										
	135	7-Jul-00										
	136	10-Jul-00										
	137	11-Jul-00										
	138	12-Jul-00										
	139	13-Jul-00										
	140	14-Jul-00										
	141	17-Jul-00										
	142	18-Jul-00										
	143	19-Jul-00										
	144	20-Jul-00										
	145	21-Jul-00										
	146	24-Jul-00										
	147	25-Jul-00										
	148	26-Jul-00										
	149	27-Jul-00										
		28-Jul-00										
		31-Jul-00										
		1-Aug-00										
		2-Aug-00										

Figure 12.5   (continued)

How to Run Successful Projects in Web Time

"Week 18. Charlie's still catching a tan. Coding finishes on Monday or Tuesday for everybody. Ted edits endlessly. We can obviously move the bug fixing up." You do it, pointing out that you've taken some of the time Charlie was allotted to bug fixing. Charlie says he wouldn't have needed it anyway. Everyone laughs. Charlie was serious. "Bug fixing pass #1 begins for you three engineers, and you get three days in before the weekend. The testers run test pass #1."

"Week 19. You four engineers finish the bug fixing from test pass #1. Ted does yet another week's editing. The testers begin test pass #2 on Wednesday."

There are some small gaps in the strip board between test passes and bug fixing. You know in reality that these will be used, and you remind yourself to fill these in before this afternoon's presentation to the higher-ups.

"Week 20. You engineers are bug fixing from test pass #2. Ted is doing the final pull-together of his Online Help stuff. The testers are testing."

"Week 21 will, I'm sure, be another quiet week." Loud guffaws. "And let's knock a day off Ted's schedule, so that the thing completes by Friday 2 June." You note with a certain amount of satisfaction, that this has the added effect of bringing the final, including contingency, date inside the June 30 boundary. It isn't 30 days after the particular Comdex they wanted, but at least it's in this half of the year.

"I want to say a word about contingency," you say. "This afternoon, I'm going to commit to delivering this product on 30 June."

"They'll never buy it," somebody says.

"You let me worry about that. I'm going to commit to 30 June. Can we make an agreement amongst ourselves that we'll try to be in a position to ship on 2 June?"

After some thought and discussion, there is general agreement. "So what about the contingency," someone asks, "are you gonna give it away?"

"Hell no," you say.

"Might save your job," ventures Charlie.

"You let me worry about my job. No, the contingency stays. If it turns out we need it, then we'll have saved our bacon. And if not ... well, if not, we can all go to the beach for the three weeks. Agreed?"

It's agreed. But not before someone else has offered some fears for your job. You find their concern touching.

You take them through the risk analysis. You give the "let's make every day count" speech. Then, just to tidy up you note that the project management calculation is now 60/130 which is closer to half a day every day or half a week every week. As you're instructing the Scribe to note this, somebody says "This plan's all wrong." You glance round. As you do so, you realize you're not in the slightest bit anxious. You *know* the plan is a good one.

It's Engineer #2 who spoke.

"You haven't included weekends," he said.

You fix his gaze.

"That's the thing," you say, "there aren't going to be any weekends."

"Now your job is definitely gone," somebody mutters.

As you leave the meeting with your Scribe, you're happy that you did a good job. A lot of the shortenings that you "discovered" during the briefing, you knew about beforehand. Or, at least you were aware that there was potential for further savings. However, you've found that it's better to do at least some of them during the kickoff / briefing meeting. For some reason, it seems to give everyone a much greater sense of ownership in the plan.

It's early but you're hungry. And you're going to need to prepare yourself for this afternoon.

Worked Example — Pitching to the Higher-Ups

It's the most prestigious gathering of higher-ups you've ever pitched to. Filing into the room are the CEO, the Chief Financial Officer (CFO), the Head of Engineering (your boss's boss), the Head of Sales, the Head of Marketing. You've got your PowerPoint presentation and handouts, updated as a result of this morning's meeting. You begin as before (see Figure 12.6).

"The aim of this project is to release to Beta Test a version of the Killer Product version 1.0. The Killer Product will have these features and we have sized them as shown on the slide."

"And that really is the bare-ass minimum functionality. We just about have a product there," says the Head of Marketing. Thanks for the support, you think sarcastically. You say nothing.

"We estimate there are 610 person-days in this project, or about 3 person-years. If you give us the go ahead today and we start tomorrow,

Figure 12.6
Features list.

| 11. Pricing (S) |
| 12. Foreign exchange (M) |
| 13. Euro support (M) |
| 14. 3rd party payments (M) |
| 15. Settlement (S) |
| 16. Reporting (S) |
| 17. Web interface (L) |
| 18. Security (L) |
| 19. Tutorial (M) |
| 20. Online help (L). |

then we'll have a prototype for Comdex available for the end of February. We'll deliver product to Beta test on 30 June."

The Head of Sales freaks. I'm assuming you've seen such performances before and that I don't have to reproduce one here. The product has to be ready by the end of March or else the window of opportunity will be lost. The CFO reminds us that if this opportunity is lost, then *all* will be lost. The CEO glares at your boss's boss. He glares at you.

"If you let me take you through the plan," you say, as soon as things have quieted down a bit, "I'll show you how we arrived at this date."

You give them an abbreviated version of what you did this morning.

"We can't live with it," says the Head of Sales. He had been standing up watching your presentation, but now he flops back theatrically into his chair. You say nothing. Finally, the CEO speaks. He is reason personified.

"We knock out the contingency and work the holidays and weekends, that saves a month for starters. That gets us back into May."

You're pleased. Firstly, you were expecting this contingency one, but more importantly, he's begun talking in terms of the plan. He's going to fight on your ground. Provided you can keep them here, you have them.

"We can't take out the contingency."

Your boss's boss looks like he's going to explode.

"Sure we can," the CEO tries, still in his reasonable voice.

"No," you say, and you're amazed at the commanding tone that came out of your mouth. (You realize, yet again, how much the success of this kind of presentation is down to their perception of you. That perception and the amateur dramatic society you joined in school!) "We can't take out the contingency because the plan is based on estimates. The estimates could be wrong. We could have underestimated, in which case, I'll need every piece of contingency I can get. Sure, we'll be trying to aim for 2 June (the date minus the contingency), but at this stage I can only guarantee 30 June."

"I think you've *over*estimated everything," says the Head of Engineering. "Take Settlement, for example, it could never take that long."

You've never really liked your boss's boss, and now you proceed to destroy him. You take him through the line items (see Figure 8.1) that make up the 8 day's effort. "It's never 4 days," he says weakly. "You're right," you say, "it could be 2. Then that would make the whole thing 6 days. But we don't know, do we?" You may have ruined your promotion prospects but what the hell, it was worth it. And anyway, there are plenty of jobs out there.

"Is this schedule based on a 5 day week?" asks the Head of Sales.

This is it—the all-out assault.

"Yes."

"So work the weekends."

"No."

Most people in the room are apoplectic, at this stage.

"Extended overtime doesn't buy you anything. In fact, extended overtime is a productivity reduction tactic."

"Says who?" they chorus.

"Says him. Chapter 15." You throw a copy of Tom DeMarco's *The Deadline* [6] onto the table. A yellow Post-it marks the relevant spot. People look at it like it's contagious. They're speechless. They quite literally don't know what to say. You let the silence deepen for another few moments. Then, speaking very softly and slowly, you say, "I can *guarantee*"—you eyeball each of them in turn—"delivery of this product on 30 June. (Your stomach churns as you make this pronouncement.) I may even do so beforehand. I can *not* do it within 30 days of Comdex."

"Do you have somebody who can?" the CEO asks the Head of Engineering. It's the final counter-attack. You interrupt.

"There may be people who will promise to make Comdex. I can tell you now they won't succeed, whatever they promise. The only guarantee you've got is here, with this plan." Awesome, you think to yourself. If you were in the audience you'd be applauding yourself.

It's time to finish the meeting. You've got work to do.

"Here's my final offer. You want 30 days from Comdex. I'm saying it can't be done. Of course none of us know for sure because all of this is based on estimates and assumptions. I guarantee 30 June—you could build your sales and marketing and promotion plans on that date. You could bet your house on that date. (Oh my God, did you really say that?) However, I understand you would like it sooner. In my opinion, it can't be done sooner. However, as the project unrolls, I'll give you weekly status updates in which I'll report if we're making any progress towards the date you want." Long pause. "That's the best I can do."

They are deathly quiet. When they realize you're finished speaking, it's almost as though they're happy to be let off the hook. There are dark mutterings, but the general message is that if that's the best offer on the table, they'll just have to take it.

"Anything else," you ask brightly.

There's nothing else.

"So that's a go?" You're rubbing it in a bit now.

"That's a go," says the CEO.

"Thank you," you say, and walk out, in search of your team. Fight from the plan and don't back down. To quote Tom Petty and the Heartbreakers [7], "they can stand you up at the gates of Hell and you won't back down." It works every time.

After you've left the conference room, the CEO says to the Head of Engineering "She's good. Got any more like her?"

References

1. O'Connell, F., *How To Run Successful Projects II—The Silver Bullet*, Hemel Hempstead, England: Prentice Hall, 1996.

2. O'Connell, F., *How To Run Successful High-Tech Project-Based Organizations*, Boston: Artech House, 1999.

3. Anderson, M., (director) *The Dam Busters*, 1954.

4. Caton-Jones, M., (director) *Memphis Belle*, 1990.

5. Cooper, A., *The Lunatics Are Running The Asylum*, Indianapolis: Sams Publishing, 1999.

6. DeMarco, T., *The Deadline—A Novel About Project Management*, New York: Dorset House, 1997.

7. Tom Petty and the Heartbreakers, *Greatest Hits*, MCA, 1993.

PART FIVE
Execute the Plan

In this part of the book we describe how to execute the shortened plan. Chapter 13 deals with monitoring and control against the plan, along with status reporting. Chapter 14 describes how to do a post-mortem, or audit, on a completed project.

13 Monitor, Control, and Report

➤ This chapter shows how monitoring and control is enormously simplified when using the techniques described earlier.

➤ It shows that the project execution phase provides further opportunities to shorten the project.

➤ Knowing where precisely to spend your project management effort is the key to your personal effectiveness. This chapter tells you what to do. You also need to continue to manage the stakeholders' expectations via status reporting.

➤ We illustrate all of these concepts using the worked example.

Monitoring and Control

Traditionally, one of the biggest problems in projects has not been so much the putting together of the plan, but rather what happens immediately after that. It's true to say that hardly is the ink dry on the plan when it is out of date. The project starts rolling. Reality intrudes on our dreams. Then, the dual issues of (a) understanding what is happening out in the world and (b) reflecting this correctly in the plan (i.e., updating the plan), can cause a huge project FUD[1] Factor to develop.

Running the project using a strip board representation of the plan, a lot of these issues disappear. It is very clear, for example, who should be working on what on what day. This can be checked against reality on the ground. There is no uncertainty about deadlines. The strip board is (depressingly!) clear about them. The targets for the week are obvious. Slippage is obvious.

---

1 FUD is an acronym for Fear, Uncertainty, and Doubt.

We will illustrate all of these claims in our worked example later in this chapter. It may have seemed to you that the whole business of building the strip board was a monster waste of time for only marginal benefit. I believe this not to be the case. As further proof of this, I hope you will see here how straightforward monitoring, control, and reporting become in our new scheme of things.

Continue to Shorten the Project

We have seen in the two preceding chapters, that there are a number of things we can do to shorten the project. At the risk of stating the obvious, these are not things that we just get to do once when we plan the project. Rather they are things we can look at doing *every day*—so that we develop a culture that encourages looking for any gain, no matter how small. So let's put together in one place, our definitive list of the things we can do.

Everybody on the team should be encouraged to do the following:

1. Make every day count. Don't do it tomorrow if it can be done today. Another way of thinking of this is to ask each day "can I finish this today?"

2. Be hypersensitive to changes that increase the scope of the project. Encourage everybody to keep an eagle eye out for changes to the scope of the project.

3. If they find themselves waiting for somebody else, raise an alert. This way somebody can do something about it.

4. If they're aware of a potential delay coming up, flag it as soon as it's known.

5. Keep Dance Cards up to date. This way people will know if they've over-allocated themselves. Better still is to use the Dance Card to avoid over-allocating themselves in the first place.

6. If they can start a job early, do so.

7. If they can finish a job early without compromising quality, do so.

8. If a piece of functionality can be achieved using a simpler or quicker approach, then do so.

9. If the elapsed time for a task can be reduced without compromising quality, do so. (This is not quite the same thing as 7).

We will see all of these things in action in the worked example at the end of this chapter.

Where to Put Your Project Management Effort

You may recall from Chapter 7 that we introduced the notion of trying to understand where our team's strengths and weaknesses lay. We described a classification scheme where once we assigned a person to a job, we could classify the assignment as follows:

1. The person has the necessary skill and experience to do the job and likes to do it.

2. The person has the necessary skill and experience to do the job and is prepared to do it.

3. The person has the necessary skill and experience to do the job but is not prepared to do it.

4. The person can be trained or instructed into doing the job.

5. The person cannot do the job.

You may have wondered at the time why we did this, since we didn't seem to do anything useful with it. The answer is that here is where we are going to do useful things with it. Basically, our project is going to require very little project management effort with the type 1's, a little more with the 2's, plenty with the 4's (i.e., micro-management), and the 3's and 5's could end up consuming enormous amounts of our management time. If we are conscious of this as our project unfolds, then we can ensure that we put the time in where it counts and leave things alone where we know things are pretty much under control. "If it ain't broke, don't fix it," the old saw goes. It applies here. Leave those who know what they're doing to get on with the job and focus your efforts on where the problems either are, or are likely to crop up. (If you're interested in a more complete discussion of this, you can read about it in either of my previous two books [1, 2]).

Status Reporting

The previous chapter was all about setting the expectations of the stakeholders. Setting them correctly at the beginning of the project is obviously crucial to its success. (It would be hard to imagine anything more crucial.) As the project unfolds, however, it is your job to ensure that the expectations continue to be managed. A weekly status report is, in my view, the single most effective way of doing this—provided, of course, it tells them something useful, which many status reports don't.

Many status reports, either intentionally or otherwise, do not make the status of the project particularly clear. Obfuscation is the order of the day. There are rambling accounts of all kinds of activity on the project, and a feeling that though things are running pretty close to the wind, we'll be alright on the night. Status reports have a lot in common with fairy stories—two things notably. One is that almost all status reports have a happy ending. There is a feeling that despite all our trials and tribulations things are going to turn out okay. The other similarity is that lots of the status reports I've seen in my time *are* fairy stories, i.e., the things described in them never happened or happened only in the author's mind.

In each of my previous books [1, 2], I've given some simple and effective guidelines for status reporting. Rather then regurgitating all of that here, I have instead chosen to illustrate the application of those guidelines in the worked example which follows.

Worked Example

It's Wednesday 12 January. You're on your way to work. Yesterday you looked them in the eye and told them that it was going to happen exactly like you were predicting in your plan. (You were squirming inside, but you let none of that show.) They said they'd buy it. Now you have to deliver.

Week 1

You get off to a good start. The jobs for 11 January (see Figure 12.4) have already been achieved on target. Charlie gets all the necessary competitive info together and reviews it with Marketing on Wednesday 12th. Fairly effortlessly, Charlie completes the user questionnaires in a day, and Anna gets them distributed. Marketing are so surprised to see something coming in early from Engineering, that when you call up and ask if the review of the competitive info can take place a day early (i.e., on Friday rather than Monday), they say yes. All of this first week requires not a lot of project management from you.

The status report for week 1 is described and bits of it are illustrated in Figures 13.1 through 13.3.

You send this status report to all of the stakeholders. You know yourself, of course, that you've *saved* a little bit of time. You've saved a person-day, in fact. Charlie is going to be able to start his analysis (task 12) on Monday, rather than Tuesday. This isn't necessarily going to translate into an elapsed day saved on the project as a whole. For us to see that we would need to shunt all of Charlie's tasks up the strip board and see what the effect of that would be. We'll obviously do that in due course, but whether it saved an elapsed day or not, we wouldn't tell the powers that be.

The rationale for this is that if no elapsed day were saved, then nothing has changed. And if an elapsed day has been saved, then that's a little bit of extra contingency that we will tuck happily away, tell nobody about, and see whether we need it in the fullness of time.

Week 2

On Monday morning, first thing, you get with Charlie over a cup of coffee. Your purpose is to make sure he's clear on what has to be done for the week. But it's a one minute insert slipped into a conversation about the weekend, technology, families, and global warming. Charlie is one of your superstars (he's a 1 in our categorization scheme). The last thing on earth he would want to feel is that you were managing him, that you

Figure 13.1   Status report at Week 1.

The project is on target for delivery of Beta units on 30 June. Status is Green.
An up to date schedule for the project is attached. (You attach the strip board shown in figure 13.2.)

Just to remind them, and so there is no doubt as to what was agreed, you provide the following information.

The date you asked for:	25 March	(Prototype availability plus 30 days)
The earliest date we said was possible:	30 June	
The date we're showing today:	30 June	

This is an *instantaneous* reading of the state of the project. You also provide them with the beginnings of an historic or cumulative view. This is done using the graph in Figure 13.3.

Week #	Day #	Date	Charlie	Engineer #2	Engineer #3	Engineer #4	Technical author	Marketing people (3)	Anna	Tester #1	Tester #2	Project management	Actual Effort (PD)	Based on (PD)
1	1	11-Jan-00	Project	Project	Project ki	Project	Project	Project	Project	Project	Project kickoff		5.5	9 x 1/2 + 1 Proj. Mgmt.
	2	12-Jan-00	6 Gath						8 Identify users				2.57	1 + (3 x 1/2)
	3	13-Jan-00	9 Prepare user questionnaires						10 Distribute user questionnaires				4	1 + 3
	4	14-Jan-00	7 Review competitive info with Marketing					7 Review with Marketing				236 Project management [up to 1/2 day]	4.5	1 + 3 + 1/2 PD Proj. Mgmt
2	5	17-Jan-00							11 Retrieve questionnair			236 Project management [up to 1/2 day]		
	6	18-Jan-00	12 Analyse information									236 Project management [up to 1/2 day]		
	7	19-Jan-00	13 Write requirements document									236 Project management [up to 1/2 day]		
	8	20-Jan-00	13 Write requirements document									236 Project management [up to 1/2 day]		
	9	21-Jan-00	13 Write requirements document									236 Project management [up to 1/2 day]		
3	10	24-Jan-00	13 Write requirements document									236 Project management [up to 1/2 day]		
	11	25-Jan-00	13 Write requirements document									236 Project management [up to 1/2 day]		
	12	26-Jan-00	13 Write requirements document									236 Project management [up to 1/2 day]		
	13	27-Jan-00	13 Write requirements document									236 Project management [up to 1/2 day]		
	14	28-Jan-00	13 Write requirements document									236 Project management [up to 1/2 day]		
4	15	31-Jan-00	13 Write requirements document						15 Circulate document			236 Project management [up to 1/2 day]		
	16	1-Feb-00	17,18 Review meeting / changes to docum				16, 17 Individual review [1/2 day ea					236 Project management [up to 1/2 day]		
	17	2-Feb-00	18 Changes to document									236 Project management [up to 1/2 day]		
	18	3-Feb-00	18,19 Changes to document (inc. circulate again)									236 Project management [up to 1/2 day]		
5	19	4-Feb-00	20-22 Second review / Signoff / Reqs comp				Reqs comp		20-22 Se	20-22 Second review / Si	236 Project management [up to 1/2 day]		
	20	7-Feb-00	58 Prot	58 Prot	58 Prot	58 Prot	209 Research tech. writing			24 Research inf	236 Project management [up to 1/2 day]		
	21	8-Feb-00	58 Prot	58 Prot	58 Prot	58 Prototype	209 Research tech. writing			24 Research inf	236 Project management [up to 1/2 day]		
	22	9-Feb-00	58, 60,	58 Prot	58 Prot	58 Prototype	209 Research tech. writing			24 Research inf	236 Project management [up to 1/2 day]		
	23	10-Feb-00	58 Prot	58 Prot	58 Prot	58 Prototype	209 Research tech. writing			24 Research inf	236 Project management [up to 1/2 day]		
	24	11-Feb-00	58 Prot	58 Prot	58 Prot	58 Prototype	209 Research tech. writing			24 Research inf	236 Project management [up to 1/2 day]		
6	25	14-Feb-00	58 Prot	58 Prot	58 Prot	58 Prototype	210 Set up environment an		25 Writ	37 Writ	236 Project management [up to 1/2 day]		
	26	15-Feb-00	58 Prot	58 Prot	58 Prot	58 Prototype	210 Set up environment an		25 Writ	37 Writ	236 Project management [up to 1/2 day]		
	27	16-Feb-00	58 Prot	58 Prot	58 Prot	58 Prototype	210 Set up environment an		25 Writ	37 Writ	236 Project management [up to 1/2 day]		
	28	17-Feb-00	58 Prot	58 Prot	58 Prot	58 Prototype	210 Set up environment an		29 Writ	41 Writ	236 Project management [up to 1/2 day]		
	29	18-Feb-00	58 Prot	58 Prot	58 Prot	58 Prototype	210 Set up environment an		29 Writ	41 Writ	236 Project management [up to 1/2 day]		
7	30	21-Feb-00	58 Prot	58 Prot	58 Prot	58 Prototype	211 Define style sheet & pre		29 Writ	41 Writ	236 Project management [up to 1/2 day]		
	31	22-Feb-00	58 Prot	58 Prot	58 Prot	58 Prototype	211 Define style sheet & pre		33 Writ	45 Writ	236 Project management [up to 1/2 day]		
	32	23-Feb-00	58, 60,	58 Prot	58 Prot	58 Prototype	211 Define style sheet & pre		33 Writ	45 Writ	236 Project management [up to 1/2 day]		
	33	24-Feb-00	58 Prot	58 Prot	58 Prot	58 Prototype	211 Define style sheet & pre		33 Writ	45 Writ	236 Project management [up to 1/2 day]		
	34	25-Feb-00	58 Prot	58 Prot	58 Prot	58 Prototype	211 Define style at 50 Circulate all Tests				236 Project management [up to 1/2 day]		

Figure 13.2   Strip board at Week 1.

Week #	Day #	Date	Charlie	Engineer #2	Engineer #3	Engineer #4	Technical author	Marketing people (3)	Anna	Tester #1	Tester #2	Project management	Actual Effort [PD]	Based on (PD)
8	35	28-Feb-00	60 Pric	73 Settl	86 Repc	99 Fore	212 Write documentation/			Help text		236 Project management [up to 1/2 day]		
	36	29-Feb-00	60 Pric	73 Settl	86 Repc	99 Fore	212 Write documentation/			Help text		236 Project management [up to 1/2 day]		
	37	1-Mar-00	60 Pric	73 Settl	86 Repc	99 Fore	212 Write documentation/			Help text		236 Project management [up to 1/2 day]		
	38	2-Mar-00	51 Indiv	51 Indiv	86 Repc	51 Indiv	212 Write documentation/			Help text		236 Project management [up to 1/2 day]		
9	39	3-Mar-00	52 Revi	52 Revi	52 Revi	52 Revi	212 Write documentation/			Help text	52 Revi	236 Project management [up to 1/2 day]		
	40	6-Mar-00	60 Pric	73 Settl	86 Repc	99 Fore	212 Write documentation/			Help text	53 Cha	236 Project management [up to 1/2 day]		
	41	7-Mar-00	60 Pric	73 Settl	86 Repc	99 Fore	212 Write documentation/			Help text	53 Cha	236 Project management [up to 1/2 day]		
	42	8-Mar-00	60 Pric	73 Settl	86 Repc	99 Fore	212 Write documentation/			53, 54 (	53, 54 (	236 Project management [up to 1/2 day]		
	43	9-Mar-00	55-57,	55-57, 5	86 Repc	99 Fore	212 Write documentation/			55-57 5	55-57 5	236 Project management [up to 1/2 day]		
10	44	10-Mar-00	60 Pric	73 Settl	86 Repc	99 Fore	212 Write documentation/			Help text		236 Project management [up to 1/2 day]		
	45	13-Mar-00	60 Pric	73 Settl	86 Repc	99 Fore	212 Write documentation/			Help text		236 Project management [up to 1/2 day]		
	46	14-Mar-00	151 Wc	170 Sec	138 Tut	99 Fore	212 Write documentation/			Help text		236 Project management [up to 1/2 day]		
	47	15-Mar-00	151 Wc	170 Sec	138 Tut	99 Fore	212 Write documentation/			Help text		236 Project management [up to 1/2 day]		
	48	16-Mar-00	151 Wc	170 Sec	138 Tut	99 Fore	212 Write documentation/			Help text		236 Project management [up to 1/2 day]		
11	49	17-Mar-00	151 Wc	170 Sec	138 Tut	99 Fore	212 Write documentation/			Help text		236 Project management [up to 1/2 day]		
	50	20-Mar-00	151 Wc	170 Sec	138 Tut	99 Fore	212 Write documentation/			Help text		236 Project management [up to 1/2 day]		
	51	21-Mar-00	151 Wc	170 Sec	138 Tut	99 Fore	212 Write documentation/			Help text		236 Project management [up to 1/2 day]		
	52	22-Mar-00	151 Wc	170 Sec	138 Tut	99 Fore	212 Write documentation/			Help text		236 Project management [up to 1/2 day]		
	53	23-Mar-00	151 Wc	170 Sec	138 Tut	99 Fore	212 Write documentation/			Help text		236 Project management [up to 1/2 day]		
12	54	24-Mar-00	151 Wc	170 Sec	138 Tut	112 Eur	212 Write documentation/			Help text		236 Project management [up to 1/2 day]		
	55	27-Mar-00	151 Wc	170 Sec	138 Tut	112 Eur	212 Write documentation/			Help text		236 Project management [up to 1/2 day]		
	56	28-Mar-00	151 Wc	170 Sec	138 Tut	112 Eur	212 Write documentation/			Help text		236 Project management [up to 1/2 day]		
	57	29-Mar-00	151 Wc	170 Sec	138 Tut	112 Eur	212 Write documentation/			Help text		236 Project management [up to 1/2 day]		
	58	30-Mar-00	151 Wc	170 Sec	138 Tut	112 Eur	212 Write documentation/			Help text		236 Project management [up to 1/2 day]		
13	59	31-Mar-00	151 Wc	170 Sec	138 Tut	112 Eur	212 Write documentation/			Help text		236 Project management [up to 1/2 day]		
	60	3-Apr-00	151 Wc	170 Sec	138 Tut	112 Eur	212 Write documentation/			Help text		236 Project management [up to 1/2 day]		
	61	4-Apr-00	151 Wc	170 Sec	138 Tut	112 Eur	212 Write documentation/			Help text		236 Project management [up to 1/2 day]		
	62	5-Apr-00	151 Wc	170 Sec	138 Tut	112 Eur	212 Write documentation/			Help text		236 Project management [up to 1/2 day]		
	63	6-Apr-00	151 Wc	170 Sec	138 Tut	112 Eur	212 Write documentation/			Help text		236 Project management [up to 1/2 day]		
14	64	7-Apr-00	151 Wc	170 Sec	189 Onl	112 Eur	212 Write documentation/			Help text		236 Project management [up to 1/2 day]		
	65	10-Apr-00	151 Wc	170 Sec	189 Onl	112 Eur	212 Write documentation/			Help text		236 Project management [up to 1/2 day]		
	66	11-Apr-00	151 Wc	170 Sec	189 Onl	112 Eur	212 Write documentation/			Help text		236 Project management [up to 1/2 day]		
	67	12-Apr-00	151 Wc	170 Sec	189 Onl	112 Eur	212 Write documentation/			Help text		236 Project management [up to 1/2 day]		
	68	13-Apr-00	151 Wc	170 Sec	189 Onl	112 Eur	212 Write documentation/			Help text		236 Project management [up to 1/2 day]		
	69	14-Apr-00	151 Wc	170 Sec	189 Onl	112 Eur	212 Write documentation/			Help text		236 Project management [up to 1/2 day]		

Figure 13.2 (continued)

Week #	Day #	Date	Charlie	Engineer #2	Engineer #3	Engineer #4	Technical author	Marketing people (3)	Anna	Tester #1	Tester #2	Project management	Actual Effort [PD]	Based on [PD]
15	70	17-Apr-00	151 Wc	170 Se	189 Onl	125 3rd	212 Write documentation / Help text					236 Project management [up to 1/2 day]		
	71	18-Apr-00	151 Wc	170 Se	189 Onl	125 3rd	212 Write documentation / Help text					236 Project management [up to 1/2 day]		
	72	19-Apr-00	151 Wc	170 Se	189 Onl	125 3rd	212 Write documentation / Help text					236 Project management [up to 1/2 day]		
	73	20-Apr-00	151 Wc	170 Se	189 Onl	125 3rd	212 Write documentation / Help text					236 Project management [up to 1/2 day]		
	74	21-Apr-00	151 Wc	170 Se	189 Onl	125 3rd	212 Write documentation / Help text					236 Project management [up to 1/2 day]		
16	75	24-Apr-00	151 Wc	170 Se	189 Onl	125 3rd	217 Edit documentation / Help text					236 Project management [up to 1/2 day]		
	76	25-Apr-00	151 Wc	170 Se	189 Onl	125 3rd	217 Edit documentation / Help text					236 Project management [up to 1/2 day]		
	77	26-Apr-00	151 Wc	170 Se	189 Onl	125 3rd	217 Edit documentation / Help text					236 Project management [up to 1/2 day]		
	78	27-Apr-00		189 Onl	189 Onl	125 3rd	217 Edit documentation / Help text					236 Project management [up to 1/2 day]		
	79	28-Apr-00		189 Onl	189 Onl	125 3rd	217 Edit documentation / Help text					236 Project management [up to 1/2 day]		
17	80	1-May-00	Vacati	189 Onl	189 Onl	125 3rd	217 Edit documentation / H			225 Te	225 Te	236 Project management [up to 1/2 day]		
	81	2-May-00	Vacati	189 Onl	189 Onl	125 3rd	217 Edit documentation / H			225 Te	225 Te	236 Project management [up to 1/2 day]		
	82	3-May-00	Vacati	189 Onl	189 Onl	125 3rd	217 Edit documentation / H			225 Te	225 Te	236 Project management [up to 1/2 day]		
	83	4-May-00	Vacati	189 Onl	189 Onl	125 3rd	217 Edit documentation / H			225 Te	225 Te	236 Project management [up to 1/2 day]		
	84	5-May-00	Vacati	189 Onl	189 Onl	125 3rd	217 Edit documentation / H			225 Te	225 Te	236 Project management [up to 1/2 day]		
18	85	8-May-00	Vacati	189 Onl	189 Onl	125 3rd	217 Edit documentation / H			225 Te	225 Te	236 Project management [up to 1/2 day]		
	86	9-May-00	Vacati	189 Online help	189 Onl	125 3rd	217 Edit documentation / H			225 Te	225 Te	236 Project management [up to 1/2 day]		
	87	10-May-00	Vacati	226 Te	226 Te	226 Te	217 Edit documentation / H			225 Te	225 Te	236 Project management [up to 1/2 day]		
	88	11-May-00	Vacati	226 Te	226 Te	226 Te	217 Edit documentation / H			225 Te	225 Te	236 Project management [up to 1/2 day]		
	89	12-May-00	Vacati	226 Te	226 Te	226 Te	217 Edit documentation / H			225 Te	225 Te	236 Project management [up to 1/2 day]		
19	90	15-May-00	226 Te	226 Te	226 Te	226 Te	217 Edit documentation / H			225 Te	225 Te	236 Project management [up to 1/2 day]		
	91	16-May-00	226 Te	226 Te	226 Te	226 Te	217 Edit documentation / H			225 Te	225 Te	236 Project management [up to 1/2 day]		
	92	17-May-00	226 Te	226 Te	226 Te	226 Te	217 Edit documentation / H			225 Te	225 Te	236 Project management [up to 1/2 day]		
	93	18-May-00					217 Edit documentation / H			228 Te	228 Te	236 Project management [up to 1/2 day]		
	94	19-May-00					217 Edit documentation / H			228 Te	228 Te	236 Project management [up to 1/2 day]		
20	95	22-May-00					217 Edit documentation / H			228 Te	228 Te	236 Project management [up to 1/2 day]		
	96	23-May-00	229 Te	229 Te	229 Te	229 Te	221 Final integration of Online Help			228 Te	228 Te	236 Project management [up to 1/2 day]		
	97	24-May-00	229 Te	229 Te	229 Te	229 Te	221 Final integration of Online Help					236 Project management [up to 1/2 day]		
	98	25-May-00	229 Te	229 Te	229 Te	229 Te	221 Final integration of Online Help					236 Project management [up to 1/2 day]		
	99	26-May-00	229 Te	229 Te	229 Te	229 Te	221 Final integration of Onl			231 Te	231 Te	236 Project management [up to 1/2 day]		
21	100	29-May-00					221 Final integration of Onl			231 Te	231 Te	236 Project management [up to 1/2 day]		
	101	30-May-00	232 Te	232 Te	232 Te	232 Test #3 - make corrections						236 Project management [up to 1/2 day]		
	102	31-May-00	232 Te	232 Te	232 Te	232 Test #3 - make corrections			233 Finalize tes			236 Project management [up to 1/2 day]		
	103	1-Jun-00					222 Final pre-production of manuals					236 Project management [up to 1/2 day]		
	104	2-Jun-00					222 Final pre-production of manuals					236 Project management [up to 1/2 day]		

Figure 13.2 (continued)

Week #	Day #	Date	Charlie	Engineer #2	Engineer #3	Engineer #4	Technical author	Marketing people (3)	Anna	Tester #1	Tester #2	Project management	Actual Effort (PD)	Based on (PD)
22	105	5-Jun-00	235 En|	235 En|	235 En|	235 En|	235 End of project review		235 End of project review	235 En|	235 En|	236 Project management [up to 1/2 day]		
	106	6-Jun-00	237 Contingency									236 Project management [up to 1/2 day]		
	113	7-Jun-00	237 Contingency									236 Project management [up to 1/2 day]		
	114	8-Jun-00	237 Contingency									236 Project management [up to 1/2 day]		
	115	9-Jun-00	237 Contingency									236 Project management [up to 1/2 day]		
23	116	12-Jun-00	237 Contingency									236 Project management [up to 1/2 day]		
	117	13-Jun-00	237 Contingency									236 Project management [up to 1/2 day]		
	118	14-Jun-00	237 Contingency									236 Project management [up to 1/2 day]		
	119	15-Jun-00	237 Contingency									236 Project management [up to 1/2 day]		
	120	16-Jun-00	237 Contingency									236 Project management [up to 1/2 day]		
24	121	19-Jun-00	237 Contingency									236 Project management [up to 1/2 day]		
	122	20-Jun-00	237 Contingency									236 Project management [up to 1/2 day]		
	123	21-Jun-00	237 Contingency									236 Project management [up to 1/2 day]		
	124	22-Jun-00	237 Contingency									236 Project management [up to 1/2 day]		
	125	23-Jun-00	237 Contingency									236 Project management [up to 1/2 day]		
25	126	26-Jun-00	Public holiday									236 Project management [up to 1/2 day]		
	127	27-Jun-00	Public holiday									236 Project management [up to 1/2 day]		
	128	28-Jun-00	Public holiday									236 Project management [up to 1/2 day]		
	129	29-Jun-00	Public holiday									236 Project management [up to 1/2 day]		
	130	30-Jun-00	Public holiday									236 Project management [up to 1/2 day]		
	131	3-Jul-00												
	132	4-Jul-00												
	133	5-Jul-00												
	134	6-Jul-00												
	135	7-Jul-00												
	136	10-Jul-00												
	137	11-Jul-00												
	138	12-Jul-00												
	139	13-Jul-00												
	140	14-Jul-00												
	141	17-Jul-00												

Figure 13.2 (continued)

Figure 13.3   Promised
versus requested
deadline.

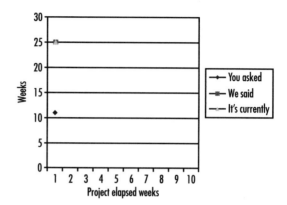

Figure 13.3   Promised versus requested deadline.

didn't trust him. But you still just want to check that there's no confusion. Charlie is hot to trot. It's only him on the project this week. Your parting words are that if he can find any way to peel a day off it, it'd be great. Having planted this seed, you both finish up your muffins and go about your business.

Mid-afternoon on Friday you check in on Charlie and he says he's doing "fine." Based on that you issue an "all quiet on the Western Front" sort of status report—status Green, everything on target. The status report, the Friday afternoon chat, and the coffee with Charlie has been about the extent of your project management this week. You call it half a day on your timesheet on the basis that there is no smaller unit of work.

Week 3

Charlie is grinning from ear to ear when you meet him on Monday. He got on a roll, he tells you, and worked the weekend. The result is that the requirements document is finished *a full 6 days* ahead of schedule. You could kiss him—except for the sexual harassment laws. Instead you treat him to a triple espresso and arrange to buy him lunch later that day. As soon as you get back to your desk, you find Anna and she starts to distribute the document. (Because this is the 21st Century, Charlie has already e-mailed the document to everybody. He did this around midnight on Sunday night—part of him was showing off! Anna's job though, is to make sure everybody got it and that nobody plays the "I never got that e-mail" game.) Now you've got to start some serious project management. You've got some rearranging to do. Otherwise, the value of Charlie's noble effort will be lost. And that could be worse than if he'd never done it in the first place.

You go to your strip board, and pull the phone nearer to you. It takes you most of the day to sort things out. The result you get for your efforts is this. Marketing agrees to review the document and hold the review meeting tomorrow, Tuesday, instead of a week from now. They give you a lot of grief for this. They have other meetings tomorrow that you and Anna end up having to rearrange for them. Of course it's not your job, but you stand to make a big saving on this—that's why it's worth the effort. Just how big a saving it is you don't know—you haven't had time to figure out yet. And you may well have more legwork to do before you can fully exploit those savings. But one thing at a time.

What you actually persuade Marketing to do is to bring forward all of their tasks related to the requirements document. You do this by vaguely implying that you had met the CEO (you didn't) and had told him that there was the potential to save a week on the project, if Marketing can "rearrange their schedules a bit." The upside of this is that Marketing suddenly becomes as submissive as a dog on its back with its paws in the air. The downside is that now you're going to have to make some reference to this in this week's status report. You return to your strip board.

The problem is crystal clear and is shown in Figure 13.4.

If you can get everyone (i.e., the two other engineers and technical writer) on the project a week sooner, you will have saved a week. If not, it'll all have been for nothing.

It ends up you manage to get nothing and nobody early. Discussing it with Charlie, he assures you it's enough. He'll get the prototype rolling by himself. Ted, the tech. writer, just can't get off the project he's completing. Over a separate coffee, you show him the strip board, and the effect that could have been achieved if he had come on a week sooner. Ted looks you in the eye, and says that you can cut a week off his schedule and he'll still deliver. "You sure, Ted?" you ask uncertainly. He nods. (If Ted were in a Western movie, he'd be the strong silent type.) You extend your hand and say "deal." He clasps it in a bone-crushing handshake that causes your fingers to crunch.

Your status report on Friday looks like the one in Figure 13.5. You resolve to give up coffee.

Week 4

Charlie turns in another barnstorming week, and builds the first cut of the prototype by himself, reviews it with Marketing and does the second

2.5 + (3 x 1/2)

Week	Day	Date	Charlie	Engineer #2	Engineer #3	Engineer #4	Technical author	Marketing people (3)	Anna	Tester #1	Tester #2	Project management	Actual Effort (PD)	Based on (PD)
1	1	11-Jan-00	Projec	Project	Project	Project	Project	Project	Project	Project	Project	Project kickoff	5.5	9 x 1/2 + 1 Proj. Mgmt.
	2	12-Jan-00	6 Gantt										2.5	1 + (3 x 1/2)
	3	13-Jan-00	9 Prepare user questionnaires					8 Identify users	10 Distribute user questionnaires				4	1 + 3
	4	14-Jan-00	7 Review competitive info with Marketir					7 Review with Marketing				236 Project management [up to 1/2 day]	4.5	1 + 3 + 1/2 PD Proj. Mgmt
2	5	17-Jan-00	12 Analyze information						11 Retrieve questionnaires				1.5	1.5 + 0.5
	6	18-Jan-00	13 Write requirements document										1	
	7	19-Jan-00	13 Write requirements document										1	
	8	20-Jan-00	13 Write requirements document										1	
	9	21-Jan-00	13 Write requirements document									236 Project management [up to 1/2 day]	1	
3	10	24-Jan-00							15 Circulate document			236 Project management [up to 1/2 day]	3.5	1(Fri) + 2(Weekend)+0.5 Proj. Mgmt.
	11	25-Jan-00	17,18 Review meeting / changes to doc						16, 17 Individual review [1/2 day]			236 Project management [up to 1/2 day]	1.5	0.5 + 1 Proj. Mgmt.
	12	26-Jan-00	18 Changes to document									236 Project management [up to 1/2 day]		
	13	27-Jan-00	18,19 Changes to document (inc. circulate again)									236 Project management [up to 1/2 day]		
	14	28-Jan-00	20-22 Second review / Signoff / Reqs c	20-22 Se					20-22 Second review again			236 Project management [up to 1/2 day]		
4	15	31-Jan-00										236 Project management [up to 1/2 day]		
	16	1-Feb-00										236 Project management [up to 1/2 day]		
	17	2-Feb-00										236 Project management [up to 1/2 day]		
	18	3-Feb-00										236 Project management [up to 1/2 day]		
	19	4-Feb-00										236 Project management [up to 1/2 day]		
5	20	7-Feb-00	58 Pro	58 Prot	58 Prot	58 Prototype	209 Research tech. writir			24 Research i		236 Project management [up to 1/2 day]		
	21	8-Feb-00	58 Pro	58 Prot	58 Prot	58 Prototype	209 Research tech. writir			24 Research i		236 Project management [up to 1/2 day]		
	22	9-Feb-00	58 Pro	58 Prot	58 Prot	58 Prototype	209 Research tech. writir			24 Research i		236 Project management [up to 1/2 day]		
	23	10-Feb-00	58 Pro	58 Prot	58 Prot	58 Prototype	209 Research tech. writir			24 Research i		236 Project management [up to 1/2 day]		
	24	11-Feb-00	58 Pro	58 Prot	58 Prot	58 Prototype	209 Research tech. writir			24 Research i		236 Project management [up to 1/2 day]		
6	25	14-Feb-00	58 Pro	58 Prot	58 Prot	58 Prototype	210 Set up environment			25 Wri	37 Wri	236 Project management [up to 1/2 day]		
	26	15-Feb-00	58 Pro	58 Prot	58 Prot	58 Prototype	210 Set up environment			25 Wri	37 Wri	236 Project management [up to 1/2 day]		
	27	16-Feb-00	58 Pro	58 Prot	58 Prot	58 Prototype	210 Set up environment			25 Wri	37 Wri	236 Project management [up to 1/2 day]		
	28	17-Feb-00	58 Pro	58 Prot	58 Prot	58 Prototype	210 Set up environment			29 Wri	41 Wri	236 Project management [up to 1/2 day]		
	29	18-Feb-00	58 Pro	58 Prot	58 Prot	58 Prototype	210 Set up environment			29 Wri	41 Wri	236 Project management [up to 1/2 day]		
7	30	21-Feb-00	58 Pro	58 Prot	58 Prot	58 Prototype	211 Define style sheet &			33 Wri	45 Wri	236 Project management [up to 1/2 day]		
	31	22-Feb-00	58 Pro	58 Prot	58 Prot	58 Prototype	211 Define style sheet &			33 Wri	45 Wri	236 Project management [up to 1/2 day]		
	32	23-Feb-00	58, 60,	58 Prot	58 Prot	58 Prototype	211 Define style sheet &			33 Wri	45 Wri	236 Project management [up to 1/2 day]		
	33	24-Feb-00	58 Pro	58 Prot	58 Prot	58 Prototype	211 Define style sheet &			33 Wri	45 Wri	236 Project management [up to 1/2 day]		
	34	25-Feb-00	58 Pro	58 Prot	58 Prot	58 Prototype	211 Define style			50 Circulate all Tests		236 Project management [up to 1/2 day]		
8	35	28-Feb-00	60 Pric	73 Sett	86 Rep	99 Forc	212 Write documentation / Help text					236 Project management [up to 1/2 day]		
	36	29-Feb-00	60 Pric	73 Sett	86 Rep	99 Forc	212 Write documentation / Help text					236 Project management [up to 1/2 day]		
	37	1-Mar-00	60 Pric	73 Sett	86 Rep	99 Forc	212 Write text					236 Project management [up to 1/2 day]		
	38	2-Mar-00	51 Indi	51 Indi	51 Indi		212 Write text / Help text					236 Project management [up to 1/2 day]		
	39	3-Mar-00	52 Rev	52 Rev	52 Rev	52 Rev	212 Write documentation					236 Project management [up to 1/2 day]		

Figure 13.4 Strip board at Week 3.

Week	Day # Date	Charlie	Engineer #2	Engineer #3	Engineer #4	Technical author	Marketing people (3)	Anna	Tester #1	Tester #2	Project management	Actual Effort (PD)	Based on (PD)
9	40 6-Mar-00	60 Prid	73 Set	86 Rep	99 For	212 Write documentation			53 Ch	53 Ch	236 Project management [up to 1/2 day]		
	41 7-Mar-00	60 Prid	73 Set	86 Rep	99 For	212 Write documentation			53 Ch	53 Ch	236 Project management [up to 1/2 day]		
	42 8-Mar-00	60 Prid	73 Set	86 Rep	99 For	212 Write documentation			53, 54	53, 54	236 Project management [up to 1/2 day]		
	43 9-Mar-00	55-57	55-57	55-57	99 For	212 Write documentation			55-57	55-57	236 Project management [up to 1/2 day]		
	44 10-Mar-00	60 Prid	73 Set	86 Rep	99 For	212 Write documentation					236 Project management [up to 1/2 day]		
10	45 13-Mar-00	151 W	170 Se	138 Tu	99 For	212 Write documentation / Help text					236 Project management [up to 1/2 day]		
	46 14-Mar-00	151 W	170 Se	138 Tu	99 For	212 Write documentation / Help text					236 Project management [up to 1/2 day]		
	47 15-Mar-00	151 W	170 Se	138 Tu	99 For	212 Write documentation / Help text					236 Project management [up to 1/2 day]		
	48 16-Mar-00	151 W	170 Se	138 Tu	99 For	212 Write documentation / Help text					236 Project management [up to 1/2 day]		
	49 17-Mar-00	151 W	170 Se	138 Tu	99 For	212 Write documentation / Help text					236 Project management [up to 1/2 day]		
11	50 20-Mar-00	151 W	170 Se	138 Tu	112 Eu	212 Write documentation / Help text					236 Project management [up to 1/2 day]		
	51 21-Mar-00	151 W	170 Se	138 Tu	112 Eu	212 Write documentation / Help text					236 Project management [up to 1/2 day]		
	52 22-Mar-00	151 W	170 Se	138 Tu	112 Eu	212 Write documentation / Help text					236 Project management [up to 1/2 day]		
	53 23-Mar-00	151 W	170 Se	138 Tu	112 Eu	212 Write documentation / Help text					236 Project management [up to 1/2 day]		
	54 24-Mar-00	151 W	170 Se	138 Tu	112 Eu	212 Write documentation / Help text					236 Project management [up to 1/2 day]		
12	55 27-Mar-00	151 W	170 Se	138 Tu	112 Eu	212 Write documentation / Help text					236 Project management [up to 1/2 day]		
	56 28-Mar-00	151 W	170 Se	138 Tu	112 Eu	212 Write documentation / Help text					236 Project management [up to 1/2 day]		
	57 29-Mar-00	151 W	170 Se	138 Tu	112 Eu	212 Write documentation / Help text					236 Project management [up to 1/2 day]		
	58 30-Mar-00	151 W	170 Se	138 Tu	112 Eu	212 Write documentation / Help text					236 Project management [up to 1/2 day]		
	59 31-Mar-00	151 W	170 Se	138 Tu	112 Eu	212 Write documentation / Help text					236 Project management [up to 1/2 day]		
13	60 3-Apr-00	151 W	170 Se	138 Tu	112 Eu	212 Write documentation / Help text					236 Project management [up to 1/2 day]		
	61 4-Apr-00	151 W	170 Se	138 Tu	112 Eu	212 Write documentation / Help text					236 Project management [up to 1/2 day]		
	62 5-Apr-00	151 W	170 Se	138 Tu	112 Eu	212 Write documentation / Help text					236 Project management [up to 1/2 day]		
	63 6-Apr-00	151 W	170 Se	138 Tu	112 Eu	212 Write documentation / Help text					236 Project management [up to 1/2 day]		
	64 7-Apr-00	151 W	170 Se	138 Tu	112 Eu	212 Write documentation / Help text					236 Project management [up to 1/2 day]		
14	65 10-Apr-00	151 W	170 Se	189 Or	112 Eu	212 Write documentation / Help text					236 Project management [up to 1/2 day]		
	66 11-Apr-00	151 W	170 Se	189 Or	112 Eu	212 Write documentation / Help text					236 Project management [up to 1/2 day]		
	67 12-Apr-00	151 W	170 Se	189 Or	112 Eu	212 Write documentation / Help text					236 Project management [up to 1/2 day]		
	68 13-Apr-00	151 W	170 Se	189 Or	112 Eu	212 Write documentation / Help text					236 Project management [up to 1/2 day]		
	69 14-Apr-00	151 W	170 Se	189 Or	112 Eu	212 Write documentation / Help text					236 Project management [up to 1/2 day]		
15	70 17-Apr-00	151 W	170 Se	189 Or	112 Eu	212 Write documentation / Help text					236 Project management [up to 1/2 day]		
	71 18-Apr-00	151 W	170 Se	189 Or	112 Eu	212 Write documentation / Help text					236 Project management [up to 1/2 day]		
	72 19-Apr-00	151 W	170 Se	189 Or	112 Eu	212 Write documentation / Help text					236 Project management [up to 1/2 day]		
	73 20-Apr-00	151 W	170 Se	189 Or	112 Eu	212 Write documentation / Help text					236 Project management [up to 1/2 day]		
	74 21-Apr-00	151 W	170 Se	189 Or	112 Eu	212 Write documentation / Help text					236 Project management [up to 1/2 day]		
16	75 24-Apr-00	151 W	170 Se	189 Or	125 3c	217 Edit documentation / Help text					236 Project management [up to 1/2 day]		
	76 25-Apr-00	151 W	170 Se	189 Or	125 3c	217 Edit documentation / Help text					236 Project management [up to 1/2 day]		
	77 26-Apr-00	151 W	170 Se	189 Or	125 3c	217 Edit documentation / Help text					236 Project management [up to 1/2 day]		
	78 27-Apr-00		189 Or	189 Or	125 3c	217 Edit documentation / Help text					236 Project management [up to 1/2 day]		
	79 28-Apr-00		189 Or	189 Or	125 3c	217 Edit documentation / Help text					236 Project management [up to 1/2 day]		

Figure 13.4   (continued)

Week	Day	Date	Charlie	Engineer #2	Engineer #3	Engineer #4	Technical author	Marketing people (3)	Anna	Tester #1	Tester #2	Project management	Actual Effort (PD)	Based on (PD)
17	80	1-May-00	Vacati	189 Or		125 3rd	217 Edit documentation			225 Te	225 Te	236 Project management [up to 1/2 day]		
	81	2-May-00	Vacati	189 Or		125 3rd	217 Edit documentation			225 Te	225 Te	236 Project management [up to 1/2 day]		
	82	3-May-00	Vacati	189 Or		125 3rd	217 Edit documentation			225 Te	225 Te	236 Project management [up to 1/2 day]		
	83	4-May-00	Vacati	189 Or		125 3rd	217 Edit documentation			225 Te	225 Te	236 Project management [up to 1/2 day]		
	84	5-May-00	Vacati	189 Or		125 3rd	217 Edit documentation			225 Te	225 Te	236 Project management [up to 1/2 day]		
18	85	8-May-00	Vacati	189 Or		125 3rd	217 Edit documentation			225 Te	225 Te	236 Project management [up to 1/2 day]		
	86	9-May-00	Vacati	189 Online help			217 Edit documentation			225 Te	225 Te	236 Project management [up to 1/2 day]		
	87	10-May-00	Vacati	226 Te	226 Te	226 Te	217 Edit documentation			225 Te	225 Te	236 Project management [up to 1/2 day]		
	88	11-May-00	Vacati	226 Te	226 Te	226 Te	217 Edit documentation			225 Te	225 Te	236 Project management [up to 1/2 day]		
	89	12-May-00	Vacati	226 Te	226 Te	226 Te	217 Edit documentation			225 Te	225 Te	236 Project management [up to 1/2 day]		
19	90	15-May-00	226 Te	226 Te		226 Te	217 Edit documentation			225 Te	225 Te	236 Project management [up to 1/2 day]		
	91	16-May-00	226 Te	226 Te		226 Te	217 Edit documentation			225 Te	225 Te	236 Project management [up to 1/2 day]		
	92	17-May-00	226 Te	226 Te		226 Te	217 Edit documentation			225 Te	225 Te	236 Project management [up to 1/2 day]		
	93	18-May-00					217 Edit documentation			228 Te	228 Te	236 Project management [up to 1/2 day]		
	94	19-May-00					217 Edit documentation			228 Te	228 Te	236 Project management [up to 1/2 day]		
20	95	22-May-00					217 Edit documentation			228 Te	228 Te	236 Project management [up to 1/2 day]		
	96	23-May-00	229 Te	229 Te		229 Te	221 Final integration of Online Help			228 Te	228 Te	236 Project management [up to 1/2 day]		
	97	24-May-00	229 Te	229 Te		229 Te	221 Final integration of Online Help			228 Te	228 Te	236 Project management [up to 1/2 day]		
	98	25-May-00	229 Te	229 Te		229 Te	221 Final integration of Online Help			228 Te	228 Te	236 Project management [up to 1/2 day]		
	99	26-May-00					221 Final integration of C			231 Te	231 Te	236 Project management [up to 1/2 day]		
21	100	29-May-00					221 Final integration of C			231 Te	231 Te	236 Project management [up to 1/2 day]		
	101	30-May-00	232 Te			232 Te	232 Test #3 - make corrections			231 Te	231 Te	236 Project management [up to 1/2 day]		
	102	31-May-00					222 Final pre-production		233 Finalise te			236 Project management [up to 1/2 day]		
	103	1-Jun-00					222 Final pre-production of manuals					236 Project management [up to 1/2 day]		
	104	2-Jun-00					222 Final pre-production of manuals					236 Project management [up to 1/2 day]		
22	105	5-Jun-00	235 En			235 En	235 End of project review			235 Er		236 Project management [up to 1/2 day]		
	106	6-Jun-00	237 Contingency									236 Project management [up to 1/2 day]		
	113	7-Jun-00	237 Contingency									236 Project management [up to 1/2 day]		
	114	8-Jun-00	237 Contingency									236 Project management [up to 1/2 day]		
	115	9-Jun-00	237 Contingency									236 Project management [up to 1/2 day]		
23	116	12-Jun-00	237 Contingency									236 Project management [up to 1/2 day]		
	117	13-Jun-00	237 Contingency									236 Project management [up to 1/2 day]		
	118	14-Jun-00	237 Contingency									236 Project management [up to 1/2 day]		
	119	15-Jun-00	237 Contingency									236 Project management [up to 1/2 day]		
	120	16-Jun-00	237 Contingency									236 Project management [up to 1/2 day]		

Figure 13.4   (continued)

Week #	Day #	Date	Charlie	Engineer #2	Engineer #3	Engineer #4	Technical author	Marketing people (3)	Anna	Tester #1	Tester #2	Project management	Actual Effort (PD)	Based on (PD)
25	126	26-Jun-00	Public holiday									236 Project management [up to 1/2 day]		
	127	27-Jun-00	Public holiday									236 Project management [up to 1/2 day]		
	128	28-Jun-00	Public holiday									236 Project management [up to 1/2 day]		
	129	29-Jun-00	Public holiday									236 Project management [up to 1/2 day]		
	130	30-Jun-00	Public holiday									236 Project management [up to 1/2 day]	24.5	
	131	3-Jul-00												
	132	4-Jul-00												
	133	5-Jul-00												
	134	6-Jul-00												
	135	7-Jul-00												
	136	10-Jul-00												
	137	11-Jul-00												
	138	12-Jul-00												
	139	13-Jul-00												
	140	14-Jul-00												
	141	17-Jul-00												
	142	18-Jul-00												
	143	19-Jul-00												
	144	20-Jul-00												
	145	21-Jul-00												
	146	24-Jul-00												
	147	25-Jul-00												
	148	26-Jul-00												
	149	27-Jul-00												
		28-Jul-00												
		31-Jul-00												
		1-Aug-00												
		2-Aug-00												
		3-Aug-00												
		4-Aug-00												
		7-Aug-00												
		8-Aug-00												
		9-Aug-00												
		10-Aug-00												
		11-Aug-00												

Figure 13.4 (continued)

Figure 13.5   Status
report at Week 3.

The project is slightly ahead of target for delivery of Beta units on 30 June. Status is Green.
An up to date schedule for the project is attached. (You attach the strip board.)

Delivery Date—Change History

Date	Reason for change	Revised date
11 Jan	Original date committed to	30 Jun
28 Jan	Shortened time to write requirements doc.	23 Jun

The date you asked for: 25 March
The earliest date we said was possible: 30 June
The date we're showing today: 23 June

cut. Thus, the prototype remains on target. (It takes another of Charlie's weekends. You tell him how grateful you are. He shrugs it off.) You spend a reasonable amount of time this week ensuring that everything is set for next week, when lots of people (Engineers #2 and #3, Ted and Tester #1) are due to join your project. You status report as always. No change to 23 June.

Week 5

First thing Monday morning, you meet with your massively increased team. You again run through with them what has to be done each day and make sure everyone's clear. Friday afternoon, as you gather the data for the status report, you find out that it all panned out exactly like you predicted. A nice week. You feel great. You're down to six cups of coffee a day—even if, on Fridays, they're all large espressos.

Week 6

Monday morning, disaster strikes. An exposure 9 risk goes live. And not just any old exposure 9 risk. An ashen-faced Charlie comes into your office and opens the conversation with "A friend of mine works for a new dot.com startup." He doesn't have to say any more. You're hardly aware of anything he says after that. Charlie will be gone later today.

Not only is that what he wants, it's your company's policy. You ask Charlie not to say anything until you've had a chance to tell everybody. He nods, says he's sorry, and goes out. You stare out the window into the parking lot where the CEO is getting out of his Porsche. He looks very grumpy. You wonder momentarily whether Charlie's friend's company is looking for burnt out project managers. You decide it probably isn't.

You go to the bathroom to think in peace. On your way there you pass down a corridor with a series of framed photographs lining the wall. They are pretty pictures with inspirational messages on them about things like success and teamwork. You've passed them a thousand times before and never paid much attention to them. You find them a bit mawkish. But this time one catches your eye. It's about determination. It's a quote from Calvin Coolidge.

"Press on," it says. "Nothing in the world can take the place of persistence. Talent will not: nothing is more common than unsuccessful men with talent. Genius will not: unrewarded genius is almost a proverb. Education will not: the world is full of educated derelicts. Persistence and determination alone are omnipotent."

Sitting in the bathroom you ponder all of this. Engineer #2 will take over from Charlie. If Engineers #2 and #3 could work some late hours, then they might keep the prototype on schedule, and so enable Engineering to meet the "bookings" they made with Marketing for reviews during the building of the prototype. Ted and the Testers are OK. You'll have to find another engineer. A contractor? Does HR have any resumes? You'll have to go see.

Of course, the other huge concern is that there'll be a stampede— that Charlie won't be the only one who goes to the new dot.com startup. Or even if people don't go there they'll go some placeelse. You'll have to tell them pretty damn quick. Okay, so what's the plan?

You leave the bathroom and start by telling Engineer #2 that he's about to have greatness thrust on him. Engineer #2 who, now that he's about to achieve a starring role in our story, had better get a real name, is called Albert. You point out what a career opportunity it is, to end up being the guy who delivered the Killer product. You're unsure whether this cuts any ice. Albert is just not in the same league as Charlie, even if his heart is in the right place—which you're unsure about anyway.

You call the Monday meeting. You tell them that Charlie's leaving, about Albert's new role, and about getting resumes. There's a flurry of panic. They point out that, generally, it takes at least three months to hire somebody, from the moment you make a decision to go look. Even normally solid Ted gives the impression of a man who's suddenly realized he's on a sinking ship. You do your best to reassure them.

Then you go through the normal "does everyone know what they're doing every day this week" thing. It's a muted exercise, unlike previous weeks when everybody had a feeling they were on a real winner. When you're finished, you simply say this: "I don't know if we can make this happen or not. The odds are against us now. We have a plan and all we can do is try to stick to that. Every day that passes that we stay on target, is a day closer to the end. Sure it takes three months to hire somebody. Sure Charlie was a good engineer. But you're *all* good at what you do. You know the targets for the week. Let's just see if we can achieve those and I'll see if I can track down a replacement. As always, let's keep looking for ways to shorten this thing. If nothing else, they may help to stop it taking any longer than our plan says."

As you leave the room you're unsure if any of this had any effect. You go and tell your boss who freaks and Marketing who also freak—though not quite as flamboyantly as your boss. HR gives you some resumes, but Helen in HR isn't very hopeful. "You know what the market's like," she sighs.

Come Friday, Albert and Engineer #3 have managed to keep the prototype on target. They have burnt some midnight oil to do it, and seem to be looking at you reproachfully every time you see them. Aside from this, you note that their completing on time means that the estimates for the prototype were reasonably accurate, which is somewhat reassuring. Ted and the testers are okay. Incredibly, it's still on target.

But you know that the problem comes next week when coding is due to start. Engineer #4 joins, but there just won't be enough people to shift the volume of work required. There are 184 days coding work. With four engineers it was going to take a little over 9 weeks. With three it'll take an additional three weeks or so. That would eat up 10 out of your 14 days contingency plus the week you saved, and would essentially return you to your 30 June date. The alternative is the whole business of hiring somebody else, even a contractor, and getting him or her up to speed so that they become productive. It's a lousy choice.

Momentarily, you brighten up when you realize that what's happened with Charlie leaving is a change control event. You'd be within your rights to go back to the powers that be, point this out to them, and say you've got to revise the plan and end date. Sure. And pigs might fly! Your momentary brightness passes.

You've got to make a decision, and so you do. You go for the three-engineer solution plus you'll begin recruitment anyway, in case somebody else leaves. Your rationale is that this removes uncertainty from the team that—in your judgment—is what they need more than anything else right now.

Are you right? You haven't a clue. It seems to you that things like this are an inexact science. Anyway, the decision is made now. You go to inform the team. In your status report, you record green / on target for 30 June, but note the serious implications of Charlie's having left. You say something to the effect that you don't know if the contingency will be enough to deal with this. If nothing else, this serves to remind everybody about the importance of contingency, and is a satisfying dig at those people who wanted to remove it.

Week 7

You decide that for the present you won't change the running order of the coding. Your theme of "business as usual without Charlie" seems to be a good one. You get the occasional vibe that the team are feeling it too, that a life without Charlie is possible. You'll see if you can't build more on this embryonic confidence.

You set the targets on Monday as always, and on Friday you report. This is what you discover.[2] Everything the strip board (see Figure 13.6) said would get done gets done. Another week on target for 30 June, you report amazedly.

Week 8

It's all seems to have been too good to be true since Charlie's departure, but the chickens start coming home to roost this week. Albert reports that Settlement, which was meant to take 8 days, is going to take 10. But the big problems occur in Reporting and Foreign exchange which now

---

2   Perhaps I should have said before now, how the story of this project unfolded. I didn't have the story fixed in my head before I started to write the chapter. Rather, in order to try to provide a realistic simulation of life, I used a dice when I came to any decision point in the story. I rolled the dice and depending on what number came up, acted according to the following scheme:
    1 = Got a lucky break on the project;
    2 or 3 = Things happened according to plan;
    4 or 5 = Things went a little bit awry;
    6 = Disaster.

Week	Day	Date	Charlie	Engineer #2	Engineer #3	Engineer #4	Technical author	Marketing people (3)	Anna	Tester #1	Tester #2	Project management	Actual Effort (PD)	Based on (PD)	Total this week
1	1	11-Jan-00	Project Project Project Project Project Project Project Project kickoff										5.5	9 x 1/2 + 1 Proj. Mgmt.	16
	2	12-Jan-00	6 Gatr										2.5	1 + (3 x 1/2)	
	3	13-Jan-00	9 Prepare user questionnaires					8 Identify users					4	1 + 3	
	4	14-Jan-00	7 Review competitive info with Marketir					7 Review with Marketing	10 Distribute user questionnaires			236 Project management [up to 1/2 day]	4.5	1 + 3 + 1/2 PD Proj.	
2	5	17-Jan-00	12 Analyse information						11 Retrieve questionnaires			236 Project management [up to 1/2 day]	1.5	1 + 0.5	
	6	18-Jan-00	13 Write requirements document										1	1	
	7	19-Jan-00	13 Write requirements document										1	1	
	8	20-Jan-00	13 Write requirements document										1	1	
	9	21-Jan-00	13 Write requirements document									236 Project management [up to 1/2 day]	3.5	1 (Fri) + 2 (Weekend	7.5
3	10	24-Jan-00	58 Prototype					15 Circulate document				236 Project management [up to 1/2 day]	2.5	1 + 0.5 + 1 Proj. Mgmt.	
	11	25-Jan-00	58 Prototype					17,18 Review meeting/ changes to dox	16, 17 Individual review [1/2 day			236 Project management [up to 1/2 day]	4.5	1 + 3 + 0.5 PM	
	12	26-Jan-00	58 Prototype					18 Changes to document				236 Project management [up to 1/2 day]	1.5	1 + 0.5 PM	
	13	27-Jan-00	58 Prototype					18,19 Changes to document (inc. circulate agair	15 Circulate document			236 Project management [up to 1/2 day]	2	1 + 0.5 + 0.5 PM	
	14	28-Jan-00	58 Prototype					20-22 Second review / Signoff / Reqs c	20-22 Se	20-22 Second review/		236 Project management [up to 1/2 day]	3	0.5 + 1.5 + 0.5 + 0.5	13.5
4	15	31-Jan-00	58 Prototype									236 Project management [up to 1/2 day]	1.5	1 + 0.5	
	16	1-Feb-00	58 Prototype										1	1	
	17	2-Feb-00	58 Prototype									236 Project management [up to 1/2 day]	1.5	1 + 0.5	
	18	3-Feb-00	58 Prototype										1	1	
	19	4-Feb-00	58 Prototype									236 Project management [up to 1/2 day]	3	1 (Fri) + 2 (Weekend	8.5
5	20	7-Feb-00	58 Pro	58 Prot	58 Prot	58 Prot	209 Research tech. writir		24 Research			236 Project management [up to 1/2 day]	5.5	5 + 0.5 PM	
	21	8-Feb-00	58 Pro	58 Prot	58 Prot	58 Prot	209 Research tech. writir		24 Research			236 Project management [up to 1/2 day]	5.5	5 + 0.5 PM	
	22	9-Feb-00	58 Pro	58 Prot	58 Prot	58 Prot	210 Set up environment		24 Research			236 Project management [up to 1/2 day]	5.5	5 + 0.5 PM	
	23	10-Feb-00	58 Pro	58 Prot	58 Prot	58 Prot	210 Set up environment		24 Research			236 Project management [up to 1/2 day]	5.5	5 + 0.5 PM	
	24	11-Feb-00	58 Pro	58 Prot	58 Prot	58 Prot	210 Set up environment		24 Research			236 Project management [up to 1/2 day]	5.5	5 + 0.5 PM	27.5
6	25	14-Feb-00		58 Prot	58 Prot	58 Prot	211 Define style sheet &		25 Wri	37 Wri		236 Project management [up to 1/2 day]	5.5	5 + 0.5 PM	
	26	15-Feb-00		58 Prot	58 Prot	58 Prot	211 Define style sheet &		25 Wri	37 Wri		236 Project management [up to 1/2 day]	5.5	5 + 0.5 PM	
	27	16-Feb-00		58 Prot	58 Prot	58 Prot	211 Define style sheet &		25 Wri	37 Wri		236 Project management [up to 1/2 day]	5.5	5 + 0.5 PM	
	28	17-Feb-00		58 Prot	58 Prot	58 Prot	211 Define style sheet &		29 Wri	41 Wri		236 Project management [up to 1/2 day]	5.5	5 + 0.5 PM	
	29	18-Feb-00		58 Prot	58 Prot	58 Prot	211 Define style	50 Circ	29 Wri	41 Wri		236 Project management [up to 1/2 day]	5.5	5 + 0.5 PM	27.5
7	30	21-Feb-00	60 Pric	73 Set	86 Rep	99 Forc	212 Write documentation		29 Wri	41 Wri		236 Project management [up to 1/2 day]	6.5	6 + 0.5 PM	
	31	22-Feb-00	60 Pric	73 Set	86 Rep	99 Forc	212 Write documentation		33 Wri	45 Wri		236 Project management [up to 1/2 day]	6.5	6 + 0.5 PM	
	32	23-Feb-00	60 Pric	73 Set	86 Rep	99 Forc	212 Write documentation		33 Wri	45 Wri		236 Project management [up to 1/2 day]	6.5	6 + 0.5 PM	
	33	24-Feb-00	51 Indi	51 Indi	51 Indi		212 Write documentation		33 Wri	45 Wri		236 Project management [up to 1/2 day]	6.5	6 + 0.5 PM	
	34	25-Feb-00	52 Rev	52 Rev	52 Rev		212 Write documentation					236 Project management [up to 1/2 day]	4.5	4 + 0.5 PM	30.5
8	35	28-Feb-00	60 Pric	73 Set	86 Rep	99 Forc	212 Write documentation / Help text					236 Project management [up to 1/2 day]			
	36	29-Feb-00	60 Pric	73 Set	86 Rep	99 Forc	212 Write documentation / Help text					236 Project management [up to 1/2 day]			
	37	1-Mar-00	60 Pric	73 Set	86 Rep	99 Forc	212 Write documentation / Help text					236 Project management [up to 1/2 day]			
	38	2-Mar-00	55-57,	55-57,	55-57,		212 Write documentation					236 Project management [up to 1/2 day]			
	39	3-Mar-00	60 Pric	73 Set	86 Rep	99 Forc	212 Write documentation [up to 1/2 day]					236 Project management [up to 1/2 day]			

Figure 13.6   Strip board at Week 7.

Week #	Day #	Date	Charlie	Engineer #2	Engineer #3	Engineer #4	Technical author	Marketing people (3)	Anna	Tester #1	Tester #2	Project management	Actual Effort (PD)	Based on (PD)	Total this week
9	40	6-Mar-00	60 Pric	73 Set	86 Rep	99 For	212 Write documentation			53 Cha	53 Cha	236 Project management	[up to 1/2 day]		
	41	7-Mar-00	151 W	170 Se	138 Tu	99 For	212 Write documentation			53 Cha	53,54	236 Project management	[up to 1/2 day]		
	42	8-Mar-00	151 W	170 Se	138 Tu	99 For	212 Write documentation			53,54	53,54	236 Project management	[up to 1/2 day]		
	43	9-Mar-00	151 W	170 Se	138 Tu	99 For	212 Write documentation			55-57	55-57	236 Project management	[up to 1/2 day]		
	44	10-Mar-00	151 W	170 Se	138 Tu	99 For	212 Write document			Help text	Help text	236 Project management	[up to 1/2 day]		
10	45	13-Mar-00	151 W	170 Se	138 Tu	99 For	212 Write documentation			Help text	Help text	236 Project management	[up to 1/2 day]		
	46	14-Mar-00	151 W	170 Se	138 Tu	99 For	212 Write documentation			Help text	Help text	236 Project management	[up to 1/2 day]		
	47	15-Mar-00	151 W	170 Se	138 Tu	99 For	212 Write documentation			Help text	Help text	236 Project management	[up to 1/2 day]		
	48	16-Mar-00	151 W	170 Se	138 Tu	99 For	212 Write documentation			Help text	Help text	236 Project management	[up to 1/2 day]		
	49	17-Mar-00	151 W	170 Se	138 Tu	99 For	212 Write documentation			Help text	Help text	236 Project management	[up to 1/2 day]		
11	50	20-Mar-00	151 W	170 Se	138 Tu	112 Eu	212 Write documentation			Help text	Help text	236 Project management	[up to 1/2 day]		
	51	21-Mar-00	151 W	170 Se	138 Tu	112 Eu	212 Write documentation			Help text	Help text	236 Project management	[up to 1/2 day]		
	52	22-Mar-00	151 W	170 Se	138 Tu	112 Eu	212 Write documentation			Help text	Help text	236 Project management	[up to 1/2 day]		
	53	23-Mar-00	151 W	170 Se	138 Tu	112 Eu	212 Write documentation			Help text	Help text	236 Project management	[up to 1/2 day]		
	54	24-Mar-00	151 W	170 Se	138 Tu	112 Eu	212 Write documentation			Help text	Help text	236 Project management	[up to 1/2 day]		
12	55	27-Mar-00	151 W	170 Se	138 Tu	112 Eu	212 Write documentation			Help text	Help text	236 Project management	[up to 1/2 day]		
	56	28-Mar-00	151 W	170 Se	138 Tu	112 Eu	212 Write documentation			Help text	Help text	236 Project management	[up to 1/2 day]		
	57	29-Mar-00	151 W	170 Se	138 Tu	112 Eu	212 Write documentation			Help text	Help text	236 Project management	[up to 1/2 day]		
	58	30-Mar-00	151 W	170 Se	138 Tu	112 Eu	212 Write documentation			Help text	Help text	236 Project management	[up to 1/2 day]		
	59	31-Mar-00	151 W	170 Se	138 Tu	112 Eu	212 Write documentation			Help text	Help text	236 Project management	[up to 1/2 day]		
13	60	3-Apr-00	151 W	170 Se	189 Or	112 Eu	212 Write documentation			Help text	Help text	236 Project management	[up to 1/2 day]		
	61	4-Apr-00	151 W	170 Se	189 Or	112 Eu	212 Write documentation			Help text	Help text	236 Project management	[up to 1/2 day]		
	62	5-Apr-00	151 W	170 Se	189 Or	112 Eu	212 Write documentation			Help text	Help text	236 Project management	[up to 1/2 day]		
	63	6-Apr-00	151 W	170 Se	189 Or	112 Eu	212 Write documentation			Help text	Help text	236 Project management	[up to 1/2 day]		
	64	7-Apr-00	151 W	170 Se	189 Or	112 Eu	212 Write documentation			Help text	Help text	236 Project management	[up to 1/2 day]		
14	65	10-Apr-00	151 W	170 Se	189 Or	125 St	212 Write documentation			Help text	Help text	236 Project management	[up to 1/2 day]		
	66	11-Apr-00	151 W	170 Se	189 Or	125 St	212 Write documentation			Help text	Help text	236 Project management	[up to 1/2 day]		
	67	12-Apr-00	151 W	170 Se	189 Or	125 St	212 Write documentation			Help text	Help text	236 Project management	[up to 1/2 day]		
	68	13-Apr-00	151 W	170 Se	189 Or	125 St	212 Write documentation			Help text	Help text	236 Project management	[up to 1/2 day]		
	69	14-Apr-00	151 W	170 Se	189 Or	125 St	212 Write documentation			Help text	Help text	236 Project management	[up to 1/2 day]		
15	70	17-Apr-00	151 W	170 Se	189 Or	125 St	217 Edit documentation			Help text	Help text	236 Project management	[up to 1/2 day]		
	71	18-Apr-00	151 W	170 Se	189 Or	125 St	217 Edit documentation			Help text	Help text	236 Project management	[up to 1/2 day]		
	72	19-Apr-00	151 W	170 Se	189 Or	125 St	217 Edit documentation			Help text	Help text	236 Project management	[up to 1/2 day]		
	73	20-Apr-00		189 Or	189 Or	125 St	217 Edit documentation			Help text	Help text	236 Project management	[up to 1/2 day]		
	74	21-Apr-00		189 Or	189 Or	125 St	217 Edit documentation			Help text	Help text	236 Project management	[up to 1/2 day]		
16	75	24-Apr-00	Vacati	189 Or	189 Or	125 St	217 Edit documentation			225 Te	225 Te	236 Project management	[up to 1/2 day]		
	76	25-Apr-00	Vacati	189 Or	189 Or	125 St	217 Edit documentation			225 Te	225 Te	236 Project management	[up to 1/2 day]		
	77	26-Apr-00	Vacati	189 Or	189 Or	125 St	217 Edit documentation			225 Te	225 Te	236 Project management	[up to 1/2 day]		
	78	27-Apr-00	Vacati	189 Or	189 Or	125 St	217 Edit documentation			225 Te	225 Te	236 Project management	[up to 1/2 day]		
	79	28-Apr-00	Vacati	189 Or	189 Or	125 St	217 Edit documentation			225 Te	225 Te	236 Project management	[up to 1/2 day]		

Figure 13.6 (continued)

Week #	Day #	Date	Charlie	Engineer #2	Engineer #3	Engineer #4	Technical author	Marketing people (3)	Anna	Tester #1	Tester #2	Project management	Actual Effort (PD)	Based on (PD)	Total this week
17	80	1-May-00	Vacati 189	Or 189		Or 125 3c	217 Edit documentation			225 Te	225 Te	236 Project management [up to 1/2 day]			
	81	2-May-00	Vacati 189	Online help			217 Edit documentation			225 Te	225 Te	236 Project management [up to 1/2 day]			
	82	3-May-00	Vacati 226 Te	226 Te			217 Edit documentation			225 Te	225 Te	236 Project management [up to 1/2 day]			
	83	4-May-00	Vacati 226 Te	226 Te	226 Te		217 Edit documentation			225 Te	225 Te	236 Project management [up to 1/2 day]			
	84	5-May-00	Vacati 226 Te	226 Te	226 Te		217 Edit documentation			225 Te	225 Te	236 Project management [up to 1/2 day]			
18	85	8-May-00	226 Te	226 Te	226 Te		217 Edit documentation			225 Te	225 Te	236 Project management [up to 1/2 day]			
	86	9-May-00	226 Te	226 Te	226 Te		217 Edit documentation			225 Te	225 Te	236 Project management [up to 1/2 day]			
	87	10-May-00	226 Te	226 Te	226 Te		217 Edit documentation			225 Te	225 Te	236 Project management [up to 1/2 day]			
	88	11-May-00					217 Edit documentation			228 Te	228 Te	236 Project management [up to 1/2 day]			
	89	12-May-00					217 Edit documentation			228 Te	228 Te	236 Project management [up to 1/2 day]			
19	90	15-May-00					217 Edit documentation			228 Te	228 Te	236 Project management [up to 1/2 day]			
	91	16-May-00		229 Te	229 Te	229 Te	221 Final integration of Online Help			228 Te		236 Project management [up to 1/2 day]			
	92	17-May-00		229 Te	229 Te	229 Te	221 Final integration of Online Help					236 Project management [up to 1/2 day]			
	93	18-May-00		229 Te	229 Te	229 Te	221 Final integration of Online Help					236 Project management [up to 1/2 day]			
	94	19-May-00										236 Project management [up to 1/2 day]			
20	95	22-May-00					221 Final integration of C			231 Te	231 Te	236 Project management [up to 1/2 day]			
	96	23-May-00		232 Te	232 Te	232 Te	232 Test #3 - make corrections			231 Te	231 Te	236 Project management [up to 1/2 day]			
	97	24-May-00					222 Final pre-production		233 Finalise te			236 Project management [up to 1/2 day]			
	98	25-May-00					222 Final pre-production of manuals					236 Project management [up to 1/2 day]			
	99	26-May-00					222 Final pre-production of manuals					236 Project management [up to 1/2 day]			
21	100	29-May-00		235 En	235 En	235 En	235 End of project review		235 Er			236 Project management [up to 1/2 day]			
	101	30-May-00		237 Contingency								236 Project management [up to 1/2 day]			
	102	31-May-00		237 Contingency								236 Project management [up to 1/2 day]			
	103	1-Jun-00		237 Contingency								236 Project management [up to 1/2 day]			
	104	2-Jun-00		237 Contingency								236 Project management [up to 1/2 day]			
22	105	5-Jun-00		237 Contingency								236 Project management [up to 1/2 day]			
	106	6-Jun-00		237 Contingency								236 Project management [up to 1/2 day]			
	113	7-Jun-00		237 Contingency								236 Project management [up to 1/2 day]			
	114	8-Jun-00		237 Contingency								236 Project management [up to 1/2 day]			
	115	9-Jun-00		237 Contingency								236 Project management [up to 1/2 day]			
23	116	12-Jun-00		237 Contingency								236 Project management [up to 1/2 day]			
	117	13-Jun-00		237 Contingency								236 Project management [up to 1/2 day]			
	118	14-Jun-00		237 Contingency								236 Project management [up to 1/2 day]			
	119	15-Jun-00		237 Contingency								236 Project management [up to 1/2 day]			
	120	16-Jun-00		237 Contingency								236 Project management [up to 1/2 day]			
24	121	19-Jun-00	Public holiday									236 Project management [up to 1/2 day]			
	122	20-Jun-00	Public holiday									236 Project management [up to 1/2 day]			
	123	21-Jun-00	Public holiday									236 Project management [up to 1/2 day]			
	124	22-Jun-00	Public holiday									236 Project management [up to 1/2 day]			
	125	23-Jun-00	Public holiday									236 Project management [up to 1/2 day]			
	126	26-Jun-00	Public holiday										131		

Figure 13.6   (continued)

look like taking close to 50% more than what was originally estimated. The new estimates are Reporting (12 days, not 8) and Foreign exchange (25 days, not 16). If this trend continues in the other bits, and the estimate for "Write Code" turns out to be half as much again as was originally estimated, then it's all over.

In your status report, you mention the unpalatable fact of the estimates and actuals, but your report is still green for 30 June. (Notice that you are not misleading anybody here. In fact, quite the contrary, you are being completely accurate and honest. The project *is* on target, but things are anything but rosy. You have successfully communicated all of this in your status report.)

Week 9

And now, out of the blue, like the kiss of a summer wind, you get a lucky break. Albert comes trundling in one morning, semi-hysterical and waving a printout of some stuff from a Web site. You calm him down and give him some water. (You're down to one coffee a day with Friday being the exception, when you're allowed to drink all you want. At least your coffee reduction diet is going well, even if nothing else is.) You find out that the reason Albert is so excited is that he has discovered a Security library that will do a lot of the things your Security module is going to have to do. Except now, you can buy it and bundle it, instead of having to develop it. When you do the estimates with him, you find that the new estimate for Security is now 10 person-days including all and any re-design. It's the kind of thing Charlie would have done. But you never would have expected Albert to do it. You look at him with a new-found admiration.

You get the legal and purchasing people on the case, negotiating a deal with the supplier of the Security package and go tell the troops. You resolve not to tell anybody else. The strip board now looks like the one in Figure 13.7. Status is green for 30 June.

Week 10

Albert hammers away on Security, Engineer #3 works on the Tutorial, Engineer #4 on Foreign exchange, Ted writes, and you trailboss[3] the lot. Status is green for 30 June.

---

3   It means project manage. See [2] if you're still puzzled!

Week	Day	Date	Cast (Jobs)	Actual Effort (PD)	Based on (PD)	Total this week
1	1	11-Jan-00	Project kickoff (all) — 236 Project kickoff	5.5	9 x 1/2 + 1 Proj. Mgmt.	
	2	12-Jan-00	Charlie: 6 Gather; Marketing: 8 Identify users	2.5	1 + (3 x 1/2)	
	3	13-Jan-00	Charlie: 9 Prepare user questionnaires; 10 Distribute user questionnaires	4	1 + 3	
	4	14-Jan-00	Charlie: 7 Review competitive info with Marketir; Marketing: 7 Review with Marketing; 236 Project management (up to 1/2 day)	4.5	1 + 3 + 1/2 PD Proj.	16
2	5	17-Jan-00	Charlie: 12 Analyse information; 11 Retrieve questionnaires; 236 Project management (up to 1/2 day)	1.5	1 + 0.5	
	6	18-Jan-00	13 Write requirements document	1	1	
	7	19-Jan-00	13 Write requirements document	1	1	
	8	20-Jan-00	13 Write requirements document	1	1	
	9	21-Jan-00	13 Write requirements document; 236 Project management (up to 1/2 day)	3.5	1(Fri) + 2(Weekend	7.5
3	10	24-Jan-00	58 Prototype; 15 Circulate document; 236 Project management (up to 1/2 day)	2.5	1 + 0.5 + 1 Proj. Mgmt.	
	11	25-Jan-00	17,18 Review meeting / changes to doc; 16, 17 Individual review (1/2 day; 236 Project management (up to 1/2 day)	4.5	1 + 3 + 0.5 PM	
	12	26-Jan-00	18 Changes to document; 236 Project management (up to 1/2 day)	1.5	1 + 0.5 PM	
	13	27-Jan-00	18,19 Change to document (inc. circulate agair; 15 Circulate document; 236 Project management (up to 1/2 day)	2	1 + 0.5 + 0.5 PM	
	14	28-Jan-00	20-22 Second review / Signoff / Reqc; 20-22 St; 20-22 Second review /; 236 Project management (up to 1/2 day)	3	0.5 + 1.5 + 0.5 + 0.5	13.5
4	15	31-Jan-00	58 Prototype; 236 Project management (up to 1/2 day)	1.5	1 + 0.5	
	16	1-Feb-00	58 Prototype	1	1	
	17	2-Feb-00	58 Prototype; 236 Project management (up to 1/2 day)	1.5	1 + 0.5	
	18	3-Feb-00	58 Prototype	1	1	
	19	4-Feb-00	58 Prototype; 236 Project management (up to 1/2 day)	3.5	1(Fri) + 2(Weekend	8.5
5	20	7-Feb-00	58 Pro / 58 Prot / 58 Prototype; 209 Research tech. writir; Tester #1: 24 Research i; Tester #2: 24 Research i; 236 Project management (up to 1/2 day)	5.5	5 + 0.5 PM	
	21	8-Feb-00	58 Pro / 58 Prot / 58 Prototype; 209 Research tech. writir; 24 Research; 24 Research; 236 Project management (up to 1/2 day)	5.5	5 + 0.5 PM	
	22	9-Feb-00	58 Pro / 58 Prot / 58 Prototype; 210 Set-up environment; 24 Research; 24 Research; 236 Project management (up to 1/2 day)	5.5	5 + 0.5 PM	
	23	10-Feb-00	58 Pro / 58 Prot / 58 Prototype; 210 Set-up environment; 24 Research; 24 Research; 236 Project management (up to 1/2 day)	5.5	5 + 0.5 PM	
	24	11-Feb-00	58 Pro / 58 Prot / 58 Prototype; 210 Set-up environment; 24 Research; 24 Research; 236 Project management (up to 1/2 day)	5.5	5 + 0.5 PM	27.5
6	25	14-Feb-00	58 Prot / 58 Prototype; 211 Define style sheet &; 25 Wri 37 Wri; 25 Wri 37 Wri; 236 Project management (up to 1/2 day)	5.5	5 + 0.5 PM	
	26	15-Feb-00	58 Prot / 58 Prototype; 211 Define style sheet &; 25 Wri 37 Wri; 25 Wri 37 Wri; 236 Project management (up to 1/2 day)	5.5	5 + 0.5 PM	
	27	16-Feb-00	58 Prot / 58 Prototype; 211 Define style sheet &; 25 Wri 37 Wri; 25 Wri 37 Wri; 236 Project management (up to 1/2 day)	5.5	5 + 0.5 PM	
	28	17-Feb-00	58 Prot / 58 Prototype; 211 Define style sheet &; 29 Wri 41 Wri; 29 Wri 41 Wri; 236 Project management (up to 1/2 day)	5.5	5 + 0.5 PM	
	29	18-Feb-00	58 Prot / 58 Prototype; 211 Define style / 50 Circu; 29 Wri 41 Wri; 29 Wri 41 Wri; 236 Project management (up to 1/2 day)	5.5	5 + 0.5 PM	27.5
7	30	21-Feb-00	60 Pric / 73 Sett 86 Rep 99 Forc; 212 Write documentatior; 29 Wri 41 Wri; 29 Wri 41 Wri; 236 Project management (up to 1/2 day)	6.5	6 + 0.5 PM	
	31	22-Feb-00	60 Pric / 73 Sett 86 Rep 99 Forc; 212 Write documentation; 33 Wri 45 Wri; 33 Wri 45 Wri; 236 Project management (up to 1/2 day)	6.5	6 + 0.5 PM	
	32	23-Feb-00	60 Pric / 73 Sett 86 Rep 99 Forc; 212 Write documentation; 33 Wri 45 Wri; 33 Wri 45 Wri; 236 Project management (up to 1/2 day)	6.5	6 + 0.5 PM	
	33	24-Feb-00	51 Indi / 51 Indi 51 Indi; 212 Write documentation; 33 Wri 45 Wri; 33 Wri 45 Wri; 236 Project management (up to 1/2 day)	6.5	6 + 0.5 PM	30.5
8	34	25-Feb-00	52 Rev / 52 Rev 52 Rev; 212 Write documentation/ Help text; 236 Project management (up to 1/2 day)	4.5	4 + 0.5 PM	
	35	28-Feb-00	60 Pric / 73 Sett 86 Rep 99 Forc; 212 Write documentation/ Help text; 236 Project management (up to 1/2 day)	4.5	4 + 0.5 PM	
	36	29-Feb-00	60 Pric / 73 Sett 86 Rep 99 Forc; 212 Write documentation/ Help text; 236 Project management (up to 1/2 day)	4.5	4 + 0.5 PM	
	37	1-Mar-00	60 Pric / 73 Sett 86 Rep 99 Forc; 212 Write documentation/ Help text; 236 Project management (up to 1/2 day)	4.5	4 + 0.5 PM	
	38	2-Mar-00	55-57, 55-57, 55-57,; 212 Write documentation/ Help text; 236 Project management (up to 1/2 day)	4.5	4 + 0.5 PM	
	39	3-Mar-00	60 Pric / 73 Sett 86 Rep 99 Forc; 212 Write documentatior; 52 Rev 52 Rev; 236 Project management (up to 1/2 day)	6.5	6+ 0.5 PM	24.5

Cast (Jobs) column headings: Charlie, Engineer #2, Engineer #3, Engineer #4, Technical author, Marketing people (3), Anna, Tester #1, Tester #2, Project management

Figure 13.7   Strip board at Week 9.

Week #	Day #	Date	Charlie	Engineer #2	Engineer #3	Engineer #4	Technical author	Marketing people (3)	Anna	Tester #1	Tester #2	Project management	Actual Effort (PD)	Based on (PD)	Total this week
9	40	6-Mar-00	73 Set	86 Rep		99 For	212 Write documentation		53 Chi	53 Chi	53 Chi	236 Project management (up to 1/2 day)	6.5	6+ 0.5 PM	
	41	7-Mar-00	73 Set	86 Rep		99 For	212 Write documentation		53 Chi	53 Chi	53 Chi	236 Project management (up to 1/2 day)	6.5	6+ 0.5 PM	
	42	8-Mar-00	73 Set	86 Rep		99 For	212 Write documentation		53, 54	53, 54	53, 54	236 Project management (up to 1/2 day)	6.5	6+ 0.5 PM	
	43	9-Mar-00	170 Se	86 Rep		99 For	212 Write documentation		55-57	55-57	55-57	236 Project management (up to 1/2 day)	6.5	6+ 0.5 PM	
	44	10-Mar-00	170 Se	86 Rep		99 For	212 Write documentation / Help text					236 Project management (up to 1/2 day)	4.5	4+ 0.5 PM	30.5
10	45	13-Mar-00	170 Security			99 For	212 Write documentation / Help text					236 Project management (up to 1/2 day)			
	46	14-Mar-00	170 Security			99 For	212 Write documentation / Help text					236 Project management (up to 1/2 day)			
	47	15-Mar-00	170 Security			99 For	212 Write documentation / Help text					236 Project management (up to 1/2 day)			
	48	16-Mar-00	170 Security			99 For	212 Write documentation / Help text					236 Project management (up to 1/2 day)			
	49	17-Mar-00	170 Security				212 Write documentation / Help text					236 Project management (up to 1/2 day)			
11	50	20-Mar-00	60 Pric	170 Security		99 For	212 Write documentation / Help text					236 Project management (up to 1/2 day)			
	51	21-Mar-00	151 w	170 Se	138 Tu	99 For	212 Write documentation / Help text					236 Project management (up to 1/2 day)			
	52	22-Mar-00	151 w	170 Se	138 Tu	99 For	212 Write documentation / Help text					236 Project management (up to 1/2 day)			
	53	23-Mar-00	151 Web interf		138 Tu	99 For	212 Write documentation / Help text					236 Project management (up to 1/2 day)			
	54	24-Mar-00	151 Web interf		138 Tu	99 For	212 Write documentation / Help text					236 Project management (up to 1/2 day)			
12	55	27-Mar-00	151 Web interf		138 Tu	99 For	212 Write documentation / Help text					236 Project management (up to 1/2 day)			
	56	28-Mar-00	151 Web interf		138 Tu	99 For	212 Write documentation / Help text					236 Project management (up to 1/2 day)			
	57	29-Mar-00	151 Web interf		138 Tu	99 For	212 Write documentation / Help text					236 Project management (up to 1/2 day)			
	58	30-Mar-00	151 Web interf		138 Tu	99 For	212 Write documentation / Help text					236 Project management (up to 1/2 day)			
	59	31-Mar-00	151 Web interf		138 Tu	99 For	212 Write documentation / Help text					236 Project management (up to 1/2 day)			
13	60	3-Apr-00	151 Web interf		138 Tu	112 Eu	212 Write documentation / Help text					236 Project management (up to 1/2 day)			
	61	4-Apr-00	151 Web interf		138 Tu	112 Eu	212 Write documentation / Help text					236 Project management (up to 1/2 day)			
	62	5-Apr-00	151 Web interf		138 Tu	112 Eu	212 Write documentation / Help text					236 Project management (up to 1/2 day)			
	63	6-Apr-00	151 Web interf		138 Tu	112 Eu	212 Write documentation / Help text					236 Project management (up to 1/2 day)			
	64	7-Apr-00	151 Web interf		138 Tu	112 Eu	212 Write documentation / Help text					236 Project management (up to 1/2 day)			
14	65	10-Apr-00	151 Web interf		138 Tu	112 Eu	212 Write documentation / Help text					236 Project management (up to 1/2 day)			
	66	11-Apr-00	151 Web interf		189 Or	112 Eu	212 Write documentation / Help text					236 Project management (up to 1/2 day)			
	67	12-Apr-00	151 Web interf		189 Or	112 Eu	212 Write documentation / Help text					236 Project management (up to 1/2 day)			
	68	13-Apr-00	151 Web interf		189 Or	112 Eu	212 Write documentation / Help text					236 Project management (up to 1/2 day)			
	69	14-Apr-00	151 Web interf		189 Or	112 Eu	212 Write documentation / Help text					236 Project management (up to 1/2 day)			
15	70	17-Apr-00	151 Web interf		189 Or	112 Eu	212 Write documentation / Help text					236 Project management (up to 1/2 day)			
	71	18-Apr-00	151 Web interf		189 Or	112 Eu	212 Write documentation / Help text					236 Project management (up to 1/2 day)			
	72	19-Apr-00	151 Web interf		189 Or	112 Eu	212 Write documentation / Help text					236 Project management (up to 1/2 day)			
	73	20-Apr-00	151 Web interf		189 Or	112 Eu	212 Write documentation / Help text					236 Project management (up to 1/2 day)			
	74	21-Apr-00	151 Web interf		189 Or	112 Eu	212 Write documentation / Help text					236 Project management (up to 1/2 day)			
16	75	24-Apr-00	151 Web interf		189 Or	125 3r	212 Write documentation / Help text					236 Project management (up to 1/2 day)			
	76	25-Apr-00	151 Web interf		189 Or	125 3r	212 Write documentation / Help text					236 Project management (up to 1/2 day)			
	77	26-Apr-00	151 Web interf		189 Or	125 3r	212 Write documentation / Help text					236 Project management (up to 1/2 day)			
	78	27-Apr-00	151 Web interf		189 Or	125 3r	212 Write documentation / Help text					236 Project management (up to 1/2 day)			
	79	28-Apr-00	151 Web interf		189 Or	125 3r	212 Write documentation / Help text					236 Project management (up to 1/2 day)			

Figure 13.7   (continued)

Week #	Day #	Date	Charlie	Engineer #2	Engineer #3	Engineer #4	Technical author	Marketing people (3)	Anna	Tester #1	Tester #2	Project management	Actual Effort (PD)	Based on (PD)	Total this week
17	80	1-May-00	151 Web interf	189 Or	125 3c		217 Edit documentation / Help text					236 Project management [up to 1/2 day]			
	81	2-May-00	151 Web interf	189 Or	125 3c		217 Edit documentation / Help text					236 Project management [up to 1/2 day]			
	82	3-May-00	151 Web interf	189 Or	125 3c		217 Edit documentation / Help text					236 Project management [up to 1/2 day]			
	83	4-May-00		189 Or	125 3c		217 Edit documentation / Help text					236 Project management [up to 1/2 day]			
	84	5-May-00		189 Or	125 3c		217 Edit documentation / Help text					236 Project management [up to 1/2 day]			
18	85	8-May-00	Vacati	189 Or	125 3c		217 Edit documentation			225 Te	225 Te	236 Project management [up to 1/2 day]			
	86	9-May-00	Vacati	189 Or	125 3c		217 Edit documentation			225 Te	225 Te	236 Project management [up to 1/2 day]			
	87	10-May-00	Vacati	189 Or	125 3c		217 Edit documentation			225 Te	225 Te	236 Project management [up to 1/2 day]			
	88	11-May-00	Vacati	189 Or	125 3c		217 Edit documentation			225 Te	225 Te	236 Project management [up to 1/2 day]			
	89	12-May-00	Vacati	189 Or	125 3c		217 Edit documentation			225 Te	225 Te	236 Project management [up to 1/2 day]			
19	90	15-May-00	Vacati	189 Or	125 3c		217 Edit documentation			225 Te	225 Te	236 Project management [up to 1/2 day]			
	91	16-May-00	Vacati	189 Online help			217 Edit documentation			225 Te	225 Te	236 Project management [up to 1/2 day]			
	92	17-May-00	Vacati	226 Te	226 Te		217 Edit documentation			225 Te	225 Te	236 Project management [up to 1/2 day]			
	93	18-May-00	Vacati	226 Te	226 Te		217 Edit documentation			225 Te	225 Te	236 Project management [up to 1/2 day]			
	94	19-May-00	Vacati	226 Te	226 Te		217 Edit documentation			225 Te	225 Te	236 Project management [up to 1/2 day]			
20	95	22-May-00		226 Te	226 Te		217 Edit documentation			225 Te	225 Te	236 Project management [up to 1/2 day]			
	96	23-May-00		226 Te	226 Te		217 Edit documentation			225 Te	225 Te	236 Project management [up to 1/2 day]			
	97	24-May-00		226 Te	226 Te		217 Edit documentation			228 Te	228 Te	236 Project management [up to 1/2 day]			
	98	25-May-00					217 Edit documentation			228 Te	228 Te	236 Project management [up to 1/2 day]			
	99	26-May-00					217 Edit documentation			228 Te	228 Te	236 Project management [up to 1/2 day]			
21	100	29-May-00					217 Edit documentation			228 Te	228 Te	236 Project management [up to 1/2 day]			
	101	30-May-00		229 Te	229 Te		221 Final integration of Online Help					236 Project management [up to 1/2 day]			
	102	31-May-00		229 Te	229 Te		221 Final integration of Online Help					236 Project management [up to 1/2 day]			
	103	1-Jun-00		229 Te	229 Te		221 Final integration of Online Help					236 Project management [up to 1/2 day]			
	104	2-Jun-00					221 Final integration of O			231 Te	231 Te	236 Project management [up to 1/2 day]			
22	105	5-Jun-00					221 Final integration of O			231 Te	231 Te	236 Project management [up to 1/2 day]			
	106	6-Jun-00		232 Te	232 Te		232 Test #3 - make corrections					236 Project management [up to 1/2 day]			
	113	7-Jun-00					222 Final pre-production 233 Finalise te					236 Project management [up to 1/2 day]			
	114	8-Jun-00					222 Final pre-production of manuals					236 Project management [up to 1/2 day]			
	115	9-Jun-00					222 Final pre-production of manuals					236 Project management [up to 1/2 day]			
23	116	12-Jun-00		235 En	235 En	235 En	235 End of project review			235 Er	235 Er	236 Project management [up to 1/2 day]			
	117	13-Jun-00		237 Contingency								236 Project management [up to 1/2 day]			
	118	14-Jun-00		237 Contingency								236 Project management [up to 1/2 day]			
	119	15-Jun-00		237 Contingency								236 Project management [up to 1/2 day]			
	120	16-Jun-00		237 Contingency								236 Project management [up to 1/2 day]			
24	121	19-Jun-00		237 Contingency								236 Project management [up to 1/2 day]			
	122	20-Jun-00		237 Contingency								236 Project management [up to 1/2 day]			
	123	21-Jun-00		237 Contingency								236 Project management [up to 1/2 day]			
	124	22-Jun-00		237 Contingency								236 Project management [up to 1/2 day]			
	125	23-Jun-00		237 Contingency								236 Project management [up to 1/2 day]			

Figure 13.7   (continued)

Week #	Day #	Date	Cast (Jobs)	Charlie	Engineer #2	Engineer #3	Engineer #4	Technical author	Marketing people (3)	Anna	Tester #1	Tester #2	Project management	Actual Effort (PD)	Based on (PD)	Total this week
25	126	26-Jun-00	237 Contingency										236 Project management (up to 1/2 day)			
	127	27-Jun-00	237 Contingency										236 Project management (up to 1/2 day)			
	128	28-Jun-00	237 Contingency										236 Project management (up to 1/2 day)			
	129	29-Jun-00	237 Contingency										236 Project management (up to 1/2 day)			
	130	30-Jun-00	237 Contingency										236 Project management (up to 1/2 day)			
26	131	26-Jun-00	Public holiday										236 Project management (up to 1/2 day)			
	132	27-Jun-00	Public holiday										236 Project management (up to 1/2 day)			
	133	28-Jun-00	Public holiday										236 Project management (up to 1/2 day)			
	134	29-Jun-00	Public holiday										236 Project management (up to 1/2 day)			
	135	30-Jun-00	Public holiday										236 Project management (up to 1/2 day)	186		
	136	3-Jul-00														
	137	4-Jul-00														
	138	5-Jul-00														
	139	6-Jul-00														
	140	7-Jul-00														
	141	10-Jul-00														
	142	11-Jul-00														
	143	12-Jul-00														
	144	13-Jul-00														
	145	14-Jul-00														
	146	17-Jul-00														
	147	18-Jul-00														
	148	19-Jul-00														
	149	20-Jul-00														
		21-Jul-00														
		24-Jul-00														
		25-Jul-00														
		26-Jul-00														
		27-Jul-00														
		28-Jul-00														
		31-Jul-00														
		1-Aug-00														
		2-Aug-00														

Figure 13.7 (continued)

Week 11

The Tutorial (Engineer #3), the (seemingly endless) Foreign exchange (Engineer #4), and tech writing (Ted) continue. Al (as you now call him) completes Security on target on Wednesday and begins work on the Web interface, which is *the* killer feature of the Killer product. Al re-estimates it at 30 person-days. The way his confidence is these days, you don't doubt him. Status is green for 30 June.

Week 12

You're back in the bathroom, your favorite place for contemplation. It occurs to you that good project teams are a bit like babies. They like routine. They like the feeling of steady progress towards objectives, of biting off a neat piece of the project each week. You remember you once read Roland Huntford's book, *The Last Place On Earth* [3], about the race for the South Pole in 1912 between Scott and Amundsen. Amundsen's expedition was almost all routine; Scott's was one crisis after another.

After the seeming-disaster of Charlie's departure, things seem to have settled back into a steady routine. However, if you are interested in dramatically shortening projects, this routine can also become a problem. Things can become too comfortable, and energy can be dulled. You need to keep people with one foot in their comfort zone, and one foot in the stretch zone. That way there is creative tension balanced with security and steadiness.

It is time that you began to think again in terms of shortening things. If nothing else, it may help to restore some of your contingency which has been so depleted. At the Monday meeting you go through each of the engineer's jobs in turn. You remind them of how each of those jobs is put together and ask them to look for savings.

For example, the job to code Pricing consists—essentially—of 4.5 days to write and document the code and 3.5 days to test it. You ask them to think not in terms of "having 4.5 days to do something," but rather "can I finish it today?"

The results are modest, at first. Engineer #3 completes the Tutorial a day ahead of schedule. Engineer #4 completes Foreign exchange (finally!) and starts on Euro support. Ted writes and Al works on the Web interface. You report status green for 30 June.

Week 13

Going into week 13 the strip board looks as in Figure 13.8.

Using the "can I finish it today?" philosophy, Al peels two days off what he had to do this week on the Web interface. Engineer #3 finishes Pricing also by working the weekend. Engineer #4 cuts a whopping 3 days off Euro support. Ted reports no change in his documentation schedule. You report green for 30 June.

Week 14

Al takes another three days off where he should have been by the end of the week. In other words, on Tuesday afternoon, he is where he expected to be by Friday. Notice that this is not beyond the realm of possibility. Nor is it—necessarily!—the author just wanting to finish the writing of this chapter! Because of (a) the level of detail we went to in building the estimates originally and (b) the strip board which gives us complete clarity of the effect of savings, it is possible for people to regulate very precisely the day to day flow of their work. Without these two things, they are working in the dark. In those circumstances, any attempts by the project manager say, to encourage such productivity improvements are often seen as fairly pathetic attempts to improve morale.

Engineer #3 takes a day off Online Help. Engineer #4 finishes Euro support in week 14. Ted knocks a day off his own personal detailed schedule. You report green for June 30th.

Week 15

Al wipes out the Web interface by working the weekend. Engineer #3 peels a day off Online Help. Engineer #4 starts 3rd party payments and knocks 2 days off. Ted reports no change on Friday, but then, not wanting to be outdone by the others, he works the weekend and peels those 2 days. You report green for June 30.

Week 16

Al is unable to make any saving in normal time, but at this stage people are becoming so used to savings, that he puts in a weekend to enable him to report an unbroken run of savings. He peels 2 days. Engineer #3 peels a day, as does Engineer #4. Ted completes his writing and begins editing. Green for 30 June.

Week	Day	Date	Charlie	Engineer #2	Engineer #3	Engineer #4	Technical author	Marketing people (3)	Anna	Tester #1	Tester #2	Project management	Actual Effort (PD)	Based on (PD)	Total this week
1	1	11-Jan-00	Project	Project	Project	Project	Project	Project	Project	Project	Project	Project kickoff	5.5	9 x 1/2 + 1 Proj. Mgmt.	
	2	12-Jan-00	6 Gast					8 Identify users					2.5	1 + (3 x 1/2)	
	3	13-Jan-00	9 Prepare user questionnaires					10 Distribute user questionnaires					4	1 + 3	
	4	14-Jan-00	7 Review competitive info with Marketing					7 Review with Marketing				236 Project management (up to 1/2 day)	4.5	1 + 3 + 1/2 PD Proj.	16
2	5	17-Jan-00	12 Analyse information					11 Retrieve questionnaires					1.5	1.5 + 0.5	
	6	18-Jan-00	13 Write requirements document										1	1	
	7	19-Jan-00	13 Write requirements document										1	1	
	8	20-Jan-00	13 Write requirements document									236 Project management (up to 1/2 day)	1	1	
	9	21-Jan-00	13 Write requirements document									236 Project management (up to 1/2 day)	3.5	1(Fri) + 2(Weekend	7.5
3	10	24-Jan-00						15 Circulate document				236 Project management (up to 1/2 day)	2.5	1 + 0.5 + 1 Proj. Mgmt.	
	11	25-Jan-00	17,18 Review meeting / changes to doc					16, 17 Individual review (1/2 day				236 Project management (up to 1/2 day)	4.5	1 + 3 + 0.5 PM	
	12	26-Jan-00	18 Changes to document									236 Project management (up to 1/2 day)	1.5	1 + 0.5 PM	
	13	27-Jan-00	18,19 Changes to document (inc. circulate agair					15 Circulate document				236 Project management (up to 1/2 day)	2	1 + 0.5 + 0.5 PM	
	14	28-Jan-00	20-22 Second review / Signoff / Reqs c					20-22 Si	20-22 Second review			236 Project management (up to 1/2 day)	3	0.5 + 1.5 + 0.5 + 0.5	13.5
4	15	31-Jan-00	58 Prototype									236 Project management (up to 1/2 day)	1.5	1 + 0.5	
	16	1-Feb-00	58 Prototype										1	1	
	17	2-Feb-00	58 Prototype										1.5	1.5 + 0.5	
	18	3-Feb-00	58 Prototype										1	1	
	19	4-Feb-00	58 Prototype									236 Project management (up to 1/2 day)	3.5	1(Fri) + 2(Weekend	8.5
5	20	7-Feb-00	58 Pro	58 Prot	58 Prototype		209 Research tech. writir		24 Research			236 Project management (up to 1/2 day)	5.5	5 + 0.5 PM	
	21	8-Feb-00	58 Pro	58 Prot	58 Prototype		209 Research tech. writir		24 Research			236 Project management (up to 1/2 day)	5.5	5 + 0.5 PM	
	22	9-Feb-00	58 Pro	58 Prot	58 Prototype		210 Set up environment		24 Research			236 Project management (up to 1/2 day)	5.5	5 + 0.5 PM	
	23	10-Feb-00	58 Pro	58 Prot	58 Prototype		210 Set up environment		24 Research			236 Project management (up to 1/2 day)	5.5	5 + 0.5 PM	
	24	11-Feb-00	58 Pro	58 Prot	58 Prototype		210 Set up environment		24 Research			236 Project management (up to 1/2 day)	5.5	5 + 0.5 PM	27.5
6	25	14-Feb-00	58 Prol	58 Prototype			211 Define style sheet &		25 Wri	37 Wri		236 Project management (up to 1/2 day)	5.5	5 + 0.5 PM	
	26	15-Feb-00	58 Prol	58 Prototype			211 Define style sheet &		25 Wri	37 Wri		236 Project management (up to 1/2 day)	5.5	5 + 0.5 PM	
	27	16-Feb-00	58 Prol	58 Prototype			211 Define style sheet &		25 Wri	37 Wri		236 Project management (up to 1/2 day)	5.5	5 + 0.5 PM	
	28	17-Feb-00	58 Prol	58 Prototype			211 Define style sheet &		29 Wri	41 Wri		236 Project management (up to 1/2 day)	5.5	5 + 0.5 PM	
	29	18-Feb-00	58 Prol	58 Prototype			211 Define style		50 Circ	29 Wri	41 Wri	236 Project management (up to 1/2 day)	5.5	5 + 0.5 PM	27.5
7	30	21-Feb-00	73 Set	86 Rep	99 For	212 Write documentatior			29 Wri	41 Wri		236 Project management (up to 1/2 day)	6.5	6 + 0.5 PM	
	31	22-Feb-00	73 Set	86 Rep	99 For	212 Write documentation			33 Wri	45 Wri		236 Project management (up to 1/2 day)	6.5	6 + 0.5 PM	
	32	23-Feb-00	73 Set	86 Rep	99 For	212 Write documentation			33 Wri	45 Wri		236 Project management (up to 1/2 day)	6.5	6 + 0.5 PM	
	33	24-Feb-00	51 Indi	51 Indi	51 Indi	212 Write documentatior			33 Wri	45 Wri		236 Project management (up to 1/2 day)	6.5	6 + 0.5 PM	
	34	25-Feb-00	52 Rev	52 Rev	52 Rev	212 Write documentation						236 Project management (up to 1/2 day)	4.5	4 + 0.5 PM	30.5
8	35	28-Feb-00	73 Set	86 Rep	99 For	212 Write documentation / Help text						236 Project management (up to 1/2 day)	4.5	4 + 0.5 PM	
	36	29-Feb-00	73 Set	86 Rep	99 For	212 Write documentation / Help text						236 Project management (up to 1/2 day)	4.5	4 + 0.5 PM	
	37	1-Mar-00	73 Set	86 Rep	99 For	212 Write documentation / Help text						236 Project management (up to 1/2 day)	4.5	4 + 0.5 PM	
	38	2-Mar-00	55-57,	55-57,	55-57,	212 Write documentation / Help text						236 Project management (up to 1/2 day)	4.5	4 + 0.5 PM	
	39	3-Mar-00	73 Set	86 Rep	99 For	212 Write documentation			52 Rev			236 Project management (up to 1/2 day)	6.5	6+ 0.5 PM	24.5

Figure 13.8   Strip board at Week 13.

Week #	Day #	Date	Charlie	Engineer #2	Engineer #3	Engineer #4	Technical author	Marketing people (3)	Anna	Tester #1	Tester #2	Project management	Actual Effort (PD)	Based on (PD)	Total this week
9	40	6-Mar-00	73 Se	86 Rep	99 Forc		212 Write documentation			53 Ch	53 Ch	236 Project management [up to 1/2 day]	6.5	6+ 0.5 PM	
	41	7-Mar-00	73 Se	86 Rep	99 Forc		212 Write documentation			53 Ch	53 Ch	236 Project management [up to 1/2 day]	6.5	6+ 0.5 PM	
	42	8-Mar-00	73 Se	86 Rep	99 Forc		212 Write documentation			53, 54	53, 54	236 Project management [up to 1/2 day]	6.5	6+ 0.5 PM	
	43	9-Mar-00	170 Se	86 Rep	99 Forc		212 Write documentation			55-57	55-57	236 Project management [up to 1/2 day]	6.5	6+ 0.5 PM	
	44	10-Mar-00	170 Se	86 Rep	99 Forc		212 Write documentation / Help text					236 Project management [up to 1/2 day]			30.5
10	45	13-Mar-00	170 Se	138 Tu	99 Forc		212 Write documentation / Help text					236 Project management [up to 1/2 day]	4.5	4+ 0.5 PM	
	46	14-Mar-00	170 Se	138 Tu	99 Forc		212 Write documentation / Help text					236 Project management [up to 1/2 day]	4.5	4+ 0.5 PM	
	47	15-Mar-00	170 Se	138 Tu	99 Forc		212 Write documentation / Help text					236 Project management [up to 1/2 day]	4.5	4+ 0.5 PM	
	48	16-Mar-00	170 Se	138 Tu	99 Forc		212 Write documentation / Help text					236 Project management [up to 1/2 day]	4.5	4+ 0.5 PM	
	49	17-Mar-00	170 Se	138 Tu	99 Forc		212 Write documentation / Help text					236 Project management [up to 1/2 day]	4.5	4+ 0.5 PM	22.5
11	50	20-Mar-00	170 Se	138 Tu	99 Forc		212 Write documentation / Help text					236 Project management [up to 1/2 day]	4.5	4+ 0.5 PM	
	51	21-Mar-00	170 Se	138 Tu	99 Forc		212 Write documentation / Help text					236 Project management [up to 1/2 day]	4.5	4+ 0.5 PM	
	52	22-Mar-00	170 Se	138 Tu	99 Forc		212 Write documentation / Help text					236 Project management [up to 1/2 day]	4.5	4+ 0.5 PM	
	53	23-Mar-00	151 Wr	138 Tu	99 Forc		212 Write documentation / Help text					236 Project management [up to 1/2 day]	4.5	4+ 0.5 PM	
	54	24-Mar-00	151 Wr	138 Tu	99 Forc		212 Write documentation / Help text					236 Project management [up to 1/2 day]	4.5	4+ 0.5 PM	22.5
12	55	27-Mar-00	151 Wr	138 Tu	99 Forc		212 Write documentation / Help text					236 Project management [up to 1/2 day]	4.5	4+ 0.5 PM	
	56	28-Mar-00	151 Wr	138 Tu	99 Forc		212 Write documentation / Help text					236 Project management [up to 1/2 day]	4.5	4+ 0.5 PM	
	57	29-Mar-00	151 Wr	138 Tu	99 Forc		212 Write documentation / Help text					236 Project management [up to 1/2 day]	4.5	4+ 0.5 PM	
	58	30-Mar-00	151 Wr	138 Tu	112 Eu		212 Write documentation / Help text					236 Project management [up to 1/2 day]	4.5	4+ 0.5 PM	
	59	31-Mar-00	151 Wr	138 Tu	112 Eu		212 Write documentation / Help text					236 Project management [up to 1/2 day]	4.5	4+ 0.5 PM	22.5
13	60	3-Apr-00	151 Wr	60 Pric	112 Eu		212 Write documentation / Help text					236 Project management [up to 1/2 day]			
	61	4-Apr-00	151 Wr	60 Pric	112 Eu		212 Write documentation / Help text					236 Project management [up to 1/2 day]			
	62	5-Apr-00	151 Wr	60 Pric	112 Eu		212 Write documentation / Help text					236 Project management [up to 1/2 day]			
	63	6-Apr-00	151 Wr	60 Pric	112 Eu		212 Write documentation / Help text					236 Project management [up to 1/2 day]			
	64	7-Apr-00	151 Wr	60 Pric	112 Eu		212 Write documentation / Help text					236 Project management [up to 1/2 day]			
14	65	10-Apr-00	151 Wr	60 Pric	112 Eu		212 Write documentation / Help text					236 Project management [up to 1/2 day]			
	66	11-Apr-00	151 Wr	60 Pric	112 Eu		212 Write documentation / Help text					236 Project management [up to 1/2 day]			
	67	12-Apr-00	151 Wr	60 Pric	112 Eu		212 Write documentation / Help text					236 Project management [up to 1/2 day]			
	68	13-Apr-00	151 Wr	189 Or	112 Eu		212 Write documentation / Help text					236 Project management [up to 1/2 day]			
	69	14-Apr-00	151 Wr	189 Or	112 Eu		212 Write documentation / Help text					236 Project management [up to 1/2 day]			
15	70	17-Apr-00	151 Wr	189 Or	112 Eu		212 Write documentation / Help text					236 Project management [up to 1/2 day]			
	71	18-Apr-00	151 Wr	189 Or	112 Eu		212 Write documentation / Help text					236 Project management [up to 1/2 day]			
	72	19-Apr-00	151 Wr	189 Or	112 Eu		212 Write documentation / Help text					236 Project management [up to 1/2 day]			
	73	20-Apr-00	151 Wr	189 Or	112 Online help		212 Write documentation / Help text					236 Project management [up to 1/2 day]			
	74	21-Apr-00	151 Wr	189 Or			212 Write documentation / Help text					236 Project management [up to 1/2 day]			
16	75	24-Apr-00	151 Wr	189 Or	125 3r		212 Write documentation / Help text					236 Project management [up to 1/2 day]			
	76	25-Apr-00	151 Wr	189 Or	125 3r		212 Write documentation / Help text					236 Project management [up to 1/2 day]			
	77	26-Apr-00	151 Wr	189 Or	125 3r		212 Write documentation / Help text					236 Project management [up to 1/2 day]			
	78	27-Apr-00	151 Wr	189 Or	125 3r		212 Write documentation / Help text					236 Project management [up to 1/2 day]			
	79	28-Apr-00	151 Wr	189 Or	125 3r		212 Write documentation / Help text					236 Project management [up to 1/2 day]			

Figure 13.8   (continued)

Week #	Day #	Date	Charlie	Engineer #2	Engineer #3	Engineer #4	Technical author	Marketing people (3)	Anna	Tester #1	Tester #2	Project management	Actual Effort (PD)	Based on (PD)	Total this week
17	80	1-May-00	151 w/	189 Or		125 3r	217 Edit documentation / Help text					236 Project management [up to 1/2 day]			
	81	2-May-00	151 w/	189 Or		125 3r	217 Edit documentation / Help text					236 Project management [up to 1/2 day]			
	82	3-May-00	151 w/	189 Or		125 3r	217 Edit documentation / Help text					236 Project management [up to 1/2 day]			
	83	4-May-00	189 Or	189 Or		125 3r	217 Edit documentation / Help text					236 Project management [up to 1/2 day]			
	84	5-May-00	189 Or	189 Or		125 3r	217 Edit documentation / Help text					236 Project management [up to 1/2 day]			
18	85	8-May-00	Vacati	189 Or		125 3r	217 Edit documentation /		225 Te	225 Te	225 Te	236 Project management [up to 1/2 day]			
	86	9-May-00	Vacati	189 Or		125 3r	217 Edit documentation /		225 Te	225 Te	225 Te	236 Project management [up to 1/2 day]			
	87	10-May-00	Vacati	189 Or		125 3r	217 Edit documentation /		225 Te	225 Te	225 Te	236 Project management [up to 1/2 day]			
	88	11-May-00	Vacati	189 Or		125 3r	217 Edit documentation /		225 Te	225 Te	225 Te	236 Project management [up to 1/2 day]			
	89	12-May-00	Vacati	189 Or		125 3r	217 Edit documentation /		225 Te	225 Te	225 Te	236 Project management [up to 1/2 day]			
19	90	15-May-00	Vacati	189 Or		125 3r	217 Edit documentation /		225 Te	225 Te	225 Te	236 Project management [up to 1/2 day]			
	91	16-May-00	Vacati	189 Online help		189 Or	217 Edit documentation /		225 Te	225 Te	225 Te	236 Project management [up to 1/2 day]			
	92	17-May-00	Vacati	226 Te		226 Te	217 Edit documentation /		225 Te	225 Te	225 Te	236 Project management [up to 1/2 day]			
	93	18-May-00	Vacati	226 Te		226 Te	217 Edit documentation /		225 Te	225 Te	225 Te	236 Project management [up to 1/2 day]			
	94	19-May-00	Vacati	226 Te		226 Te	217 Edit documentation /		225 Te	225 Te	225 Te	236 Project management [up to 1/2 day]			
20	95	22-May-00	226 Te	226 Te		226 Te	217 Edit documentation /		225 Te	225 Te	225 Te	236 Project management [up to 1/2 day]			
	96	23-May-00	226 Te	226 Te		226 Te	217 Edit documentation /		225 Te	225 Te	225 Te	236 Project management [up to 1/2 day]			
	97	24-May-00	226 Te	226 Te		226 Te	217 Edit documentation /		228 Te	228 Te	228 Te	236 Project management [up to 1/2 day]			
	98	25-May-00					217 Edit documentation /		228 Te	228 Te	228 Te	236 Project management [up to 1/2 day]			
	99	26-May-00					217 Edit documentation /		228 Te	228 Te	228 Te	236 Project management [up to 1/2 day]			
21	100	29-May-00					217 Edit documentation /		228 Te	228 Te	228 Te	236 Project management [up to 1/2 day]			
	101	30-May-00	229 Te	229 Te		229 Te	221 Final integration of Online Help					236 Project management [up to 1/2 day]			
	102	31-May-00	229 Te	229 Te		229 Te	221 Final integration of Online Help					236 Project management [up to 1/2 day]			
	103	1-Jun-00	229 Te	229 Te		229 Te	221 Final integration of Online Help					236 Project management [up to 1/2 day]			
22	104	2-Jun-00				231 Te	221 Final integration of C	231 Te				236 Project management [up to 1/2 day]			
	105	5-Jun-00				231 Te	221 Final integration of C	231 Te				236 Project management [up to 1/2 day]			
	106	6-Jun-00	232 Te	232 Te	232 Te	232 Te	#3 - make corrections					236 Project management [up to 1/2 day]			
	113	7-Jun-00					233 Finalise pre-production					236 Project management [up to 1/2 day]			
	114	8-Jun-00					222 Final pre-production of manuals					236 Project management [up to 1/2 day]			
	115	9-Jun-00					222 Final pre-production of manuals					236 Project management [up to 1/2 day]			
23	116	12-Jun-00	235 Er	235 En	235 En	235 En	235 End of project review	235 Er	235 Er			236 Project management [up to 1/2 day]			
	117	13-Jun-00	237 Contingency									236 Project management [up to 1/2 day]			
	118	14-Jun-00	237 Contingency									236 Project management [up to 1/2 day]			
	119	15-Jun-00	237 Contingency									236 Project management [up to 1/2 day]			
	120	16-Jun-00	237 Contingency									236 Project management [up to 1/2 day]			
24	121	19-Jun-00	237 Contingency									236 Project management [up to 1/2 day]			
	122	20-Jun-00	237 Contingency									236 Project management [up to 1/2 day]			
	123	21-Jun-00	237 Contingency									236 Project management [up to 1/2 day]			
	124	22-Jun-00	237 Contingency									236 Project management [up to 1/2 day]			
	125	23-Jun-00	237 Contingency									236 Project management [up to 1/2 day]			

Figure 13.8 (continued)

Week #	Day #	Date	Cast (Jobs)	Charlie	Engineer #2	Engineer #3	Engineer #4	Technical author	Marketing people (3)	Anna	Tester #1	Tester #2	Project management	Actual Effort (PD)	Based on (PD)	Total this week
25	126	26-Jun-00	237 Contingency										236 Project management [up to 1/2 day]			
	127	27-Jun-00	237 Contingency										236 Project management [up to 1/2 day]			
	128	28-Jun-00	237 Contingency										236 Project management [up to 1/2 day]			
	129	29-Jun-00	237 Contingency										236 Project management [up to 1/2 day]			
	130	30-Jun-00	237 Contingency										236 Project management [up to 1/2 day]			
26	126	26-Jun-00	Public holiday										236 Project management [up to 1/2 day]			
	127	27-Jun-00	Public holiday										236 Project management [up to 1/2 day]			
	128	28-Jun-00	Public holiday										236 Project management [up to 1/2 day]			
	129	29-Jun-00	Public holiday										236 Project management [up to 1/2 day]			
	130	30-Jun-00	Public holiday										236 Project management [up to 1/2 day]			
	131	3-Jul-00												253.5		
	132	4-Jul-00														
	133	5-Jul-00														
	134	6-Jul-00														
	135	7-Jul-00														
	136	10-Jul-00														
	137	11-Jul-00														
	138	12-Jul-00														
	139	13-Jul-00														
	140	14-Jul-00														
	141	17-Jul-00														
	142	18-Jul-00														
	143	19-Jul-00														
	144	20-Jul-00														
	145	21-Jul-00														
	146	24-Jul-00														
	147	25-Jul-00														
	148	26-Jul-00														
	149	27-Jul-00														
		28-Jul-00														
		31-Jul-00														
		1-Aug-00														
		2-Aug-00														
		3-Aug-00														
		4-Aug-00														
		7-Aug-00														
		8-Aug-00														
		9-Aug-00														
		10-Aug-00														
		11-Aug-00														

Figure 13.8 (continued)

Week 17

All coding completes on Wednesday 3 May. According to the original plan (see Figure 12.4), the testers were due to come back to begin testing on May 1. You've left that arrangement unchanged, so that they do indeed start on that day, overlapping with the end of coding. The engineers begin bug fixing on Thursday. Green for 30 June.

Weeks 18–21

In the best traditions of software engineering, testing takes longer than expected (see Figure 13.9), though no weekends are used.

For week 18, you report green for 30 June. Similarly for weeks 19 and 20. Week 21, as the number of outstanding bugs becomes satisfyingly small, you report green for 30 June. However, you note on the status report that there is "a possibility we may finish a few days early. "

Sniffing that the end may be in sight, everybody works the weekend, but there are just too many outstanding bits and pieces to be resolved, so that late on Sunday night, it's acknowledged that it's going to take a bit more time.

Week 22

The project is wrapped on Tuesday evening around 11 p.m. It's Tuesday 6 June. If we assume the project took place in Ireland, then that would have added on three public holidays, so that the actual end date would have been Friday 9 June. Your final status report looks like the one in Figure 13.10.

Week #	Day #	Date	Cast (Jobs): Charlie / Engineer #2 / #3 / #4 / Technical author / Marketing people (3) / Anna / Tester #1 / Tester #2 / Project management	Effort (PD)	Based on (PD)	Total this week
1	1	11-Jan-00	Project Project Project Project Project Project kickoff	5.5	9 x 1/2 + 1 Proj. Mgmt.	
	2	12-Jan-00	6 Gath	2.5	1 + (3 x 1/2)	
	3	13-Jan-00	9 Prepare user questionnaires; 8 Identify users	4	1 + 3	
	4	14-Jan-00	7 Review competitive info with Marketir; 7 Review with Marketing; 10 Distribute user questionnaires; 236 Project management up to 1/2 day	4.5	1 + 3 + 1/2 PD Proj.	16
2	5	17-Jan-00	12 Analyze information; 11 Retrieve questionnaires	1.5	1 + 0.5	
	6	18-Jan-00	13 Write requirements document	1	1	
	7	19-Jan-00	13 Write requirements document	1	1	
	8	20-Jan-00	13 Write requirements document	1	1	
	9	21-Jan-00	13 Write requirements document; 236 Project management up to 1/2 day	3.5	1(Fri) + 2(Weekend)	7.5
3	10	24-Jan-00	58 Prototype; 15 Circulate documents; 236 Project management up to 1/2 day	2.5	1 + 0.5 + 1 Proj. Mgmt.	
	11	25-Jan-00	17,18 Review meeting / changes to doc 16, 17 Individual review [1/2 day; 236 Project management up to 1/2 day	4.5	1 + 3 + 0.5 PM	
	12	26-Jan-00	18 Changes to document; 236 Project management up to 1/2 day	1.5	1 + 0.5 PM	
	13	27-Jan-00	18,19 Changes to document (inc. circulate agair 15 Circulate document; 236 Project management up to 1/2 day	2	1 + 0.5 + 0.5 PM	13.5
4	14	28-Jan-00	20-22 Second review / Signoff / Reqc c; 20-22 Second review / 20-22 Second review; 236 Project management up to 1/2 day	3	0.5 + 1.5 + 0.5 + 0.5	
	15	31-Jan-00	58 Prototype	1.5	1.5	
	16	1-Feb-00	58 Prototype	1	1	
	17	2-Feb-00	58 Prototype	1.5	1.5	
	18	3-Feb-00	58 Prototype; 236 Project management up to 1/2 day	1	1	
	19	4-Feb-00	58 Prototype; 236 Project management up to 1/2 day	3.5	1(Fri) + 2(Weekend)	8.5
5	20	7-Feb-00	58 Pro 58 Prototype; 209 Research tech. writin; 24 Research i; 236 Project management up to 1/2 day	5.5	5 + 0.5 PM	
	21	8-Feb-00	58 Pro 58 Prototype; 209 Research tech. writir; 24 Research i; 236 Project management up to 1/2 day	5.5	5 + 0.5 PM	
	22	9-Feb-00	58 Pro 58 Prototype; 210 Set up environment; 24 Research i; 236 Project management up to 1/2 day	5.5	5 + 0.5 PM	
	23	10-Feb-00	58 Pro 58 Prototype; 210 Set up environment; 24 Research i; 236 Project management up to 1/2 day	5.5	5 + 0.5 PM	
	24	11-Feb-00	56 Pro 58 Prototype; 210 Set up environment; 24 Research i; 236 Project management up to 1/2 day	5.5	5 + 0.5 PM	27.5
6	25	14-Feb-00	58 Prol 58 Prototype; 211 Define style sheet &; 25 Wri 37 Wri; 236 Project management up to 1/2 day	5.5	5 + 0.5 PM	
	26	15-Feb-00	58 Prol 58 Prototype; 211 Define style sheet &; 25 Wri 37 Wri; 236 Project management up to 1/2 day	5.5	5 + 0.5 PM	
	27	16-Feb-00	58 Prol 58 Prototype; 211 Define style sheet &; 25 Wri 37 Wri; 236 Project management up to 1/2 day	5.5	5 + 0.5 PM	
	28	17-Feb-00	58 Prol 58 Prototype; 211 Define style sheet &; 29 Wri 41 Wri; 236 Project management up to 1/2 day	5.5	5 + 0.5 PM	
	29	18-Feb-00	58 Prol 58 Prototype; 211 Define style; 50 Circu 29 Wri 41 Wri; 236 Project management up to 1/2 day	5.5	5 + 0.5 PM	27.5
7	30	21-Feb-00	73 Set 86 Rep 99 Forc; 212 Write documentation; 29 Wri 41 Wri; 236 Project management up to 1/2 day	6.5	6 + 0.5 PM	
	31	22-Feb-00	73 Set 86 Rep 99 Forc; 212 Write documentation; 33 Wri 45 Wri; 236 Project management up to 1/2 day	6.5	6 + 0.5 PM	
	32	23-Feb-00	73 Set 86 Rep 99 Forc; 212 Write documentation; 33 Wri 45 Wri; 236 Project management up to 1/2 day	6.5	6 + 0.5 PM	
	33	24-Feb-00	51 Indi 51 Indi 99 Forc; 212 Write documentation; 33 Wri 45 Wri; 236 Project management up to 1/2 day	6.5	6 + 0.5 PM	
	34	25-Feb-00	52 Rev 52 Rev 99 Forc; 212 Write documentation; 29 Wri 41 Wri; 236 Project management up to 1/2 day	6.5	6 + 0.5 PM	30.5
8	35	28-Feb-00	73 Set 86 Rep 99 Forc; 212 Write documentation/ Help text; 236 Project management up to 1/2 day	4.5	4 + 0.5 PM	
	36	29-Feb-00	73 Set 86 Rep 99 Forc; 212 Write documentation/ Help text; 236 Project management up to 1/2 day	4.5	4 + 0.5 PM	
	37	1-Mar-00	73 Set 86 Rep 99 Forc; 212 Write documentation/ Help text; 236 Project management up to 1/2 day	4.5	4 + 0.5 PM	
	38	2-Mar-00	55-57, 55-57, 55-57; 212 Write documentation/ Help text; 236 Project management up to 1/2 day	4.5	4 + 0.5 PM	
	39	3-Mar-00	73 Set 86 Rep 99 Forc; 212 Write documentation; 52 Rev 52 Rev; 236 Project management up to 1/2 day	6.5	6+ 0.5 PM	24.5

Figure 13.9   Strip board at Week 18.

Week #	Day #	Date	Cast (Jobs) Charlie	Engineer #2	Engineer #3	Engineer #4	Technical author	Marketing people (3)	Anna	Tester #1	Tester #2	Project management	Effort (PD) Based on	Total this week
9	40	6-Mar-00		73 Set	86 Rep	99 For	212 Write documentation			53 Cht	53 Cht	236 Project management (up to 1/2 day)	6.5 6+ 0.5 PM	
	41	7-Mar-00		73 Set	86 Rep	99 For	212 Write documentation			53 Cht	53 Cht	236 Project management (up to 1/2 day)	6.5 6+ 0.5 PM	
	42	8-Mar-00		73 Set	86 Rep	99 For	212 Write documentation			53, 54	53, 54	236 Project management (up to 1/2 day)	6.5 6+ 0.5 PM	
	43	9-Mar-00		170 Se	86 Rep	99 For	212 Write documentation			53, 54	53, 54	236 Project management (up to 1/2 day)	6.5 6+ 0.5 PM	
	44	10-Mar-00		170 Se	86 Rep	99 For	212 Write documentation			55-57	55-57	236 Project management (up to 1/2 day)	4.5 4+ 0.5 PM	30.5
10	45	13-Mar-00		170 Se	138 Tu	99 For	212 Write documentation / Help text					236 Project management (up to 1/2 day)	4.5 4+ 0.5 PM	
	46	14-Mar-00		170 Se	138 Tu	99 For	212 Write documentation / Help text					236 Project management (up to 1/2 day)	4.5 4+ 0.5 PM	
	47	15-Mar-00		170 Se	138 Tu	99 For	212 Write documentation / Help text					236 Project management (up to 1/2 day)	4.5 4+ 0.5 PM	
	48	16-Mar-00		170 Se	138 Tu	99 For	212 Write documentation / Help text					236 Project management (up to 1/2 day)	4.5 4+ 0.5 PM	
	49	17-Mar-00		170 Se	138 Tu	99 For	212 Write documentation / Help text					236 Project management (up to 1/2 day)	4.5 4+ 0.5 PM	22.5
11	50	20-Mar-00		170 Se	138 Tu	99 For	212 Write documentation / Help text					236 Project management (up to 1/2 day)	4.5 4+ 0.5 PM	
	51	21-Mar-00		151 Wr	138 Tu	99 For	212 Write documentation / Help text					236 Project management (up to 1/2 day)	4.5 4+ 0.5 PM	
	52	22-Mar-00		151 Wr	138 Tu	99 For	212 Write documentation / Help text					236 Project management (up to 1/2 day)	4.5 4+ 0.5 PM	
	53	23-Mar-00		151 Wr	138 Tu	99 For	212 Write documentation / Help text					236 Project management (up to 1/2 day)	4.5 4+ 0.5 PM	
	54	24-Mar-00		151 Wr	138 Tu	99 For	212 Write documentation / Help text					236 Project management (up to 1/2 day)	4.5 4+ 0.5 PM	22.5
12	55	27-Mar-00		151 Wr	138 Tu	99 For	212 Write documentation / Help text					236 Project management (up to 1/2 day)	4.5 4+ 0.5 PM	
	56	28-Mar-00		151 Wr	138 Tu	99 For	212 Write documentation / Help text					236 Project management (up to 1/2 day)	4.5 4+ 0.5 PM	
	57	29-Mar-00		151 Wr	138 Tu	99 For	212 Write documentation / Help text					236 Project management (up to 1/2 day)	4.5 4+ 0.5 PM	
	58	30-Mar-00		151 Wr	138 Tu	112 Eu	212 Write documentation / Help text					236 Project management (up to 1/2 day)	4.5 4+ 0.5 PM	
	59	31-Mar-00		151 Wr	138 Tu	112 Eu	212 Write documentation / Help text					236 Project management (up to 1/2 day)	4.5 4+ 0.5 PM	22.5
13	60	3-Apr-00		151 Wr	112 Eu	112 Eu	212 Write documentation / Help text					236 Project management (up to 1/2 day)	4.5 4+ 0.5 PM	
	61	4-Apr-00		151 Wr	60 Pric	112 Eu	212 Write documentation / Help text					236 Project management (up to 1/2 day)	4.5 4+ 0.5 PM	
	62	5-Apr-00		151 Wr	60 Pric	112 Eu	212 Write documentation / Help text					236 Project management (up to 1/2 day)	4.5 4+ 0.5 PM	
	63	6-Apr-00		151 Wr	60 Pric	112 Eu	212 Write documentation / Help text					236 Project management (up to 1/2 day)	4.5 4+ 0.5 PM	
	64	7-Apr-00		151 Wr	60 Pric	112 Eu	212 Write documentation / Help text					236 Project management (up to 1/2 day)	6.5 4+ 2(Weekend)+0.5	24.5
14	65	10-Apr-00		151 Wr	189 Qr	112 Eu	212 Write documentation / Help text					236 Project management (up to 1/2 day)	4.5 4+ 0.5 PM	
	66	11-Apr-00		151 Wr	189 Qr	112 Eu	212 Write documentation / Help text					236 Project management (up to 1/2 day)	4.5 4+ 0.5 PM	
	67	12-Apr-00		151 Wr	189 Qr	112 Eu	212 Write documentation / Help text					236 Project management (up to 1/2 day)	4.5 4+ 0.5 PM	
	68	13-Apr-00		151 Wr	189 Qr	112 Eu	212 Write documentation / Help text					236 Project management (up to 1/2 day)	4.5 4+ 0.5 PM	
	69	14-Apr-00		151 Wr	189 Qr	112 Eu	212 Write documentation / Help text					236 Project management (up to 1/2 day)	4.5 4+ 0.5 PM	22.5
15	70	17-Apr-00		151 Wr	189 Qr	125 3r	212 Write documentation / Help text					236 Project management (up to 1/2 day)	4.5 4+ 0.5 PM	
	71	18-Apr-00		151 Wr	189 Qr	125 3r	212 Write documentation / Help text					236 Project management (up to 1/2 day)	4.5 4+ 0.5 PM	
	72	19-Apr-00		151 Wr	189 Qr	125 3r	212 Write documentation / Help text					236 Project management (up to 1/2 day)	4.5 4+ 0.5 PM	
	73	20-Apr-00		151 Wr	189 Qr	125 3r	212 Write documentation / Help text					236 Project management (up to 1/2 day)	4.5 4+ 0.5 PM	
	74	21-Apr-00		151 Wr	189 Qr	125 3r	212 Write documentation / Help text					236 Project management (up to 1/2 day)	8.5 4+ 4(2 Weekends)	26.5
16	75	24-Apr-00		151 Wr	189 Qr	125 3r	212 Write documentation / Help text					236 Project management (up to 1/2 day)	4.5 4+ 0.5 PM	
	76	25-Apr-00		189 Qr	125 3r		217 Edit documentation / Help text					236 Project management (up to 1/2 day)	4.5 4+ 0.5 PM	
	77	26-Apr-00		189 Qr	125 3r		217 Edit documentation / Help text					236 Project management (up to 1/2 day)	4.5 4+ 0.5 PM	
	78	27-Apr-00		189 Qr	125 3r		217 Edit documentation / Help text					236 Project management (up to 1/2 day)	4.5 4+ 0.5 PM	
	79	28-Apr-00		189 Qr	125 3r		217 Edit documentation / Help text					236 Project management (up to 1/2 day)	4.5 4+ 2(Weekend)+0.5	22.5

Figure 13.9 (continued)

Week #	Day #	Date	Charlie	Engineer #2	Engineer #3	Engineer #4	Technical author	Marketing people (3)	Anna	Tester #1	Tester #2	Project management	Effort (PD)	Based on (PD)	Total this week
17	80	1-May-00			189 Or	125 3r	217 Edit documentation			225 Te	225 Te	236 Project management [up to 1/2 day]	6.5 6+	0.5 PM	
	81	2-May-00			189 Or	125 3r	217 Edit documentation			225 Te	225 Te	236 Project management [up to 1/2 day]	6.5 6+	0.5 PM	
	82	3-May-00			199 Or 189 Or	125 3r	217 Edit documentation			225 Te	225 Te	236 Project management [up to 1/2 day]	6.5 6+	0.5 PM	
	83	4-May-00			226 Te	226 Te	217 Edit documentation			225 Te	225 Te	236 Project management [up to 1/2 day]	6.5 6+	0.5 PM	
	84	5-May-00			226 Te	226 Te	217 Edit documentation			225 Te	225 Te	236 Project management [up to 1/2 day]	6.5 6+	0.5 PM	32.5
18	85	8-May-00			226 Te	226 Te	217 Edit documentation			225 Te	225 Te	236 Project management [up to 1/2 day]			
	86	9-May-00			226 Te	226 Te	217 Edit documentation			225 Te	225 Te	236 Project management [up to 1/2 day]			
	87	10-May-00			226 Te	226 Te	217 Edit documentation			225 Te	225 Te	236 Project management [up to 1/2 day]			
	88	11-May-00			226 Te	226 Te	217 Edit documentation			225 Te	225 Te	236 Project management [up to 1/2 day]			
	89	12-May-00			226 Te	226 Te	217 Edit documentation			225 Te	225 Te	236 Project management [up to 1/2 day]			
19	90	15-May-00			226 Te	226 Te	217 Edit documentation			225 Te	225 Te	236 Project management [up to 1/2 day]			
	91	16-May-00			226 Te	226 Te	217 Edit documentation			225 Te	225 Te	236 Project management [up to 1/2 day]			
	92	17-May-00			226 Te	226 Te	217 Edit documentation			225 Te	225 Te	236 Project management [up to 1/2 day]			
	93	18-May-00			226 Te	226 Te	217 Edit documentation			225 Te	225 Te	236 Project management [up to 1/2 day]			
	94	19-May-00			229 Te	229 Te	217 Edit documentation			228 Te	228 Te	236 Project management [up to 1/2 day]			
20	95	22-May-00			229 Te	229 Te	217 Edit documentation			228 Te	228 Te	236 Project management [up to 1/2 day]			
	96	23-May-00			229 Te	229 Te	217 Edit documentation			228 Te	228 Te	236 Project management [up to 1/2 day]			
	97	24-May-00			232 Te	232 Te	217 Edit documentation			231 Te	231 Te	236 Project management [up to 1/2 day]			
	98	25-May-00			232 Te	232 Te	221 Final integration of C			231 Te	231 Te	236 Project management [up to 1/2 day]			
	99	26-May-00			232 Te	232 Te	221 Final integration of C			231 Te	231 Te	236 Project management [up to 1/2 day]			
21	100	29-May-00			232 Te	232 Te	221 Final integration of C			231 Te	231 Te	236 Project management [up to 1/2 day]			
	101	30-May-00			232 Te	232 Te	221 Final integration of C			231 Te	231 Te	236 Project management [up to 1/2 day]			
	102	31-May-00			232 Te	232 Te	221 Final integration of C			231 Te	231 Te	236 Project management [up to 1/2 day]			
	103	1-Jun-00			232 Te	232 Te	232 Test #3 - make corrections			231 Te	231 Te	236 Project management [up to 1/2 day]			
	104	2-Jun-00			232 Te	232 Te	222 Final pre-production			231 Te	231 Te	236 Project management [up to 1/2 day]			
22	105	5-Jun-00			232 Te	232 Te	222 Final pre-production			231 Te	231 Final pre-production	236 Project management [up to 1/2 day]			
	106	6-Jun-00			232 Te	232 Te	222 Final pre-production			233 Fi	231 Final pre-production	236 Project management [up to 1/2 day]			
	113	7-Jun-00	235 E/		235 En	235 En	235 End of project review		235 E/	235 E/	235 E/	236 Project management [up to 1/2 day]			
	114	8-Jun-00													
	115	9-Jun-00													
23	116	12-Jun-00													
	117	13-Jun-00	237 Contingency									236 Project management [up to 1/2 day]			
	118	14-Jun-00	237 Contingency									236 Project management [up to 1/2 day]			
	119	15-Jun-00	237 Contingency									236 Project management [up to 1/2 day]			
	120	16-Jun-00	237 Contingency									236 Project management [up to 1/2 day]			
24	121	19-Jun-00	237 Contingency									236 Project management [up to 1/2 day]			
	122	20-Jun-00	237 Contingency									236 Project management [up to 1/2 day]			
	123	21-Jun-00	237 Contingency									236 Project management [up to 1/2 day]			
	124	22-Jun-00	237 Contingency									236 Project management [up to 1/2 day]			
	125	23-Jun-00	237 Contingency									236 Project management [up to 1/2 day]			

Figure 13.9 (continued)

Week #	Day #	Date	Charlie	Engineer #2	Engineer #3	Engineer #4	technical author	Marketing people (3)	Anna	Tester #1	Tester #2	Project management	Effort (PD)	Based on (PD)	Total this week
25	126	26-Jun-00	237 Contingency									236 Project management (up to 1/2 day)			
	127	27-Jun-00	237 Contingency									236 Project management (up to 1/2 day)			
	128	28-Jun-00	237 Contingency									236 Project management (up to 1/2 day)			
	129	29-Jun-00	237 Contingency									236 Project management (up to 1/2 day)			
	130	30-Jun-00	237 Contingency									236 Project management (up to 1/2 day)			
26	126	26-Jun-00	Public holiday									236 Project management (up to 1/2 day)			
	127	27-Jun-00	Public holiday									236 Project management (up to 1/2 day)			
	128	28-Jun-00	Public holiday									236 Project management (up to 1/2 day)			
	129	29-Jun-00	Public holiday									236 Project management (up to 1/2 day)			
	130	30-Jun-00	Public holiday									236 Project management (up to 1/2 day)			
	131	3-Jul-00												382	
	132	4-Jul-00													
	133	5-Jul-00													
	134	6-Jul-00													
	135	7-Jul-00													
	136	10-Jul-00													
	137	11-Jul-00													
	138	12-Jul-00													
	139	13-Jul-00													
	140	14-Jul-00													
	141	17-Jul-00													
	142	18-Jul-00													
	143	19-Jul-00													
	144	20-Jul-00													
	145	21-Jul-00													
	146	24-Jul-00													
	147	25-Jul-00													
	148	26-Jul-00													
	149	27-Jul-00													
		28-Jul-00													
		31-Jul-00													
		1-Aug-00													
		2-Aug-00													
		3-Aug-00													
		4-Aug-00													
		7-Aug-00													
		8-Aug-00													
		9-Aug-00													
		10-Aug-00													
		11-Aug-00													

Figure 13.9   (continued)

Figure 13.10   Final
status report.

The project completed and the Beta product shipped on Friday 9 June, 3 weeks ahead of schedule.
An up to date schedule for the project is attached. (You attach the strip board.)

Delivery Date—Change History

Date	Reason for change	Revised date
11 Jan	Original date committed to	30 Jun
28 Jan	Shortened time to write requirements doc.	23 Jun
9 Jun	Completion	9 Jun

The date you asked for:	25 March
The earliest date we said was possible:	30 June
The date we're showing today:	9 June

(You insert the graph just to rub it in.)

References

1. O'Connell, F., *How To Run Successful Projects II—The Silver Bullet*, Hemel Hempstead, England: Prentice Hall, 1996.

2. O'Connell, F., *How To Run Successful High-Tech Project-Based Organizations*, Boston: Artech House, 1999.

3. Huntford, R., *The Last Place On Earth*, London: Pan Books, 1985.

14 Do a Post-Mortem

➤ This chapter shows how recording what actually happens on a project is essential to improving your project management.

➤ We do a post-mortem on the worked example.

Introduction

Traditionally, people rarely do this. That being the case, there was a time when I probably would have written "and this is a real pity." These days, I have to be much more vehement. Not to do a post-mortem or audit on a completed project is completely unforgivable. Knowledge management is trendy these days. To quite literally throw away all of the knowledge you have gathered on a project is little short of a crime.

After all, when you have completed a project, no matter how elegantly or otherwise it was carried out, you have a map through the great unknown. You have a complete account of how one of these projects was actually done. Look at what this means. This now means that the next time you undertake a project, you have one possible way it could be done. Thus, rather than having to make it all up from scratch, you have a blueprint. You have either a blueprint for how to do another project, that is, adhere to this as much as possible or a blueprint for how not to do another project (i.e., avoid this as much as possible). In either case, you're in much better shape than when you were starting the first time.

In my previous book [1], I suggested that in building your knowledge base, you first needed to gather the basic data about the project—who actually did what when. One of the nice things about using a strip boarded plan, is that when the project ends, all of that data is automatically available to you. (See Figure 14.1.)

209

Week	Day	Date	Cast (Jobs)	Project management	Effort (P[Based on (PD)]	Total this week
1	1	11-Jan-00	Projec Projec Projec Projec Projec Projec Project kickoff		5.5 9 × 1/2 + 1 Proj. Mgmt.	
	2	12-Jan-00	6 Gantt		2.5 1 + (3 × 1/2)	
	3	13-Jan-00	9 Prepare user questionnaires; 8 Identify users		4 1 + 3	
	4	14-Jan-00	7 Review competitive info with Marketir; 7 Review with Marketing; 10 Distribute user questionnaires; 236 Project management up to 1/2 day		4.5 1 + 3 + 1/2 PD Proj.	16
2	5	17-Jan-00	12 Analyze information; 11 Retrieve questionnaires		1.5 1 + 0.5	
	6	18-Jan-00	13 Write requirements document		1	
	7	19-Jan-00	13 Write requirements document		1	
	8	20-Jan-00	13 Write requirements document		1	
	9	21-Jan-00	13 Write requirements document; 236 Project management up to 1/2 day		3.5 1(Fri) + 2(Weekend	7.5
3	10	24-Jan-00	15 Circulate document; 236 Project management up to 1/2 day		2.5 1 + 0.5 + 1 Proj. Mgmt.	
	11	25-Jan-00	17,18 Review meeting/ changes to do; 16, 17 Individual review (1/2 day; 236 Project management up to 1/2 day		4.5 1 + 3 + 0.5 PM	
	12	26-Jan-00	16 Changes to document; 236 Project management up to 1/2 day		1.5 1 + 0.5 PM	
	13	27-Jan-00	18,19 Changes to document(inc. circulate agair; 15 Circulate documen; 236 Project management up to 1/2 day		2 1 + 0.5 + 0.5 PM	
4	14	28-Jan-00	20-22 Second review/ Signoff Reqs c; 20-22 Si; 20-22 Second review/; 236 Project management up to 1/2 day		3 0.5 + 1.5 + 0.5 + 0.5	13.5
	15	31-Jan-00	58 Prototype; 236 Project management up to 1/2 day		1.5 1 + 0.5	
	16	1-Feb-00	58 Prototype		1 1	
	17	2-Feb-00	58 Prototype; 236 Project management up to 1/2 day		1.5 1 + 0.5	
	18	3-Feb-00	58 Prototype		1 1	
	19	4-Feb-00	58 Prototype; 236 Project management up to 1/2 day		3.5 1(Fri) + 2(Weekend	8.5
5	20	7-Feb-00	58 Pro 58 Pro 58 Prototype; 209 Research tech. writir; 24 Research i; 236 Research i; 236 Project management up to 1/2 day		5.5 5 + 0.5 PM	
	21	8-Feb-00	58 Pro 58 Prototype; 209 Research tech. writir; 24 Research i; 236 Research i; 236 Project management up to 1/2 day		5.5 5 + 0.5 PM	
	22	9-Feb-00	58 Pro 58 Prototype; 210 Set up environment; 24 Research i; 236 Research i; 236 Project management up to 1/2 day		5.5 5 + 0.5 PM	
	23	10-Feb-00	58 Pro 58 Prototype; 210 Set up environment; 24 Research i; 236 Research i; 236 Project management up to 1/2 day		5.5 5 + 0.5 PM	
	24	11-Feb-00	58 Pro 58 Prototype; 210 Set up environment; 24 Research i; 236 Research i; 236 Project management up to 1/2 day		5.5 5 + 0.5 PM	27.5
6	25	14-Feb-00	58 Prototype; 211 Define style sheet &; 25 Wri; 37 Wri; 236 Project management up to 1/2 day		5.5 5 + 0.5 PM	
	26	15-Feb-00	58 Prototype; 211 Define style sheet &; 25 Wri; 37 Wri; 236 Project management up to 1/2 day		5.5 5 + 0.5 PM	
	27	16-Feb-00	58 Prototype; 211 Define style sheet &; 25 Wri; 37 Wri; 236 Project management up to 1/2 day		5.5 5 + 0.5 PM	
	28	17-Feb-00	58 Prototype; 211 Define style sheet &; 29 Wri; 41 Wri; 236 Project management up to 1/2 day		5.5 5 + 0.5 PM	
	29	18-Feb-00	58 Prototype; 211 Define style; 50 Circ; 29 Wri; 41 Wri; 236 Project management up to 1/2 day		5.5 5 + 0.5 PM	27.5
7	30	21-Feb-00	73 Se 86 Rep 99 Fo; 212 Write documentation; 29 Wri; 41 Wri; 236 Project management up to 1/2 day		6.5 6 + 0.5 PM	
	31	22-Feb-00	73 Se 86 Rep 99 Fo; 212 Write documentation; 45 Wri; 45 Wri; 236 Project management up to 1/2 day		6.5 6 + 0.5 PM	
	32	23-Feb-00	73 Se 86 Rep 99 Fo; 212 Write documentation; 33 Wri; 45 Wri; 236 Project management up to 1/2 day		6.5 6 + 0.5 PM	
	33	24-Feb-00	51 Indi 51 Indi; 212 Write documentation; 33 Wri; 45 Wri; 236 Project management up to 1/2 day		6.5 6 + 0.5 PM	
	34	25-Feb-00	52 Rev 52 Rev; 212 Write documentation/ Help text; 236 Project management up to 1/2 day		4.5 4 + 0.5 PM	30.5
8	35	28-Feb-00	73 Se 86 Rep 99 Fo; 212 Write documentation/ Help text; 236 Project management up to 1/2 day		4.5 4 + 0.5 PM	
	36	29-Feb-00	73 Se 86 Rep 99 Fo; 212 Write documentation/ Help text; 236 Project management up to 1/2 day		4.5 4 + 0.5 PM	
	37	1-Mar-00	73 Se 86 Rep 99 Fo; 212 Write documentation/ Help text; 236 Project management up to 1/2 day		4.5 4 + 0.5 PM	
	38	2-Mar-00	55-57, 55-57, 55-57; 212 Write documentation/ Help text; 236 Project management up to 1/2 day		4.5 4 + 0.5 PM	
	39	3-Mar-00	73 Se 86 Rep 99 Fo; 212 Write documentation; 52 Res; 52 Res; 236 Project management up to 1/2 day		6.5 6+ 0.5 PM	24.5

Figure 14.1　Final strip board.

Week #	Day #	Date	Charlie	Engineer #2	Engineer #3	Engineer #4	Technical author	Marketing people (3)	Anna	Tester #1	Tester #2	Project management	Effort (P[	Based on (PD)	Total this week
9	40	6-Mar-00	73 Set	86 Rep	99 Forc		212 Write documentation		53 Chr	53 Chr	53, 54	236 Project management [up to 1/2 day]	6.5	6+ 0.5 PM	
	41	7-Mar-00	73 Set	86 Rep	99 Forc		212 Write documentation		53 Chr	53 Chr	53, 54	236 Project management [up to 1/2 day]	6.5	6+ 0.5 PM	
	42	8-Mar-00	73 Set	86 Rep	99 Forc		212 Write documentation		53 Chr	53 Chr	53, 54	236 Project management [up to 1/2 day]	6.5	6+ 0.5 PM	
	43	9-Mar-00	170 Se	86 Rep	99 Forc		212 Write documentation		55-57	55-57		236 Project management [up to 1/2 day]	6.5	6+ 0.5 PM	
	44	10-Mar-00	170 Se	86 Rep	99 Forc		212 Write documentation					236 Project management [up to 1/2 day]	4.5	4+ 0.5 PM	30.5
10	45	13-Mar-00	170 Se	138 Tu	99 Forc		212 Write documentation/Help text					236 Project management [up to 1/2 day]	4.5	4+ 0.5 PM	
	46	14-Mar-00	170 Se	138 Tu	99 Forc		212 Write documentation/Help text					236 Project management [up to 1/2 day]	4.5	4+ 0.5 PM	
	47	15-Mar-00	170 Se	138 Tu	99 Forc		212 Write documentation/Help text					236 Project management [up to 1/2 day]	4.5	4+ 0.5 PM	
	48	16-Mar-00	170 Se	138 Tu	99 Forc		212 Write documentation/Help text					236 Project management [up to 1/2 day]	4.5	4+ 0.5 PM	
	49	17-Mar-00	170 Se	138 Tu	99 Forc		212 Write documentation/Help text					236 Project management [up to 1/2 day]	4.5	4+ 0.5 PM	22.5
11	50	20-Mar-00	170 Se	138 Tu	99 Forc		212 Write documentation/Help text					236 Project management [up to 1/2 day]	4.5	4+ 0.5 PM	
	51	21-Mar-00	170 Se	138 Tu	99 Forc		212 Write documentation/Help text					236 Project management [up to 1/2 day]	4.5	4+ 0.5 PM	
	52	22-Mar-00	170 Se	138 Tu	99 Forc		212 Write documentation/Help text					236 Project management [up to 1/2 day]	4.5	4+ 0.5 PM	
	53	23-Mar-00	151 Wr	138 Tu	99 Forc		212 Write documentation/Help text					236 Project management [up to 1/2 day]	4.5	4+ 0.5 PM	
	54	24-Mar-00	151 Wr	138 Tu	99 Forc		212 Write documentation/Help text					236 Project management [up to 1/2 day]	4.5	4+ 0.5 PM	22.5
12	55	27-Mar-00	151 Wr	138 Tu	99 Forc		212 Write documentation/Help text					236 Project management [up to 1/2 day]	4.5	4+ 0.5 PM	
	56	28-Mar-00	151 Wr	138 Tu	99 Forc		212 Write documentation/Help text					236 Project management [up to 1/2 day]	4.5	4+ 0.5 PM	
	57	29-Mar-00	151 Wr	138 Tu	99 Forc		212 Write documentation/Help text					236 Project management [up to 1/2 day]	4.5	4+ 0.5 PM	
	58	30-Mar-00	151 Wr	112 Eu	60 Pric		212 Write documentation/Help text					236 Project management [up to 1/2 day]	4.5	4+ 0.5 PM	
	59	31-Mar-00	151 Wr	112 Eu	60 Pric		212 Write documentation/Help text					236 Project management [up to 1/2 day]	4.5	4+ 0.5 PM	22.5
13	60	3-Apr-00	151 Wr	112 Eu	60 Pric		212 Write documentation/Help text					236 Project management [up to 1/2 day]	4.5	4+ 0.5 PM	
	61	4-Apr-00	151 Wr	112 Eu	60 Pric		212 Write documentation/Help text					236 Project management [up to 1/2 day]	4.5	4+ 0.5 PM	
	62	5-Apr-00	151 Wr	112 Eu	60 Pric		212 Write documentation/Help text					236 Project management [up to 1/2 day]	4.5	4+ 0.5 PM	
	63	6-Apr-00	151 Wr	112 Eu	60 Pric		212 Write documentation/Help text					236 Project management [up to 1/2 day]	4.5	4+ 0.5 PM	
	64	7-Apr-00	151 Wr	112 Eu	60 Pric		212 Write documentation/Help text					236 Project management [up to 1/2 day]	6.5	4+ 2(Weekend)+0.5	24.5
14	65	10-Apr-00	151 Wr	112 Eu	60 Pric		212 Write documentation/Help text					236 Project management [up to 1/2 day]	4.5	4+ 0.5 PM	
	66	11-Apr-00	189 Or	112 Eu	112 Eu		212 Write documentation/Help text					236 Project management [up to 1/2 day]	4.5	4+ 0.5 PM	
	67	12-Apr-00	189 Or	112 Eu	112 Eu		212 Write documentation/Help text					236 Project management [up to 1/2 day]	4.5	4+ 0.5 PM	
	68	13-Apr-00	189 Or	112 Eu	112 Eu		212 Write documentation/Help text					236 Project management [up to 1/2 day]	4.5	4+ 0.5 PM	
	69	14-Apr-00	189 Or	112 Eu	112 Eu		212 Write documentation/Help text					236 Project management [up to 1/2 day]	4.5	4+ 0.5 PM	22.5
15	70	17-Apr-00	151 Wr	189 Or	125 3r		212 Write documentation/Help text					236 Project management [up to 1/2 day]	4.5	4+ 0.5 PM	
	71	18-Apr-00	151 Wr	189 Or	125 3r		212 Write documentation/Help text					236 Project management [up to 1/2 day]	4.5	4+ 0.5 PM	
	72	19-Apr-00	151 Wr	189 Or	125 3r		212 Write documentation/Help text					236 Project management [up to 1/2 day]	4.5	4+ 0.5 PM	
	73	20-Apr-00	151 Wr	189 Or	125 3r		212 Write documentation/Help text					236 Project management [up to 1/2 day]	4.5	4+ 0.5 PM	
	74	21-Apr-00	151 Wr	189 Or	125 3r		212 Write documentation/Help text					236 Project management [up to 1/2 day]	8.5	4+ 4(2 Weekends)+0.5	26.5
16	75	24-Apr-00	189 Or	189 Or	125 3r		212 Write documentation/Help text					236 Project management [up to 1/2 day]	4.5	4+ 0.5 PM	
	76	25-Apr-00	189 Or	189 Or	125 3r		212 Write documentation/Help text					236 Project management [up to 1/2 day]	4.5	4+ 0.5 PM	
	77	26-Apr-00	189 Or	189 Or	125 3r		217 Edit documentation/Help text					236 Project management [up to 1/2 day]	4.5	4+ 0.5 PM	
	78	27-Apr-00	189 Or	189 Or	125 3r		217 Edit documentation/Help text					236 Project management [up to 1/2 day]	4.5	4+ 0.5 PM	
	79	28-Apr-00	189 Or	189 Or	125 3r		217 Edit documentation/Help text					236 Project management [up to 1/2 day]	4.5	4+ 2(Weekend)+0.5	22.5

Figure 14.1   (continued)

Week #	Day #	Date	Charlie	Engineer #2	Engineer #3	Engineer #4	Technical author	Marketing people (3)	Anna	Tester #1	Tester #2	Project management	Effort (P	Based on (PD)	Total this week
17	80	1-May-00		189 Or	189 Or	125 3x	217 Edit documentation			225 Te	225 Te	236 Project management [up to 1/2 day]	6.5	6+ 0.5 PM	
	81	2-May-00		189 Or	189 Or	125 3x	217 Edit documentation			225 Te	225 Te	236 Project management [up to 1/2 day]	6.5	6+ 0.5 PM	
	82	3-May-00		189 Or	189 Or	125 3x	217 Edit documentation			225 Te	225 Te	236 Project management [up to 1/2 day]	6.5	6+ 0.5 PM	
	83	4-May-00		226 Te			217 Edit documentation			225 Te	225 Te	236 Project management [up to 1/2 day]	6.5	6+ 0.5 PM	
	84	5-May-00		226 Te			217 Edit documentation			225 Te	225 Te	236 Project management [up to 1/2 day]	6.5	6+ 0.5 PM	32.5
18	85	8-May-00		226 Te			217 Edit documentation			225 Te	225 Te	236 Project management [up to 1/2 day]	6.5	6+ 0.5 PM	
	86	9-May-00		226 Te			217 Edit documentation			225 Te	225 Te	236 Project management [up to 1/2 day]	6.5	6+ 0.5 PM	
	87	10-May-00		226 Te			217 Edit documentation			225 Te	225 Te	236 Project management [up to 1/2 day]	6.5	6+ 0.5 PM	
	88	11-May-00		226 Te			217 Edit documentation			225 Te	225 Te	236 Project management [up to 1/2 day]	6.5	6+ 0.5 PM	
	89	12-May-00		226 Te			217 Edit documentation			225 Te	225 Te	236 Project management [up to 1/2 day]	6.5	6+ 0.5 PM	32.5
19	90	15-May-00		226 Te			217 Edit documentation			225 Te	225 Te	236 Project management [up to 1/2 day]	6.5	6+ 0.5 PM	
	91	16-May-00		226 Te			217 Edit documentation			225 Te	225 Te	236 Project management [up to 1/2 day]	6.5	6+ 0.5 PM	
	92	17-May-00		226 Te			217 Edit documentation			228 Te	228 Te	236 Project management [up to 1/2 day]	6.5	6+ 0.5 PM	
	93	18-May-00		226 Te			217 Edit documentation			228 Te	228 Te	236 Project management [up to 1/2 day]	6.5	6+ 0.5 PM	
	94	19-May-00		226 Te			217 Edit documentation			228 Te	228 Te	236 Project management [up to 1/2 day]	6.5	6+ 0.5 PM	32.5
20	95	22-May-00		229 Te			217 Edit documentation			228 Te	228 Te	236 Project management [up to 1/2 day]	6.5	6+ 0.5 PM	
	96	23-May-00		229 Te			217 Edit documentation			228 Te	228 Te	236 Project management [up to 1/2 day]	6.5	6+ 0.5 PM	
	97	24-May-00		229 Te			217 Edit documentation			228 Te	228 Te	236 Project management [up to 1/2 day]	6.5	6+ 0.5 PM	
	98	25-May-00		232 Te			221 Final integration of C			228 Te	228 Te	236 Project management [up to 1/2 day]	6.5	6+ 0.5 PM	
	99	26-May-00		232 Te			221 Final integration of C			231 Te	231 Te	236 Project management [up to 1/2 day]	6.5	6+ 0.5 PM	32.5
21	100	29-May-00		232 Te			221 Final integration of C			231 Te	231 Te	236 Project management [up to 1/2 day]	6.5	6+ 0.5 PM	
	101	30-May-00		232 Te			221 Final integration of C			231 Te	231 Te	236 Project management [up to 1/2 day]	6.5	6+ 0.5 PM	
	102	31-May-00		232 Te #3 make corrections			221 Final integration of C			231 Te	231 Te	236 Project management [up to 1/2 day]	6.5	6+ 0.5 PM	
	103	1-Jun-00		232 Te			222 Final pre-production			231 Te	231 Te	236 Project management [up to 1/2 day]	6.5	6+ 0.5 PM	
	104	2-Jun-00		232 Te			222 Final pre-production			231 Te	231 Te	236 Project management [up to 1/2 day]	6.5	6+ 0.5 PM	32.5
22	105	5-Jun-00		232 Te			222 Final pre-production			233 Fi	231 Te	236 Project management [up to 1/2 day]	6.5	6+ 0.5 PM	
	106	6-Jun-00		232 Te			222 Final pre-production			233 Fi	231 Te	236 Project management [up to 1/2 day]	6.5	6+ 0.5 PM	
	107	7-Jun-00		235 En			235 End of project review			235 Ex	235 Ex	236 Project management [up to 1/2 day]	9		
	108	8-Jun-00	Public holiday										6.5	6+ 0.5 PM	
	109	9-Jun-00	Public holiday										6.5	6+ 0.5 PM	
23	110	12-Jun-00	Public holiday										6.5	6+ 0.5 PM	
	111	13-Jun-00										**Total**	553.5		
	112	14-Jun-00													
	119	15-Jun-00													
	120	16-Jun-00													
24	121	19-Jun-00													
	122	20-Jun-00													
	123	21-Jun-00													
	124	22-Jun-00													
	125	23-Jun-00													

Figure 14.1   (continued)

In particular, you have a template for your next project. This means that you can build your future project plans much more quickly, and that those plans are likely to be much more accurate than any you would have done previously. You can also extract from this data high level estimates versus actuals, which will be of immense value to you in assessing future plans—either your own or other people's.

Again, as I've mentioned in [1], the best post-mortems, in my opinion, are ones where there is both an objective account of the project, and also everybody gets to have a say. This is the kind we follow in the post-mortem of the worked example. In conclusion, it's also worth pointing out that many projects leave behind useful things which can also be valuable. Examples are test harnesses, test data, scripts to simplify the use of configuration management tools, and so on.

Worked Example — The Informal Post-Mortem

It's Friday, 9 June, as you drive home. Monday you will do the real post-mortem, but tonight, you're doing a sort of informal one in your head.

Your first reaction is that you did it! You brought it in not just on time, but ahead of target. The former is still unusual enough in the software world to be worthy of mention; the second is rare to the point of being unheard of. You brought it in 3 weeks ahead of the published schedule. However, if you compare the final result to the original MS Project plan, it showed a completion date of 11 August. On that basis, you brought the project in 9 weeks ahead of schedule, and this on a schedule of 31 weeks, a saving of 30%.

And you did it with very little overtime. Sure, people worked a few weekends. But everybody didn't work every weekend. And nobody griped. In fact, several people commented on the fact that you seemed to be making so much progress with so little overtime. Of course, the begrudgers will be saying that if you had worked continuous overtime, then the project would have come in even sooner. You know this is not true.

You remember that you turned in this performance in the face of great adversity. Charlie leaving seemed like a hammer blow at the time. In retrospect, it almost didn't seem to matter. Like all good projects, for much of it, it seemed like there was only going to be one outcome.[1]

---

1   Thanks to Phil Chambers of the Institute of Business Analysts and Consultants for this fine phrase.

Mohammed Ali used to call it "future history." You said what was going to happen and then you made it happen.

You remember again how important routine turned out to be. That, and the "can we get it done today?" mentality. These turned out to be the two killer things on the project, in your view.

You arrive home. As you get out of the car, you see stars shining overhead. You stay for a long time watching them. It's good to be alive.

Worked Example—The Real Post-Mortem

Getting Everybody Else's Input

It's Monday. You get your team together, call up Marketing, send an e-mail to the CEO, CFO, Head of Engineering, and anyone else you can think of who was involved in the project. To all of them you say the same thing.

You're planning to do a post-mortem on the project you tell them. You explain that you will write the factual account of the project, and gather the appropriate metrics. What you would like them to do is to write a "how was it for you?" memo. You tell them you're expecting 1–3 pages, and that you would like them to be blunt. You would like them to say both the things that were done well and the things that, in their view, were done badly. You tell them that you're particularly interested in any rules of thumb they came up with, that may be of value to the rest of the team. You ask them to identify the three key lessons they have learned from the project. You give them a week to reply, and say that if you don't hear from them, then you'll assume that they feel the project couldn't have been done better!

On the subject of being blunt, you try to make the following as crystal clear as possible. You want them to say exactly what's on their mind. Thus, if they'd rather, they can give their contributions anonymously. However, the entire collection of contributions—your factual account plus all of theirs—will be distributed to everyone who makes a contribution.

The Factual Account

Parts of the factual account are reproduced here.

Introduction

This document is a post-mortem on the project to produce the Killer product version 1.0. The project ran between January 10 and June 9, and involved the following people. (You list them.) There are two sections and an Appendix to the document.

Section 1 tells the story of the project from start to finish and contains statistics about the project. Section 2 gives a series of general recommendations resulting from things learned on this project. These recommendations could be usefully applied throughout the company. The Appendix contains accounts of the project written by all of those involved.

This project began on Monday, 10 January and ended on Friday, 9 June, a total elapsed time of 22 weeks. The project consumed 554 person-days of effort and produced (number) of lines of code. The product contained the following functionality. (You list it.)

Section 1 — The project phase by phase

Figure 14.2 shows the estimated versus actuals for this project. (The original estimates are taken from Figure 8.1, the final actuals from Figure 14.1.)

Figure 14.2
Comparison of estimates and actuals.

Phase	Estimated				Actuals				Differences			
	Elapsed (days)	% (2)	Effort (PD)	% (3)	Elapsed (days)	% (5)	Effort (PD)	%	Elapsed (days)	%	Effort (MD)	%
Requirements	40	26%	27	4%	15	14%	34	6%	−25	−63%	7	26%
Design (Prototype)	14	9%	22	4%	15	14%	33	6%	1	7%	11	50%
Coding	32	21%	184	30%	53	48%	164	30%	21	66%	−20	−11%
System Test (4)	60	39%	115	19%	47	43%	159	29%	−13	−22%	44	38%
Technical writing	84	55%	99	16%	88	80%	88	16%	4	5%	−11	−11%
Contingency	14	9%	103	17%	0	0%	0	0%	−14	−100%	−103	−100%
Project Management	140	91%	46	8%	110	100%	55	10%	−30	−21%	9	20%
Totals	(1)	(1)	596	98%	(1)	(1)	533	96%			−63	

Notes:
(1) Adding these doesn't necessarily make sense since some of the phases of the project overlapped.
(2) As a percentage of the total elapsed time, i.e., 154 days
(3) As a percentage of the total work, i.e., 610 person-days
(4) Estimated elapsed includes both writing the tests and carrying them out. Effort includes this plus bug fixing
(5) As a percentage of the total actual elapsed time, i.e., 110 days
(6) As a percentage of the total actual work, i.e., 554 person-days

Requirements

We managed to shorten the requirements phase substantially by doing a project scoping and planning session.

Design

We got the elapsed time for the prototype pretty much dead on. The effort was greater than we had anticipated.

Coding

Coding elapsed time is greater because of the fact that we only had three engineers rather than the four originally planned for. Effort was reasonably accurate.

System Test

Lower elapsed time represents effects of trying to shorten the project. Effort figure shows that we underestimated the amount of testing and bug fixing required.

Technical Writing

These figures were very accurate.

Contingency

Wasn't used—actuals reflect this.

Project Management

Smaller elapsed time figure due to shortened project. Larger effort figure perhaps due to Charlie's departure and attendant crisis.
    (Section 2 and Appendix follow, but are not reproduced here.)

Reference

1.   O'Connell, F., *How To Run Successful High-Tech Project-Based Organizations*, Norwood: Artech House, 1999.

PART SIX
Bringing It All Together

Everything we have said so far relates to a single project. It is possible to run an organization, with multiple projects, so that all projects are given the shortening treatment. This part of the book explains how to do that. It also provides a blueprint for implementing these ideas in your organization.

Chapter 15 shows that, in order to run multiple projects at all, you have to match demand (the amount of work to be done) with supply (the amount of people available to do the work). Note that this statement applies whether you are trying to shorten the project or not. Part of the process of matching supply to demand requires you to set up and maintain a priority list. Using this as a framework, you can then run each of your multiple projects in Web-time. Chapter 16 describes how to implement the ideas in the book in your organization.

15

Run Multiple Projects

➤ Many projects go wrong because the organization in which the project is being run is trying to do much work (demand) with too few resources (supply). This chapter shows, first of all, how to find out if this is the case.

➤ Next it shows that the key to running all of an organization's projects in Web-time is to establish a project priority list and a process for maintaining it.

➤ The third and final step in running all of an organization's projects in Web-time is to run (i.e. plan and execute) each of the individual projects using the techniques described in Chapters 3 through 15.

➤ We illustrate the concepts with a (different) worked example.

Introduction

If an organization wants to run all of its projects in Web-time, then an understanding of the organization-wide supply-demand is an essential first step. This statement is actually more widely true.

If your organization is serious about getting products out the door, then it is necessary that it understand whether there is enough supply (resources available) to meet the demand (work identified). If there isn't—and in my experience, in general, there isn't—then no amount of working harder, smarter project planning, or wishing things were better will make it so.

If your organization is experiencing one or more of the following symptoms:

- Marketing or senior management complaining that "we don't seem to be able to get products out the door" or "bring projects in on time";

221

- Engineering or Product Development complaining that the company keeps changing its mind;

- People working longer and longer hours;

- Projects falling further and further behind;

- Projects not getting completed.

Then there is a fair chance that the cause is that the organization-wide supply and demand is out of balance, that is, the demand exceeds (usually by a lot) the supply.

If you let this go unchecked, then things will just get worse and worse. This is because it is in the nature of things that supply tends downwards and demand tends upwards. If you tackle some of the symptoms, for example, decide that people need time management or project management training, then all you will do will be to waste effort and money while the disease remains. If you want to run successful projects, never mind if you want to run them in Web-time, you must fix this problem.

How you do it is very simple. You just get all of the guilty parties together and do the following:

1. Write down a list of all the projects that are currently being done or are intended to be done in a specified period (e.g., 6 months, 1 year) by the organization.

2. Estimate how much effort is in each of the projects. The sum of all these efforts gives the total organization-wide demand.

3. Estimate how much people effort is available in the same period to do this work.

4. Assuming demand is greater than supply, prioritize the list and make a "cut" at the point where demand is equal to supply.

5. Establish a procedure for maintaining the list, that is, how do projects get on, move up and down, and drop off?

6. Finally—to run the projects in Web-time—plan and execute the projects using the techniques we have described in Chapters 3 through 15.

In the rest of this chapter, we illustrate all of this with a new worked example.

Worked Example

Introduction

Time has moved on. So have you. You decided you'd leave in a blaze of glory, so you put in your resignation on the same day that the people came back from Comdex saying that the Killer product had gone down in a storm. They tried to make you stay—the offers were surprising—but you'd made your mind up.

So, you're hired on at a new place. At each of your interviews, people eagerly pointed out to you the "challenges" that awaited you. Once you thought you detected an amused look flicker between the Head of Marketing and the CEO when they used this expression at your final interview.

You're not in too much doubt about what you're facing. You've been around the block enough to know what it means when an organization uses phrases like "dynamic," "aggressive schedules," "market focused." To project managers, or the managers of project managers, which is what you are now, they mean the same thing—impossible deadlines.

Now you see this new company as having lots of potential. (And you've got a nice block of stock options.) You think they're really going to go places. But, if they're to do so, there are some pretty fundamental things they're going have to sort out on the product development front. You've taken the approach that you're going to face all of these upfront. In your view, there's no point in going softly. All that will happen then is that you'll preside over a disaster and you'll be out on your ear. Far better to be kicked out while you still hold the moral high ground. Barry Boehm [1] describes it as "hard-soft" rather than "soft-hard."

Your experience at your last company tells you that you could convert all of this organization to running its projects in Web-time. This was the message you sold at your interview. (This is why you were able to hold out for such a big block of stock options.) You've looked them in the eye and told them that you can make it happen for them—consistently (i.e., over and over again) and quicker than anybody else can. Once again, you felt that familiar squirming in your stomach while you said it, but you didn't show it—your gaze was steely and unflinching.

Now, it's your first week. You've arranged a meeting with all of the powers that be. The CEO will be there, the CFO, Heads of Marketing and Sales, the Head of Manufacturing (these guys make hardware and software products), and all of your senior Project Managers. Your strategy is twofold. First, you're going to show them what a big mess they're in. Then, you'll show them the way out. It's high risk. You reckon you may not have a job by the end of the month. Actually, you think, as you park your company car with its lovely smell of brand-new, you may not have a job by the end of the day.

The first thing you do when you get in is to ask your assistant to check on public transport options to your home. She looks at you quizzically.

A List of All the Projects

"Okay," you begin, as everyone settles themselves into the meeting. "Thanks for coming. Our objective here today is to build the definitive prioritized list of projects, so that I can make sure our people are working on the right things."

"I thought we already had that," says somebody.

"Hey, that's great if we have it already, then it's going to be a quick meeting." You put on a "humor me" tone. "But I'm sure you can understand. I'm new and I don't want anyone coming back in six month's time and asking where the Blah product is and me knowing nothing about it. I just want to make sure our people are developing the right products for the rest of the company."

You look around the room, meeting each pair of eyes in turn. You don't know most of these people particularly well, so it's even harder than usual to gauge the mood of the room. You turn to the flipchart, put up a new page. "OK," you say, "who can give me the list?"

"What period we looking at?" somebody sensibly asks.

"Let's look at the rest of this year and all of next year," you reply.

"So, 19 months?"

You nod.

It starts off evenly enough. The first few go flying onto the paper as fast as you can write. But then an interesting thing happens. Marketing mentions something and one of your PMs says "we're not doing that." Sales chimes in. "Of course you are, Charlie's working on it. (It's not the same Charlie!) And anyway we've sold it to the Acme Corporation." You let the discussion flow for a while and then say reasonably "Well, if it's out there, if we've promised it to somebody we'd better put it up there." You add it.

Things become even more heated and what everybody—except you—thought would be a fifteen-minute meeting turns into a two and a half-hour marathon. It's eleven o'clock by the time the final list is up in front of them. It looks like this.

1. Able (two variants—1 and 2);

2. Baker (three variants—1, 2, and 3);

3. Charlie (not the same Charlie!);

4. Dog (three variants—1, 2, and 3);

5. Easy (three variants—1, 2, and 3);

6. Fox (three variants—1, 2, and 3);

7. Golf (three variants—1, 2, and 3);

8. Hotel;

9. India (two variants—1 and 2);

10. Supporting existing products;

11. R&D;

12. Training.

The last three go in at your suggestion. Significant engineering effort also goes into supporting existing and newly released products, Research & Development of new products, and training to keep people up to speed with all the new stuff that's emerging. At this point you suggest a break for coffee. As they file out you hear two different people say, "I never realized we were doing so much." Interestingly, one is from the Sales/Marketing area and the other is one of your people.

How Much Effort Is in Each of the Projects

When they come back you're ready to spring your trap. Innocently, you begin. "Just before we prioritize the projects, it would be really helpful for me if I could get some feeling for how much work is involved in each of these things. Anyone mind if we spend a few minutes on that?"

"But doesn't Engineering already have estimates?" the CEO says. He sounds mildly exasperated. "Not for some of these we don't," one of the PMs retorts. "Today is the first we heard about some of these."

More skin and hair starts to fly. You let it continue for a minute or two and then call them back to order."

"How shall we estimate them?" you ask brightly.

Silence. After a while you suggest the following three steps as a way forward. First, you will classify each of the products as small, medium, or large. Then you will identify the major phases that each project goes through. The following end up being generally accepted:

- Requirements & Design Specs;

- Engineering Development;

- Test;

- Production.

Finally, you will modify any estimates based on where particular projects are in their life cycle.

They're a little puzzled, so you show them how it works.

"Take Baker Variant 1," you say. "Small, Medium, or Large?"

"Large," comes the reply.

"Specs?"

"You mean how long will they take?"

"No. How much work is involved? How many people are working on it for how long?"

"Three people for 4 months."

"OK, that's 48-person weeks.

"Development?"

"That's due to be 6 people for … let me see"—he checks a schedule and comes back with "6 months."

"OK, that's 6 people by 6 weeks by 4 weeks per month. That's 144 person weeks."

"Test?"

"Six people for 10 weeks."

"60," you note.

"Production?"

"What precisely does it mean?" asks the Head of Manufacturing. "What are you trying to estimate?"

A bit of a discussion ensues until finally it is established that what we meant by "Production" was actually engineering effort used during production. The estimate ends up being based on so many engineers for the time taken to get the product into production. 53 person weeks is the estimate in this case.

You write the total down as $48 + 144 + 60 + 53 = 305$ person weeks. "Got the idea?" you ask.

They do. So you proceed and eventually end up with Figure 15.1.

Figure 15.1   List of all projects.

1 Able	**8 person weeks**
Effort required to finish both variants	8 person weeks
2 Baker	**541 person weeks**
Variant 1	305 person weeks
Variant 2	172 person weeks
Variant 3	64 person weeks
3 Charlie	**48 person weeks**
Specs.	4 person weeks
Eng. Dev.	32 person weeks
Test	8 person weeks
Production	4 person weeks
4 Dog	**440 person weeks**
Variant 1	312 person weeks
Variant 2	64 person weeks
Variant 3	64 person weeks
5 Easy	**368 person weeks**
Variant 1	232 person weeks
Variant 2	68 person weeks
Variant 3	68 person weeks
6 Fox	**135 person weeks**
Variant 1	95 person weeks
Variant 2	20 person weeks
Variant 3	20 person weeks
7 Golf	**976 person weeks**
Variant 1	720 person weeks
Variant 2	128 person weeks
Variant 3	128 person weeks
8 Hotel	**1,032 person weeks**
Specs.	32 person weeks
Eng. Dev.	800 person weeks
Test	100 person weeks
Production	100 person weeks
9 India	**256 person weeks**
Variant 1	128 person weeks
Variant 2	128 person weeks
10 Product Support (Estimates based on so many weeks per product)	**392 person weeks**
Existing Products	152 person weeks
New Products	240 person weeks
R & D (Estimate based on so many people for so many weeks)	**176 person weeks**
Training (Estimate based on so much training per person)	**96 person weeks**
Sub-total	**4,468 person weeks**
Project Management Effort @ 10%	**447 person weeks**
Contingency @15%	**670 person weeks**
Total	**5,585 person weeks**

The last two items are added in at your suggestion. Project management effort is calculated at 10% of the subtotal, and contingency at 15%.

How Much People Effort Is Available

Now you close the trap.

"How many people do we have now?" you ask.

It turns out there are 19 engineers currently. For 19 months that's 359 person months. The hiring plan calls for an additional 6 engineers to be added towards the end of the year. This will give an additional 6 people for (an average of) 13 months, that is, 78 person months. The grand total is 437 person-months or 1892 person weeks. (You count the weeks in the period under consideration.) You summarize on a fresh sheet of paper:

- Demand = 5,585 person weeks;

- Supply = 1,892 person weeks.

There is a stunned silence in the room. You let it deepen for several minutes, before asking innocently if anybody would like a break. They would!

By the time they return, they have gone into denial. "That could never be that much," "How come these estimates are so different from the ones we already have?" You deal with each of their queries in turn. You're careful to do this and it takes a while. Generally, you find that the reasons for the vast discrepancy between their previous estimates and these, can be drawn from the following list:

- They hadn't included certain projects (especially to produce variants) that have now been definitively identified.

- They only identified the Engineering Development time for a certain product and forgot about all the other phases.

- They forgot about things like product support, training, and project management. They hadn't even considered contingency until you brought it up.

When the last of the objections have been dealt with, you tell them you're going to need some more time, if that's okay with them. Can you continue after lunch? It is—there isn't an objection in the house. They file out morosely.

Prioritize the List

With the supply-demand summary page on the flipchart, you continue after lunch.

"Now, to fix this problem, you can increase this"—you point to the supply—"or decrease this"—you point to the demand. You stop speaking. But they're all still looking at you as though they think you haven't finished the sentence. You say nothing, once more letting the silence deepen. Eventually, somebody cracks.

"Aren't there other things you can do?"

"Like what?" you ask.

More silence. Then the CEO says it. The line you'd been waiting to hear.

"Well you tell us, for heaven's sake. That's why we hired you."

This is it. The moment. What happens in the next minute or two will determine whether you travel home this evening by car or public transport.

Like a bell tolling, you say the words slowly.

"There's nothing else."

"What about improving our process?"

"That'll buy you five or ten percent improvement. Maybe fifteen over a couple of years. The gap you have now is"—you do the calculation while they watch in horror—"is that you have nearly three times more work than you have people to do it."

"So what can we do?"

"Increase this or decrease this," you say evenly. "Or a combination of the two."

"So what do we do?"

"Prioritize the list and make a cut at the point at which supply equals demand."

"But that means loads of projects won't get done." There is furious nodding of heads.

You do your bell tolling, Death the Grim Reaper voice again. "They won't get done anyway."

It's like you hit them. While they're still down, you add, "At least this way you decide what gets done, as opposed to letting things just happen themselves. At least this way you can be sure of what will and won't get done. The other way you have no idea."

It's a while before anyone speaks. You get the impression they're all waiting on the CEO. You actually get the impression that they're waiting for the CEO to fire you. Finally, he speaks.

"So how do we prioritize them?"

"We could rate them on cumulative profit," you suggest, mindful of the content of Chapter 3. "But there are some projects where we don't expect to make much profit, but it's important that we have that client on our list. And some where we need the project to develop technology for the future."

"So maybe we could identify these factors and then rate them Low, Medium, High, and come up with some kind of scoring scheme?"

"But surely cumulative profit is the highest priority?" says the CFO.

"Generally it is," says the CEO, "but not always."

"So then, why don't we rate by cumulative profit, and then slot the other ones onto that list?"

It's generally agreed that this is a way to go.[1]

"It's gonna take a few days while we work all the models," you say.

Make the "Cut"

It's a week later. The list is a simple one-pager. On it is the name of each project, it's cumulative profit, and the estimated effort involved. The list was originally sorted in the order of descending cumulative profit, but then a few projects were moved further up the list, depending on some of the "fuzzier" factors we spoke about, such as getting a particular client on the client list or developing technology for the future. The calls that had to get made were things like "it's more important to have the Acme Corporation on our client list than it is to make x million dollars from the Fox Variant 2 product" or "we'll have to give up Baker Variant 3 so that the guys can work on the latest Three Letter Acronym technology." Once the list is finalized, it's a simple matter to make the cut where you run out of resources.

It may be simple but that doesn't make it any less painful.

---

1   I'm not suggesting that this is the absolutely only right way to do this. I'm actually not aware of any absolutely right way. There are plenty of approaches, however. Here, in keeping with the spirit of the book, I have chosen what I believe to be a practical, simple, and reasonably effective way.

Establish a Procedure for Maintaining the List

Now that you have the list, you need to figure out how to maintain it. You quote them something from [2]: "The basic means of avoiding overload is to start fewer projects *but get them done*, then start a few more." [My italics.] This statement will be the theme underlying your maintenance of the priority list.

It's agreed that as new projects or ideas for new products appear on the radar screen they will be added to the bottom of the priority list. Somebody—and the contingency ensures that there is some resource available to do this—will do a Chapter 3 type model of the project. Then periodically, the same group of people who established the list will meet and agree where the new projects fit into the priority list. Most people are anxious that the group meets weekly. You want it to be monthly—weekly implies a level of chopping and changing that would be little better than what you have already.

The "weekly" people win out, but you're happy enough to lose that one. You know that if they try changing their minds every week—which they will in the short term—you can always win it by coming back to the supply demand calculations. You can imagine it already. "Okay, so the Brand New Project goes to number 1 slot and that means that the Fox Project, all three variants, falls off the end." It shouldn't take too long before the priority list meetings settle down to some kind of acceptable regularity.

Run the Projects in Web time

Now that you have your priority list—which, incidentally, you got the powers-that-be to sign—you're now ready to begin planning and executing the projects in Web time. You know what to do. You follow the approach that we've described already in Chapters 3 through 14. Starting from the top, you plan the projects starting with the highest priority one.

Now here comes the really important point. Remember we spoke briefly in Chapter 2 about multitasking. We said that in making movies they don't really do it. If you're to get all your projects done in Web time, then it's important that you don't do it either. Plan the highest priority project as though it was the only one you had. Flood it with resources with the intention of getting it finished as quickly as possible.

Then with the schedule (which includes contingency, of course) for that first project locked into place, plan the second one, but plan it around the first one, that is, where there is a conflict, the first one takes absolute priority.² Continue onto the third one. Lock numbers 1 and 2 in place and then plan number 3. Continue this until you have worked your way down the priority list and all projects have been strip boarded and are being executed as we described in Chapter 13.

References

1. Kruchten, P., *The Rational Unified Process*, Reading, MA: Addison-Wesley, 1998.

2. Smith, P. G., and D. G. Reinertsen, *Developing Products in Half the Time*, New York: Wiley, 1998.

3. Leach, L. P., *Critical Chain Project Management*, Norwood, MA: Artech House, 2000.

4. Jordan, N., *Michael Collins—Film Diary & Screenplay*, London, England: Vintage, 1996.

---

2   Don't just take my word for this. Look at [4], [17], or [18] in the Bibliography. All of the authors say the same thing in different ways.

16 Implementing These Ideas In Your Organization

➤ This chapter shows how to begin applying these ideas in your organization.

➤ Once begun, it provides a weekly routine to ensure that you continue to do these things.

Where Do I Start?

If you are a project manager responsible for a single project, then you start at Chapter 3 and work your project through to Chapter 14.

If you are responsible for a portfolio of projects then you need to begin at Chapter 15.

1. Write down a list of all the projects that are currently being done or are intended to be done in a specified period (e.g., 6 months, 1 year) by the organization.

2. Estimate how much effort is in each of the projects. The sum of all these efforts gives the total organization-wide demand.

3. Estimate how much people effort is available in the same period to do this work.

4. Assuming demand is greater than supply, prioritize the list and make a "cut" at the point where demand is equal to supply.

5. Establish a procedure for maintaining the list, for example, how do projects get on, move up and down, and drop off?

6. Finally—to run the projects in Web-time—plan and execute the projects using the techniques we have described in Chapters 3 through 14.

How Do I Continue?

1. Maintain Dance Cards so that you don't get overloaded.

2. On Monday first thing, set the targets for the week. Do this in project priority order, that is, set (or ensure they are set) the targets for project #1, then project #2, project #3, and so on.

3. On Fridays, for each project, report progress against the targets.

4. Best of all is to write the project Status Reports on Monday morning, and then see if you can send them out unchanged on Friday at close of business.

Bibliography

Cooper, A., *The Lunatics Are Running The Asylum*, Indianapolis: Sams Publishing, 1999.

Gardner, J., *On Becoming A Novelist*, New York: Harper & Row, 1985.

Jordan, N., *Michael Collins—Film Diary & Screenplay*, London, England: Vintage, 1996.

About the Author

Fergus O'Connell graduated with a First in mathematical physics from University College Cork, Ireland. His twenty-four years of experience—twenty-one of those in project management positions—cover commercial data processing, microprocessor-based office automation systems, computer networking, data communications, and telecommunications. He has worked with companies such as CPT, ICL, and Retix, before founding ETP in 1992. He is currently chairman and CEO of ETP. His experience covers projects in Australia, Britain, Denmark, Germany, Ireland, Luxembourg, Sweden, Switzerland, and the United States. He has taught project management on three continents.

Fergus is the author of a trio of books on project management:

- *How To Run Successful Projects II—The Silver Bullet* (Prentice Hall, 1996);

- *How To Run Successful High-Tech Project-Based Organizations* (Artech House, 1999);

- *How To Run Successful Projects in Web Time* (Artech House, 2001).

His first book, sometimes known simply as "The Silver Bullet," has become both a bestseller and a classic. He has written on project management for *The Sunday Business Post*, *Computer Weekly*, and *The Wall Street Journal*. He has lectured on project management at

University College Cork, Boston University, and on television for the National Technological University.

He lives with his wife, son, daughter, three dogs, two horses, three ponies, and a donkey beside the River Barrow in Ireland.

Index

Recent Titles in the Artech House Computing Library

Advanced ANSI SQL Data Modeling and Structure Processing,
Michael M. David

Authentication Systems for Secure Networks, Rolf Oppliger

Business Process Implementation for IT Professionals and Managers,
Robert B. Walford

*Client/Server Computing: Architecture, Applications, and Distributed Sytems
Management*, Bruce Elbert and Bobby Martyna

Computer-Mediated Communications: Multimedia Applications,
Rob Walters

Computer Telephony Integration, Second Edition, Rob Walters

Data Modeling and Design for Today's Architectures, Angelo Bobak

Data Quality for the Information Age, Thomas C. Redman

Data Warehousing and Data Mining for Telecommunications,
Rob Mattison

Designing Web Software, Stan Magee and Leonard L. Tripp

Distributed and Multi-Database Systems, Angelo R. Bobak

Electronic Payment Systems, Donal O'Mahony, Michael Peirce, and
Hitesh Tewari

Future Codes: Essays in Advanced Computer Technology and the Law,
Curtis E.A. Karnow

A Guide to Programming Languages: Overview and Comparison,
Ruknet Cezzar

Guide to Software Engineering Standards and Specifications,
Stan Magee and Leonard L. Tripp

How to Run Successful High-Tech Project-Based Organizations,
Fergus O'Connell

How to Run Successful Projects in Web Time, Fergus O'Connell

Internet and Intranet Security, Rolf Oppliger

Internet Digital Libraries: The International Dimension, Jack Kessler

Managing Computer Networks: A Case-Based Reasoning Approach,
Lundy Lewis

Metadata Management for Information Control and Business Success,
Guy Tozer

Multimedia Database Management Systems, Guojun Lu

Practical Guide to Software Quality Management, John W. Horch

Practical Process Simulation Using Object-Oriented Techniques and C++, José
Garrido

Risk Management Processes for Software Engineering Models,
Marian Myerson

Secure Electronic Transactions: Introduction and Technical Reference,
Larry Loeb

Software Process Improvement With CMM, Joseph Raynus

Software Verification and Validation: A Practitioner's Guide,
Steven R. Rakitin

Solving the Year 2000 Crisis, Patrick McDermott

User-Centered Information Design for Improved Software Usability, Pradeep
Henry

For further information on these and other Artech House titles,
including previously considered out-of-print books now available through our
In-Print-Forever® (IPF®) program, contact:

Artech House   Artech House
685 Canton Street   46 Gillingham Street
Norwood, MA 02062   London SW1V 1AH UK
Phone: 781-769-9750   Phone: +44 (0)20 7596-8750
Fax: 781-769-6334   Fax: +44 (0)20 7630-0166
e-mail: artech@artechhouse.com   e-mail: artech-uk@artechhouse.com

Find us on the World Wide Web at:
www.artechhouse.com